FRAGILE RESONANCE

FRAGILE RESONANCE

Caring for Older Family Members
in Japan and England

Jason Danely

CORNELL UNIVERSITY PRESS   ITHACA AND LONDON

First published 2022 by Cornell University Press

Library of Congress Cataloging-in-Publication Data
Names: Danely, Jason, author.
Title: Fragile resonance : caring for older family members in Japan and England / Jason Danely.
Description: Ithaca [New York] : Cornell University Press, 2022. | Includes bibliographical references and index.
Identifiers: LCCN 2021057941 (print) | LCCN 2021057942 (ebook) | ISBN 9781501765643 (hardcover) | ISBN 9781501765810 (paperback) | ISBN 9781501765834 (pdf) | ISBN 9781501765827 (epub)
Subjects: LCSH: Caregivers—Japan—Social conditions. | Caregivers—England—Social conditions. | Older people—Care—Social aspects—Japan. | Older people—Care—Social aspects—England.
Classification: LCC HV65 .D36 2022 (print) | LCC HV65 (ebook) | DDC 362/.04250942—dc23/eng/20220510
LC record available at https://lccn.loc.gov/2021057941
LC ebook record available at https://lccn.loc.gov/2021057942

Contents

Preface

In the exposure of life forms in a disaster situation, the truth of
our dependencies emerges. If this moral revelation is possible, it is
precisely because of the situation (unprecedented for many of the
present generations) of disaster, which reveals radical vulnerabilities.
Vulnerability is at the core of the ethics of care. Vulnerability of
persons, institutions, and threats to the human form of life.

Sandra Laugier, "War on Care"

I finished writing this book in the summer of 2020, during the long tail of the largest global epidemic in generations. The first things I learned about SARS Cov-2
were that it was unlikely to result in full symptomatic COVID-19 if contracted
by younger people, and that most people in good health experience only mild
symptoms. No doubt my mind sifted the stream of information for these facts
before the alarm bells started ringing and the supermarket shelves became bare.
Even as I felt relieved that my children were not immediately endangered, I was
horrified when I found out what was happening in hospitals and care homes as
older people and carers faced the peak of infection without adequate protection
or guidance. In some cases carers or health staff were told to prioritize those who
were younger and more likely to recover—a chilling instance of the inhumanity
of rationalized care in a time of political incompetence.

COVID-19 would teach us about exposure and vulnerability, the human condition of our embodied life and its microbial porosity. But as hundreds of voices
were quick to point out, vulnerability was not evenly distributed. Most commen-
tators focused on disparities between white British and Black and other minority
groups, sometimes using a proxy of "low income" citizens. But the most severely
affected were frail and disabled older people. The images were devastating: older
people locked in isolation or being ventilated in emergency room wards. I rarely
saw an image of an older person at home with family, but as adult day care services shut their doors and home help assistants became sick or quit, family carers
were taking up even more responsibility, sometimes while also trying to work or

parent, and unable to move freely. The consequences of this time of worry, stress, and exhaustion on family carers will continue for decades.

This is a time to think seriously about family carers. Times of disaster tests our morals, our institutions, and our relationships. But when the disaster moves on, the inequalities and violence that it exposed will not go with it. COVID-19 has made it harder to trust our care homes, and perhaps made us more cautious about too much reliance on paid formal care. At the same time, faith communities and volunteer groups, neighbors and local businesses, became suddenly much more visible. "Key workers" became celebrated as heroes. Yet again, family carers received little attention; they remained the invisible and unacknowledged backbone of the care system (Chan et al. 2020).

While I try to make sense of the deluge numbers and daily reports, I am also faced with the unspoken, unspeakable excess of this tragedy. Family carers know the true costs, of the loss not only of lives and livelihoods but also of the sense of security and trust. This book has tried to show that despite the heartbreaking realities that such care entails, carers endure, find meaning, and deepen their relationships. These are stories that deserve to be told in the voices of the carers themselves. They are stories of ethical commitments of shared lives, the pains and pleasures of proximity, the transcendence of compassion. Carers can teach us more than the headlines and statistics can about how to face a post-pandemic future. Perhaps this is a key moment for us to rethink the ways we care for older people and the value of carers, and to see these as part of a larger project of social justice for aging societies. Now is not the time to reduce this global event to a single war.

In this way, it is my hope that this book can do something to broaden our discussions not only beyond the boundaries of nation and culture, but also beyond mainstream gerontology. To do so would expand the possibilities for imagining relationships of care and enhance what it means to live together in our shared and fragile world.

Acknowledgments

If there is one message that returned to me most often while writing this book, it was the voice of a carer telling me, "There is nothing that teaches you more than caring." I still find these words so wonderfully simple, yet at the same time powerful; hopeful, yet also heavy with responsibility. This book would not have been possible without the many Japanese and English carers who gave their precious time to sit with me and share all the things they learned about accompanying an older family member through the long journey of care. They did so with the hope that their story might resonate with other carers or the many carers-in-waiting. In every encounter, they extended this spirit of care, and I have been moved and humbled by their sincerity and generosity. The lessons carers taught me have been invaluable, and while this book gives only the slightest glimpse of the fullness of their lives, I hold the deepest respect and gratitude for all of them. It has been a joy to learn from all of you.

This research was launched through the generous support of the Social Science Research Council (USA) and the Japan Society for the Promotion of Science Postdoctoral Fellowship program. JSPS not only provided the financial support that allowed me to spend a year conducting intensive fieldwork in Japan but also provided the care and attention to make sure that my family had peace of mind. This opportunity would have been impossible without the labor and perseverance of Professor Carl Becker, whose wisdom and kindness are matched only by his skillful expedience and dedication. I find myself enormously lucky to count him as a mentor and a friend. I would also like to extend my gratitude to the Kokoro no Mirai Research Center at Kyoto University and to its director at the time of my research, Professor Sakiko Yoshikawa, for providing such a stimulating environment for thinking creatively about care. Thanks also to Miki Nakaji and the Kokoro Center office staff for all their help arranging our housing, travel, and affiliation details. My time in Kyoto was greatly enriched by discussions about care, compassion, religion, and health, with those inside and outside the Kokoro Center, especially John and Ruth Campbell, Edward Drott, Tatsuro Fujikura, Yoko Hayami, Iza Kavedžija, Shinobu Kitayama, Makiko Morita, Aya Seike, James Mark Shields, Laura Specker Sullivan, and Yukiko Uchida.

I am deeply indebted to several individuals who, although most are not mentioned in this book, were crucial to facilitating introductions to carers and carer support groups in Kyoto. I would like to thank Misayo Shibamoto, Yukiko

Taniguchi, Noriko Washizu, Mariko Yamaguchi, and Kiyoko Yoshimura. A spe-cial thanks to Maru-chan of Tsudoi no ba Sakura-chan, Hayakawa-sensei, and to Hayashi-sensei of Dōwaen, all of whom helped sharpen my critiques and broaden my visions of a caring society. Though they are too numerous to men-tion, I am grateful to all the staff and carers who welcomed me to the various support groups and volunteer functions, day service and nursing care facilities, religious groups, and visits into their homes.

When I returned from Kyoto, I knew that the story I really wanted to tell about care had to go beyond Japan, even though I was still unsure about what to make of all the fieldwork interviews and observations I had already collected. The turning point for me came in the form of the Enhancing Life Project (ELP), funded by the John Templeton Foundation and led by William Schweiker of the University of Chicago and Günter Thomas of Ruhr University Bochum. The intellectual vibrancy and boldness of this project and its participants inspired me not only to develop and pursue many of the key ideas of this book, but also to ask big questions about how this work can connect with and enhance public life. Among all my ELP friends and interlocutors, I am especially grateful to Amit Pinchevski, who taught me new ways of thinking about echo and resonance; to Christian Chautard, Michael Ing, Monique Mitchell, Anne Mocko, Chris Scott, Heike Springhart, and Ruben Zimmermann for our many conversations about vulnerability, compassion, grief, and care; and to Pamela Sue Anderson, my men-tor in the ethics of care, grief, love, and the possibility of transformation.

Many sections in the book came together in conference sessions or invited talks and the questions and conversations that arose from them. When my writ-ing seemed to grind down to a crawl, these opportunities kept me moving for-ward. Some of the many friends and colleagues with whom I have exchanged ideas in the early days of this book include Anne Allison, Felicity Aulino, Paul Brodwin, Elana Buch, Lawrence Cohen, Jo Cook, Lone Grøn, Jolanda Linden-berg, Cheryl Mattingly, Lotte Meinert, Janelle Taylor, and Jason Throop. Thanks also to the sensitivity and hard work of research assistants Elizabeth Dunthorne and Ryoko Watanabe, who not only transcribed broken and muffled interview recordings, but also offered their kind words of support.

Portions of chapters and some ethnographic material appeared in previously published work, including "'He Wanted to Eat Eel': Food and End-of-Life Care," *Kyoto Journal* 83 (2015); "Learning Compassion: Everyday Ethics among Japa-nese Carers," *Inochi no Mirai* (Future of life) 1 (2016): 170–92; "Carer Narratives of Fatigue and Endurance in Japan and England," *Subjectivity* 10, no. 4 (2017); "Mourning and Mutuality," in *Companion to the Anthropology of Death* (2018); "Love and Imagination That Transcends Death," *Journal of Death and Life Studies and Practical Ethics* 24 (2020): 165–76; and "'It Rips You to Bits': Woundedness and Compassion in Carer Narratives," in *Vulnerability and the Politics of Care: Transdisciplinary Dialogues* (2021).

Long before the manuscript was finished, I presented the book proposal to Cornell University Press senior editor Jim Lance. It would be another three years before I finally submitted the finished draft of the manuscript. I am very grateful to Jim for his unwavering patience and support for the book over these years and for all his work shepherding it through the editorial process. It has been a privilege to work with everyone at Cornell University Press, including the talented editorial and production staff whose care and consideration for the text have been amazing. My sincere thanks to the anonymous reviewers who, despite the stress and chaos of academic life in the COVID-19 pandemic, offered a close reading and detailed suggestions that have improved the book enormously.

Finally, my greatest sources of care and resonance over this long journey have been my wife and children. I was never lonely while writing this book and never without the chance to care and be cared for. They have been with me every step, picking me up when I stumbled and grounding me when I started to float into the clouds.

Note on Terminology and Transliteration

I use the common term "carer" rather than the equivalent in the United States, "caregiver," to translate the Japanese word *kaigosha*, which I employ in this book to refer specifically to elderly care (as this is the main context where it is used in Japan). "Carer" can refer to paid/professional/formal carers (or "care workers") as well as unpaid/family/informal carers. I tend to use the terms unpaid/paid to distinguish these groups, even though I realize that in practice, such distinctions are often blurred: volunteers and paid carers often provide care that exceeds the boundaries of their compensated work, and informal carers often receive a small carer allowance or other financial support. Nonetheless, the distinction is useful for foregrounding the political and economic value typically accorded to care provided in some social contexts (through welfare schemes or corporate entities), and not in others (the family). The paid/unpaid carer distinction is also preferable to terms like formal/informal care, which imply a hierarchy of skill, expertise, and legitimacy that is demeaning to those who care.

I use "care recipient" and "cared-for" interchangeably. In Japanese this would be the equivalent of *kaigo sareru hito*, or *yōkaigosha*. I use these terms self-consciously, as I realize the roles of carer and cared-for are not static but may blend or reverse at various times. While "care recipient" is commonly used in social science literature regarding care of older people, "cared-for" is more common in the philosophical literature of the ethics of care. By adopting both, I hope to speak to both of these fields.

In England, it is more common than it is in the United States to use the word "elderly" when referring to people over the age of sixty-five (although in ordinary speech it is typically reserved for those much older). In the US, the term can carry a stigmatizing connotation of debility and obsolescence. Yet the common alternative term, "older," is also vague and can be construed as patronizingly euphemistic. While recognizing the impoverished vocabulary for describing people who have aged beyond midlife adulthood, I try to avoid overly general and reductionist language such as references to "the elderly" and adopt the "people-first" principle commonly employed in disability studies, using terms such as "elderly people" or "older people" interchangeably, as seems most appropriate. I clarify when I refer specifically to frail, disabled, or cognitively impaired and dependent older people. I also use phrases in forms such as "people living with dementia" to acknowledge that people are not defined by illness or disability, nor does an illness or disability mean that one cannot have a good and full life.

While the sample of English carers participating in this research all resided in England, I do acknowledge that they may have important cultural heritage elsewhere in the British Isles or around the world. While "English" is not an ethnic term, it can be used to delineate a national boundary; "Britain/British" is much more ambiguous. Since the policies discussed pertain mainly to England, I use the word "English" throughout. The majority of names are pseudonyms, except when individuals specifically requested their real name be used (e.g., Maru-chan and Hashimoto-sensei in chapter 7) and there were no reasons to deny their preference based on research ethics guidelines.

Choosing an appropriate form of address presented a problem. While referring to British carers as Mr. or Ms. would appear overly formal, as it would in the context of an interview, simply using a first name to refer to the Japanese carers appears too informal, even disrespectful for all except the few I was closest to. In the end, however, I have chosen to adopt a consistent form of first-name address that English-speaking readers will be most accustomed to. The exception is when referring to doctors or clergy, whom I address with the more respectful last name followed by "teacher" (-sensei).

Romanization of Japanese words throughout the book follows the Modified Hepburn system.

During the period of fieldwork, the exchange rate for Japanese yen (¥) was approximately ¥105 to the US$1.00 and British pound £0.75.

FRAGILE RESONANCE

INTRODUCTION

"I want to get up!"

Tomomi was already on her feet, moving quickly, watching closely as her mother strained to lift herself from the bulky adjustable hospital bed that occupied almost half of the small living room.

"I want to get up!"

In an instant, she was by her mother's side, studying her expression, the searching eyes, heaving chest, gasping mouth. Tomomi gently placed a hand behind her mother's shoulder, but patiently hesitated from lifting her up. Her mother strained, barely lifting her body from the bed, then exhaled and relaxed onto the mattress again. Her breathing was labored, but she was still intent, and the next time she pushed herself up, Tomomi slipped her hand farther behind her back, placing it flat between the shoulder blades to support her. In slow motion, Tomomi helped her mother sit upright on the bed.

"How are you feeling, Mum? You have some energy today?" Tomomi asked in a calm but friendly tone, helping her mother swivel her heavy legs to the side of the bed. But her mother wasn't looking at her. She was hanging on tightly with both hands to the bed behind her, growing nervous and hesitant. The legs didn't seem to want to get up.

She tried again to will her body to move. Her hands gripped the bed as she tried to push herself forward, but her body wouldn't budge. Tomomi dropped her hand from her mother's back and stood back, watching at arm's length. "You're doing really well!" she chimed encouragingly. "Nearly there." But after another attempt, her mother gave a sigh of resignation.

"Hmm, it's a little tiring I suppose, huh? Maybe your energy is a little low today. We might try again after you've had a little more to eat, what do you say?" Tomomi's mother responded with a feeble, mumbled agreement. "I'm tired." Tomomi leaned into her mother's body, wrapping herself around the thin frame as she helped her to slowly recline back into bed again. "Maybe we can try to get up later. You did really well. Just need a little more rest."

Confident that her mother was settled in again, Tomomi returned to her housework. Tomomi didn't tell her mother that she could no longer walk. Indeed, her mother had not been able to walk since they returned from the hospital three months earlier. The afternoon dragged on, hot, humid, and heavy.

"I want to get up!"

The same voice called out again:

"I want to get up!"

"Okay, wait just a moment!" Tomomi stood and shuffled back to her mother's side. "How are you feeling?"

When Tomomi and I recalled this moment five months later, not long after her mother had died, she told me that it was one of the moments when she felt her mother was most alive:

> She didn't know any better, but she tried so hard to get up on her own. She really wanted to do it. I had to let her do that herself, to figure it out on her own. I couldn't tell her that she can't stand. I'd just say, "Maybe you have to eat something or rest," or something like that. I'd have my hand behind her [*she reaches behind me and places her palm on my back, leaning in close*], and she would try so hard. . . . Then she'd lie back down, and ten minutes later she would try again!

Tomomi smiled, but the tears were starting to well up along the bottom ridge of her eyes. Her voice wavered but didn't crack. "It would be like that all day long. I don't know how long . . ." Her voice trailed off. On the recording, I could hear the long pause open up and the soft music of the café drift in and fill it up, neither one of us feeling the need to say anything more.

Halfway around the world, in a hospital in England, I ran into Russell. He was off his crutches but still limping slightly from a bicycle accident a month earlier. Over the last ten years, Russell and his two younger brothers had been caring for their mother. I guessed by the humorless and expectant look on his face that he knew I was going to ask about her, and before I could say anything, he breathed out a sigh that seemed to drain the color from his face.

"My brothers and I are all at our end. We've been having [paid] carers come in, but we can't do it anymore. She can barely walk, barely speak, barely swallow."

A year earlier, when I had visited Russell in his mother's home, I saw that she was having trouble climbing the stairs unaided, and although her speech was stuttering and often left phrases incomplete, Russell could more or less figure out what she was trying to say. He installed a wet-room on the ground floor once it was clear his mother would no longer be able to use the upstairs bathroom, and later, paid carers started coming in every day to look after her. Now Russell and his brother were starting to feel that they had run out of options. "My brother said to me, we're relatively young guys, but we're living the life of an eighty-seven-year-old, you know? We're living *her* life. We move at her pace, we eat at her pace, we watch the same rubbish telly, we just sit there in silence because there's no more conversation. You're not caring for the person anymore, really. It's like a shell."

Although moving her to a nursing home could have relieved some of the burden, the cost would be considerable, and after they had already done so much, it felt like abandoning her in her last days. Russell and his brothers' decision was to hire a full-time in-home care professional.

"Twenty-four-hour care means that we get to be sons again," he said. "When you're washing your mum, you're not a son, you're a carer. When I do that I have to forget she's my mum. I just pretend she is someone else." We looked at each other for a long moment, not really waiting for the other to respond. I'm not sure who looked away first.

Fragile Resonance

Back at home, in front of my computer screen, I set these two episodes in front of me and read them over again. Each struck me as profoundly significant in the moment, fragments of life that went to the heart of what it means to care for an older family member today. Why did I feel these two moments were so worthy of reflection? What did they mean individually, and how did they relate to each other?

I made a few false starts at trying to address these questions, each time the strands of the argument falling apart again like the knot of a magician's rope. "Every carer's story is unique. No one has the same experience." I heard variations of this statement on countless occasions during my fieldwork, both in Japan and in England, and now they echoed in my head. I sensed the narratives resisting my efforts to draw analytical comparisons, each one exceeding the boundaries of cultural categories of difference, demanding that I pay attention to their singularity. As I continued to reread my notes and transcripts, delving deeper into the affective contours of each relationship, I moved further away from the impulse to find patterns, and closer to the sensation of resonance. There was an undeniable resonance between the stories of carers like Tomomi and Russell, just as there was a kind of resonance between the lives of the carers and the older family members they cared for.

Resonance describes the ways people relate to each other and the world even as they maintain their singularity; it is what makes care possible.[1] I began to follow these resonances: between the carer and the person being cared for (empathetic imagination); between carers and the cultural and historical worlds they inhabited (narrative resonance); and finally, the resonances between the experiences of carers and those of other carers across different cultural and historical contexts (cosmic resonance). Each layer of resonance presupposes an encounter that emerges from a relationship of fragility and openness between carers, care recipients, and the world, a fragility that is at once the precondition for tender, responsive care, and at the same time exposes carers to exhaustion and suffering.[2] It is in this quality of fragility that the lifeworlds of carers can help us understand our human condition and its future in an aging world that needs our care.

The first type of resonance describes the intimate, vulnerable, and mutually affecting relationship between specific carers and those whom they care for, the ways carers develop and hone their sensitivity, intuition, and responsiveness.[3] Medical anthropologist Arthur Kleinman, himself a carer for a spouse living with dementia, describes this care as "a *practice* of empathic imagination, responsibility, witnessing, and solidarity with those in great need" (Kleinman 2009, 293, emphasis mine). Only in the practice, the "actually doing it" (293), does care gradually reshape affective sensitivities, emotions, and selves, but practicing care for an older family member in this way is often difficult and exhausting. As the narratives of Tomomi and Russell illustrate, care might heighten feelings of tenderness and love, but it can just as likely plunge a carer into hopelessness and despair.

Narrative resonance emerges as carers come to reflect on their experiences as moral and meaningful, having a relationship to broader cultural values and structures. Narratives give a sense of order and coherence to the volatile encounters of empathetic imagination, patching together a quilt-work of personal memories, chance encounters, public discourses, and spiritual beliefs. Carers, many times in conversation with each other, find ways not only to accept and endure their responsibility, but also to question and challenge it. When these narratives present a horizon of the future, of emergence, hope, or transcendence, I refer to them as "counter-worlds."[4] Counter-worlds are not merely a means of escaping this world, but a vantage point from which new possible selves could take shape and be embodied forth. Historical and cultural narratives can also produce resonances with worlds that are haunted and ambivalent (Lepselter 2016), carrying traces of past trauma, desire, and power that reproduce inequalities. Counterworlds often formed in response to these forces, but carers found themselves regularly faced with ethical and existential challenges with no clear answers. Caring was a project of endurance and becoming, a form of life that Biehl and Locke (2017, 3) describe as "hovering on the verge of exhaustion while also harboring the potential for things to be otherwise."[5]

While most of the carers I spoke with rarely met another unpaid family carer who came from a different cultural background, a "cosmic resonance" shone through their narratives of fragile encounters. As my own research progressed, this transcultural, cosmic resonance of care became a frequent reassuring euphony. For example, midway through my research, I was invited to give a short presentation about care in Japan to an audience in England. The talk involved a discussion of the Japanese long-term care policy along with some of the stories of carers I had spoken with. After I had delivered the talk and returned to my seat, the Englishman next to me leaned over to whisper, "You've just told my story." Slightly stunned, I thanked him, unable to think of what else to say, but intuitively feeling that it was not exactly the right reaction. After all, I had not intended or expected this sort of response, and most likely the comment was less about my conceptual musings than it was about the feelings and experiences that spilled out of the ethnographic stories I shared. Nevertheless, the reaction was humbling, and it made me realize the importance of recognizing the ways cosmic resonance, like a tuning fork on a piano, amplifies the stories of carers without collapsing them into a singly unified narrative. This book asks what might we learn from this kind of resonance, and how might it help us to radically rethink the global future of care starting from stories and connections rather than from systems and institutions of social welfare.[6]

These three layers of resonance each capture the sense of transformation that arises out of the encounter with the familiar other, the sense of connecting or relating with a new urgency or intensity, to becoming open to possibility. At the same time, the world of human relationships is, as Jerome Bruner (1991, 4) succinctly phrased it, "rich and messy"; resonance also implies limitations, or modes of dissonance and alienation. In physical terms, resonating bodies vibrate in tune with each other while remaining separate, but only if they share a resonant frequency. In other words, resonance is not to be taken as an innate, given property of every relation, but rather it will be easier for some individuals to enact and find meaning in care if they are already predisposed toward caring (for example, because of earlier life experiences or close relationship with the cared-for). For others, resonance involves a long process of attunement and responsivity as they come to embody new habits and sensitivities.[7] It is just as important, then, to pay attention to the times when carers felt alienated from the noise of the world, out of step and tune with the care recipient, or with cultural narratives of care, or with other carers. The experience of dissonance, of feeling unable to live up to the way one thinks a carer ought to feel or behave, can bring about or rekindle feelings of guilt, frustration, isolation, and invisibility for carers. But as feminist and care ethics philosophers have pointed out, this dissonance is also critical for revealing points of inequality and injustice (Dalmiya 2009; Held 2006; Kittay 2019; Tronto 1993). Women caring for in-laws and husbands in Japan, for instance, often felt a strong ambivalence toward cultural expectations of female nurturance and self-sacrifice, and may seek ways to escape or to find agency elsewhere rather than strain to resonate with gendered expectations of their generational cohort.[8] Other carers found their sense of worth and ability thrown into doubt when their own messy experience "on the ground" clashed with the stiff, rationalized approach of health and social welfare bureaucracy. The individuals who shared their stories with me wrestled with these feelings, and most of them did, over time (sometimes abruptly), either find some new capacity to adapt or some alternate ways to care by involving others. Even for those who develop a sense of resonance, that resonance is fragile and uncertain, always in need of repair—no care is ever perfect. But for Tomomi, Russell, and the other carers I got to know over the course of researching for this book, imperfect resonance was transformative, meaningful, and enduring, even after the care had ended. To understand care as resonance, then, means following this process of transformation, while at the same time situating it within the broader social, historical, and political transformations that can enhance or dampen the resonance.

Summits and Paths

I was drawn to the stories of Tomomi and Russell because in many ways their stories resonated with each other. Both spoke of uncertainties and worries, everyday intimate moments of connection to and disjuncture from the one they cared for. Both felt a sense of isolation and emotional upending in the most intense periods of care, and found it agonizing to articulate these feelings to others. Yet despite these similarities, which arose in almost every carer's narrative, Tomomi and Russell would also try to place their experiences into terms that resonated with their respective cultural orientations. In this way, they seemed to illuminate and amplify the stories of other carers that I had been following in ways that brought the cultural dimensions of care into stronger relief.

The ways Tomomi described her care, returning to its physicality, as well as feelings of empathy, fatigue, endurance, transformation, and deep connection, were all themes that arose frequently when speaking to other carers in Japan—men and women, adult children and elderly spouses, those with religious affiliations and those without. Care was first of all a matter of empathetic bodily attunement requiring touch and proximity, and so Tomomi moved in with her mother for several months at a time while she provided care. Of course, closeness and attention to the body are not unique to care in Japan, and similar descriptions can be found in ethnographic accounts of care in Thailand (Aulino 2016, 2019), India (Brijnath 2014), and even among paid carers in the UK (Twigg 2000) and the US (Buch 2018). In some cases, anthropologists have given us phenomenological accounts of the physicality of this kind of empathetic care by describing their own participation in the acts of care (Aulino 2019; Gill 2020). The meanings and values attributed to such experiences, however, differ widely across these cultural contexts; the counter-worlds they initiated and the ways they offered a sense of existential security over the course of the caring relationship reflect the historical, material, and social worlds they are situated within.

Russell's description of caring for his mother brought dimensions of English culture and society to light. For Russell, unlike Tomomi, taking on more care tasks would have meant losing rather than enhancing his ability to maintain an intimate filial relationship, widening the gap or disrupting the resonance between mother and son. While Tomomi insisted her mother stay home and receive only brief visits from nurses, Russell and his brothers were willing to invest in twenty-four-hour care in order to "be sons again." Like Russell, several of the English carers of older family members whom I spoke with tended to downplay the importance of emotions and the body in giving good care, to the point of viewing them as disruptions to maintaining a responsible relationship with the cared-for. Instead, English carers tended to emphasize their role in incorporating and managing professional care services and maintaining the dignity and independence of the relative being cared for. Again, as I will describe, these dealings with care systems are not unique to English carers, nor do I wish to downplay their importance, both for the cared-for and for the carer. But once more, it was the meanings and values associated with the family management of this care work that were most pronounced across English carers' stories, preserving a sense of having a purposeful role and creating new possible worlds to inhabit when imagination and hope were running out.

Tomomi and Russell were not taking separate paths up the same mountain, so much as emerging from what seemed like the same forest to find themselves on different peaks. While describing the vista from each of these summits would lend itself to one kind of project of cultural comparison, it also runs the risk of simply reinforcing cultural stereotypes of "the Japanese" or "the English" carer. We would only see two seemingly separate positions and not the path that separates and connects them. This kind of comparison also risks rendering the stories of individuals like Tomomi and Russell as sterile and lifeless as organs laid out on a dissection table; as Daniel Linger (2010, 218) cautioned, "you pin your butterflies to the mat at the cost of their lives." The view from the summit misses what I argue is most important for understanding care as a process of responsive resonance: the *path*.[9] A view from the path makes it difficult not only to engage in systematic comparison, but also to make simple evaluations like "Which country takes better care of the elderly?" or "Is family care better than professional care?" (both of which I have been asked on several occasions when presenting this material). These are, I think, the wrong questions—questions from the summit, rather than from the path.

What would an anthropology from the path look like?[10] Tomomi and Russell navigated their separate journeys through cultural forests to reach a point where care made sense. Making sense did not mean a complete freedom from uncertainty or doubt, nor did it give them "resilience" (in some ways it may have rendered them more vulnerable). However, making sense did offer a way to read the forest, and to accept its mysterious twists and rambles. Most carers, Tomomi and Russell included, never felt they could clearly see where they were going, often feeling they might even be heading in the wrong direction—away from "good care" rather than toward it. Both Russell and Tomomi, in their own ways, responded to care in manners that would be considered resonant with their respective cultural contexts. Yet even so, both often found their decisions fraught with ethical complications, ambivalences, and uncertainties.

As they tried to articulate what being a carer meant to them, Tomomi and Russell also reflected on the world as they have found it transformed. These transformations were not only internal reappraisals of past selves or possible future selves (Parish 2008), but also transformations in relationships with "significant others" (Mead 1934), the community, and care institutions. As the world changed, gaps emerged between what they felt and experienced, the cultural expectations they perceived, and structures of governance. But carers like Tomomi and Russell endured, not simply because they managed the practical tasks of care, but because it was meaningful. *It mattered that they cared.*[11]

The everyday stories of carers described in this book tell us *how care comes to matter* (and why that matters), and in doing so have taught me about what it means to live with complex and difficult emotions, ethical choices, and relationships. For those reading this book who have experienced caregiving directly, or who have supported someone who cared for an older family member, these stories may offer both moments of resonance and a wider frame of social and cultural experience in which to locate their own singular experience of care.

Meaning-making, after all, cannot be a solitary endeavor, since it is about connecting, relating, belonging: telling one's own stories and the stories of others. Stories of family, care, aging, and death call on us to take notice because they are also our own stories, or, perhaps more precisely, they represent various versions of our own narrative possibilities (Jackson 2002; Mattingly 2008, 2010).

Dangerous Paths

One of the most iconic images of resonance is the virtuoso opera singer whose powerful soprano voice shatters the seemingly motionless glass at the crescendo of an aria (Pinchevski 2017). If resonance is what makes care possible, it also has the capacity to break a fragile body if sustained or intensified.

For carers who spend months or years looking after very dependent family members, sometimes with little help from other relatives or without adequate support from their community or welfare institutions, this effort to resolve the contradictions of care can feel like an unending struggle. Kleinman (2009, 293) writes that caring "sucks out strength and determination. It turns simple ideas of efficacy and hope into big question marks. It can amplify anguish and desperation. It can divide the self. It can bring out family conflicts. It can separate out those who care from those who can't or won't handle it. It is very difficult."

Like Kleinman, both Japanese and English carers I spoke with described the feeling of descending into a "dark place," or the shadow-side of caring. Some mentioned having had thoughts about killing themselves or killing the person they cared for, out of "mercy," exhaustion, or hopelessness. Even if they did not mention having these thoughts, when asked, nearly everyone I spoke to in Japan indicated that they could understand and empathize with that feeling. The properties of resonance apply equally to cultural stories of violence.

On July 26, 2016, Satoshi Uematsu, a former employee of the Tsukui Lilly Garden care facility, returned with a knife, stabbing and killing nineteen and badly wounding twenty-six disabled residents before he was arrested.[12] It was the worst mass killing in modern Japanese history. Two weeks later, I was drinking an ice-cold green-tea-flavored shake at a KFC in Kyoto, talking to a group of about half a dozen older women about care. When I mentioned the incident at the care home, everyone around the table agreed that it was horrible news. One by one they started to piece together what they remembered about it: the age of the attacker, his background, the circumstances of his firing, a history of hospitalization for mental illness. The sudden somber tone clashed with the bright, cheery surroundings of the shop and our sweet, colorful drinks. Then the youngest in the group, Fumi, who looked after her mother-in-law for six years until her death only a couple of months earlier, caught my attention:

> FUMI: When I hear those sorts of stories, I understand, because I have been there! Looking after my *obāsan*,[13] I would sometimes think those sorts of things. We all have. I get it. You think about what it would be like if [you could] make them die. It's either her or me [I would think], because it is just too hard.
>
> DANELY: But then you have to change the way you feel?
>
> FUMI: Right, you have to change your feeling. It is a matter of controlling those thoughts when they come.
>
> TAKAKO: I have to get out in order to change my feelings. I have to get out and just like this, talk to someone else!
>
> ETSUKO: That's right, I can't talk about this with anyone else. You talk to a stranger, and it's no good.
>
> TAKAKO: It's really bothersome to the listeners [*kiku hō ni meiwaku*]. If you don't have the experience [of caring], you can't understand.
>
> ETSUKO: Right, the only people who understand are other people who have done [care]!

As each of the women voiced her feelings, building a common narrative identity, they voiced both horror and resonance. They found themselves in the violent thoughts that emerge from the "dark side of empathy" (Bubandt and Willerselv 2015) and a counter-world of sympathetic fellow carers who could change those feelings. In Japan, "care murders" (*kaigo satsujin*) are estimated to account for one in ten cases of homicide, or an average of about one every two weeks (Mainichi Shinbun 2016; Shimada 2016; Yuhara 2017). Carer exhaustion (*kaigo tsukare*) is considered the leading reason for suicides among people over sixty (Hamada 2009).

While data on "care homicide" is not available for England, it is known that older people are the victims of about one in four domestic homicides, an average of one every nine days (Bows 2019). Over half these incidents occurred in homes occupied by both the victim and perpetrator (most often a spouse), who may have been a carer as well. This is not limited to Japan and England; one study found that in Australia, 26 percent of family carers of people with dementia had thoughts of homicide, while another study found that about one in six carers had contemplated suicide (O'Dwyer, Moyle, Taylor, et al. 2016 and O'Dwyer, Moyle, Zimmer-Gembeck, et al. 2016). These numbers might seem alarming, but they are consistent with decades of research on "carer burden" showing that carers are more vulnerable to physical harm, mental distress, financial hardships, and social isolation (Carmichael and Ercolani 2016; Pinquart and Sorensen 2003; Schulz and Beach 1999; Schulz and Sherwood 2008; Roth et al. 2009). Even those who place a relative in full-time residential care homes continue to experience high levels of stress, including depression, guilt, anger, and loss of self (Boekhurst et al. 2008, 761). The carers I spoke with while researching this book taught me that it doesn't take much of a push for ordinary people, even those who used professional care services or drew on other sources of support, to fall over the edge. They lost jobs or partners, had frequent conflicts with family members, and experienced a variety of health problems (mental and emotional). Care is an undertaking that, at times, offers the most majestic views of human love and compassion, but look down, and you realize you're also standing at the precipice.

Despite evidence on care murder and suicide, there has been little research that looks to the stories of carers for insights on why most continue to care despite the dangers it poses. What can we say about the lives behind the numbers, not just as isolated cases, but as participants in a social and cultural world, who resonate with its meanings and stories? What is the relationship between the way care awakens a profound sense of meaning on the one hand, and the way it produces such tragic situations on the other? Concepts like "compassion fatigue," which has been applied mainly to staff working in professional health care settings rather than unpaid carers, suggest that good carers simply get worn down. While Fumi and the other women at the KFC would likely agree that fatigue can deepen the darkness, they would also add that when your body and mind are empathetically resonating deeply with someone who is suffering, someone who nobody else seems to care about, ending that suffering has a feeling of logic to it. The more you become vulnerable and open to the care recipient, the more responsive you can be to that person's needs, but also, the closer you may be to harming yourself or the care recipient. It is not the lack of compassion that is dangerous, but rather its excess.

Dangerous compassion describes how care and suffering become mutually entangled in ways that enhance carers' ability to respond and to be responsible while at the same time rendering them dangerously exposed to harm. As one Japanese social care worker told me, "Care and violence are two sides of the same coin." Each contains the other, and it is this entanglement that makes care both a moral practice and a meaningful one. Kleinman (2006, 10) argued that what makes life matter (what is moral and meaningful) is precisely the ways we define ourselves against a dangerous world.

This sentiment is echoed in Rev. Martin Luther King Jr.'s (1968) "I've Been to the Mountaintop" speech, delivered to striking city sanitation workers in Memphis, Tennessee. In his speech, King paints a picture of a global struggle before rallying his audience with a call to "develop a kind of dangerous unselfishness."

The phrase provides a hinge between the secular political message of the first half and the spiritual second half. To illustrate this notion of dangerous selfless-ness, King invoked the Christian parable of the Good Samaritan, whose actions epitomize selfless love for the "undeserving" other (an enemy, hurt, alone, poor). King's use of this cultural narrative of care to create resonant imaginaries of solidarity and social justice is powerful: the story reaches out to us, and we place our hands on the one who suffers and realize that suffering as our own (Zimmermann 2015). The mutual vulnerability of care is dangerous, but King's narrative of the Good Samaritan suggests a way of being that makes this danger *meaningful*, such that its moral value is enhanced by its vulnerability. Later in King's speech, he recounts a previous attempt on his life, which he barely sur-vived, driving home the message that a moral life must accept its exposure to danger (indeed he was assassinated the day following the speech). Yet for King, such a life also transcended danger; he had "been to the mountaintop" and "seen the Promised Land." Stories open up our capacity for such utopic visions, or counter-worlds that help us to see ourselves and our world in ways impossible to imagine otherwise (Jackson 2002), ways to endure the exposure to the existential danger of caring.

Researching Care Ecologies

The research undertaken for this book came in two stages: an initial ten-month intensive fieldwork residence in Kyoto (2013–2014), followed by eighteen months of attending carer events and conducting interviews with carers in England (2015–2017). I made an additional one-month follow-up visit to Kyoto midway through my research in England (2016), during which time I was able to ask more-focused questions arising in response to topics brought up in discussions with the English carers. The resulting balance between field sites is admittedly uneven. Immersive fieldwork in Japan afforded many more opportunities to observe a variety of care settings, participate in various volunteer activities, and build strong rapport with carers. Fieldwork in England was mainly conducted through one-on-one interviews and a few interactions with carer groups and members of the local authority. While interviews with the English sample were open-ended, they were also steered toward points made by Japanese carers I had already interviewed, so the content was more focused and originally intended mainly as a foil for the Japanese carers, similar to Lock's (1993) comparative study of menopause in Japan and North America.

While the overall sample size and regional distribution were too limited to provide a representative picture of the variety of experiences of the millions of unpaid informal carers in each of these countries, the in-depth case studies and observations yielded hundreds of hours of rich accounts of often profoundly intimate yet ordinary moments in my informants' personal lives.

Stage I: Fieldwork in Japan

Exploring what care means and how it is practiced in Japan means tracing the ways individuals link the familiar rhythms of local informal structures of kinship and community to modern, marketized, and techno-scientific systems of social welfare, insurance, and health care. As a city where deeply rooted social values and structures of urban modernity not only coincide but constantly interact and affect each other, Kyoto is an ideal site for observing how the different facets of care come together in contemporary Japan.[14]

My first task was to build relationships with the people my family and I would be living alongside on a day-to-day basis. I announced the topic of my research to anyone who would listen, whether that was the local self-governing association, the parents of my children's classmates, the owners of local cafés, or my neighbors outside their homes watering their potted flowers. It wasn't long before I was disabused of the notion that carers would be eager to share their homes and feelings the moment an anthropologist landed in their midst. Kyotoites, especially those whose family connection to the city runs several generations deep, are known for their insularity and guardedness toward "outsiders," which to those unaccustomed to local etiquette might be misinterpreted naively as polite generosity, or cynically as cold aloofness. The sort of fieldwork I hoped to carry out could only work with the interest and cooperation of my interlocutors, so I set to work on the slow, patient practice of attempting each day to start a conversation, chipping here and there at the façade, searching for cracks and fissures that might allow me to glimpse something beyond the surface. Sometimes a spontaneous chat became a regular conversation, or led to introductions to other carers or invitations to join small carer groups.

Carers have busy, irregular schedules, so finding a time to have a one-hour conversation could take weeks of regular phone calls. Even after months of regular contact or introductions from friends, it proved difficult to establish trust (*najimu*). By the end of my ten-month period of fieldwork, I had spoken with over one hundred Japanese carers or recently bereaved post-carers, twenty-five of whom I recorded more in-depth one-to-one interviews with. Most of the people I interviewed were individuals I had spoken to over several occasions and with whom I shared several acquaintances, so they were happy to participate in more lengthy private interviews or to allow me to visit their home or observe moments of care. In addition to the unpaid carers, I interviewed eleven paid, or formal, carers (nine of whom also had a personal history of unpaid care for a family member) in a range of occupations including a geriatric nurse, care home directors, day service staff, care managers, and social workers.

Although it was challenging to get to know individuals, I was immediately welcomed to participate in the activities of two local volunteer groups that ran activities for older community residents, especially those living alone. Both groups were managed by a small core group of about six local women. One group prepared and delivered freshly cooked meals to homebound or solo-dwelling older adults. The other group met once each month to run craft activities, exercise sessions, and musical practice for around a dozen older men and women (only a couple of men would attend each session). I participated in both groups every month, making conversation as I peeled apple skins or glued felt shapes onto Christmas ornaments shoulder-to-shoulder with the volunteers and older participants. The groups proved to be not only an excellent means of getting to understand the motivations and backgrounds of the volunteers, but also an opportunity to hear the community welfare gossip, as older individuals joined or dropped out of the groups. Interestingly, most of the volunteers lived locally and worked in the formal care sector as well.

Locally based volunteer groups and community leaders tended to focus their efforts on older people who lived alone and lacked regular informal care support from family (Danely 2019), so meeting carers took some additional effort. After getting to know the local groups, I was given introductions to several paid carers, who in turn invited me to join carer support groups that they facilitated. These support groups were structured meetings where attendees would state their basic information, provide updates on themselves and the cared-for, and ask for advice from the facilitators. All facilitators had professional qualifications either as social workers, geriatric nurses, or other formal care staff. Some of the carers who attended these meetings participated in informal groups as well, and invited me to come and talk to members there. In contrast to the more formal support groups, informal groups were loosely organized around a core group of current or recently bereaved carers, and participants conversed freely over food and drink, sometimes sharing practical information or venting frustrations related to caring, but at other times simply chatting and enjoying the relaxed company of others and the break from care.

In addition to neighborhood contacts and support groups, I volunteered once or twice a week at a local day service center (adult day care), where I was able to interact more frequently with service users who still lived in the community. Most of these elderly individuals attended the day service center once or twice a week, providing respite for an unpaid carer. Many also lived alone, and some lived with a spouse who required more advanced care. Although I was unable to conduct lengthy interviews, either because of the limitations of the environment or the health or cognitive limitations of the clients, I served meals, aided in leisure activities, made conversation, and gently supported mobility for individuals who needed assistance (some of whom, to my surprise, were carers themselves). Since unpaid family carers frequently used formal respite care services or eventually moved the person they cared for to a residential care home facility, I also toured three other day service facilities as well as different types of residential care homes (*shokibōtakinō* and *tokubetsu yōgo rōjin hōmu*), speaking to residents and conducting interviews with staff when possible.

Because the interviewees, whose stories interweave the fabric of this book, were selected from a range of different encounters over the course of fieldwork, they included men and women from a range of socioeconomic, occupational, and religious backgrounds. In terms of age and relationship to the care recipient, they were evenly split between adult children (most in their fifties and sixties) and spouses (most in their eighties and nineties). Twelve had provided care for more than one older adult, such as parents and in-laws, in-laws and spouse, or parents and spouse. For some, this meant taking on caring responsibilities without cease for more than two decades as relatives developed disabilities and care needs in overlapping succession. Only one interviewee was a young carer of a grandparent. Even for those who had only cared for one older relative, it was not unusual for the length of care to last between five and ten years (though it can be difficult for informal carers to pinpoint when care begins, particularly when they already co-reside or live in a mutually supportive relationship).

All the Japanese carers I interviewed provided some form of regular personal care (e.g., changing, feeding, bathing, toilet assistance, or changing diapers) in addition to other forms of companionship, financial support, and health assistance. Given how extensive and time-consuming these responsibilities were, the majority of family carers I interviewed were not working while caring, and those who did work were either self-employed or working part-time in service-sector positions (including three who worked in elderly care). While I did not collect details of socioeconomic status or class, based on a general appraisal of homes and details of education and prior employment, I estimate that around five of my key informants could be categorized as upper or upper-middle class, while the majority were from middle- or working-class backgrounds.

Each interview took place in Japanese and in a quiet environment where the person being cared for was not in the room. This was often the carer's home, but we also met at cafés, or found a private room after support group meetings. In order to give myself a better sense of processes and transformations in carers' lives as they developed and fine-tuned resonances, my interviews followed a basic narrative structure: I asked what life was like *before* becoming a carer, what caring was like at *present*, and what they anticipated things would be like in the *future*.[15] As the conversation progressed, I encouraged carers to elaborate on any instances that seemed important to them. Within this framework, narratives mapped the paths carers took, including the dead-ends and dangerous curves. The chapters of this book do not follow any one carer's timeline of care, but rather they represent places of resonance within those lines, places where the carers' stories spoke together, yet each in their own voice (Rosa 2019).

Stage II: Fieldwork in England and Return to Japan

Following fieldwork in Japan, I had originally planned to conduct comparative work in the United States, but as luck would have it, I accepted a new position based in Oxford, England, and adapted this plan to this new setting. The move proved to be fortuitous, as the many similarities between the two countries made them a much better match for comparison than Japan and the US. There were also far fewer cross-cultural studies of Japanese and English practices and attitudes toward informal care, so again, here was an opportunity to add something fresh to the conversation. In cooperation with one of the county councils in southern England, I recruited and interviewed fifteen carers, including three who were bereaved within the year prior to our meeting. Of this group, four were selected for two additional interviews scheduled at roughly six-month intervals in order to get a better sense of how their experiences changed as the health of the cared-for declined.

I initially recruited participants by circulating information about the research through an email list for a local carer support group, but I subsequently recruited additional carers through introductions at a carer support conference, through introductions from the county council, and through personal networks. While I did live and work in Oxford at the time of conducting interviews, and attended several events and formal support groups for carers, I did not volunteer or participate in the world of carer support services to the same extent that I could while conducting fieldwork in Japan. The focus instead was to collect personal narratives using the same format I used in Japan, to listen, learn, and follow the fragile resonances.

Two years after the close of my initial fieldwork in Japan, I spent one month reconnecting with research participants and their families in Kyoto. During this trip, I was able to return to several support groups, volunteer associations, and individuals to see how things had changed since we had last spoken. In the interim, four of the carers I spoke to previously had experienced the death of the person they cared for. This follow-up was crucial for my understanding of resonance as both fragile *and* durable, situated spontaneous responsiveness and deep moral commitments. While little had changed in terms of the broader social care regime, the carers seemed to have changed dramatically.

I was able to share some of my thoughts about the English care system with friends and informants in Japan. A few offered their opinions about which country was doing things better, but the majority agreed that the core of the stories of carers in England were not too different from those in Japan. There was something recognizable in the pull of responsibility, the frustrations navigating the health and welfare bureaucracy, and the arguments with other family members over care decisions. While cosmic resonance between carers in Japan and England was striking to me, when presented with specific scenarios from each country, carers were also likely to emphasize cultural differences, especially negative perceptions of the other country that were guided by preexisting generalizations. The extent to which carers in England used formal services, such as live-in carers, surprised some of the Japanese carers, and seemed to support their impressions of the value of autonomy in English culture. English carers seemed disturbed by what they saw as Japanese "codependency" and explained to me that some care responsibilities were best handled by professionals. As with Tomomi and Russell, the point of cultural difference seemed to focus primarily on the position the carer held between the limits and possibilities for resonance afforded by the state and the family.

Despite the impressions of my informants (which may say more about how they think about their own culture than the culture they are commenting on),[16] when I returned to the interviews and notes, I could not make such an easy distinction between Japan and England. Using care as a method, I did not try to explain away individuals, nor did I assume that what mattered most to them was always fully articulated in the thick stories they told (Das 1997; Kleinman 2009). Sometimes the meaning of care resided in the pauses, silences, and elisions.

Keeping the focus on the immediate tasks at hand was one way carers managed to keep a sense of narrative intact, but these narrow temporal borders would inevitably be challenged once again when the situation changed. When this happened, carers would reflect again on why they continued to do what they did, on the meaning and value of caring. For someone who has spent years engaged in care, leaving work or giving up other responsibilities along the way, the feeling that the needs of the cared-for might exceed one's capacity for caring can be very difficult to handle. The subjective experience of care has a force that constantly overflows its cultural narrative. It slips away even as it is seized by it again. It creates gaps between the individual and the social even as it attempts to resonate across other gaps: between carer and cared-for, between family and social welfare system, between an accumulated history of meanings and the immediate feelings in care. Casting one's vision beyond this moment to catch care again in some meaningful narrative often meant imagining a horizon beyond the tangle of the forest.

1

CULTURAL ECOLOGIES OF CARE

Cultural gardens have living selves in them, who slyly, stubbornly, painfully, inescapably make themselves present in their own lives. They seek some adequate response to whatever the world offers them, some way they can define self, be, live, respond, go on.

Steven Parish, *Subjectivity and Suffering in American Culture*

What better time to be thinking about narratives of care than in the midst of the COVID-19 pandemic, a global health emergency that has revealed so much to us about the fragility of our social policies and institutions meant to support older people and those who care for them (Badone 2021; Caduff 2020; Cohen 2020; Taylor 2020)?[1] Yet, even while I was conducting my fieldwork in the years before COVID-19 emerged, global population aging was already causing what Woodward (2009) calls a "statistical panic" of our media-saturated culture. Demographers predict that globally, between 2000 and 2050, the number of people eighty years and older will have quadrupled to 395 million (WHO 2021), and while many of these older men and women would be hale and hearty for many years to come, there has been little indication that the model of "successful aging" has reduced age-related dependence, frailty, or disability requiring some kind of care (Lamb, Robbins-Ruszkowski, and Corwin 2017; Rubinstein and Medeiros 2014).[2] Scenarios like these generate an atmosphere of "care crisis," not only because of a shortage of paid care workers, but also because more people than ever before in human history will take on the responsibility of unpaid care (Bunting 2020; Dowling 2021). As modern institutional care has become displaced by the liberal paradigm of "aging in place" in "age-friendly communities" (Stafford 2018), family carers find themselves organizing and managing an increasing array of home-based services or providing care directly when formal care is inadequate (Glendinning 2012). In both Japan and England, confinement of elderly people in residential care homes has been replaced by increased isolation in the community (Danely 2019). Care, it seems, is in short supply.

But what if we have the story of care all wrong? The narrative of "apocalyptic demography" (Martin-Matthews 2000) that has intensified in the dystopian spectacle of COVID-19, may call urgent attention to genuine concerns, but it also oversimplifies the complex picture of the lifeworlds of carers and those they care for (Baraitser and Brook 2021).[3] When we listen to the ways carers narrate their own experiences, it becomes clear that the narrative of the care crisis, reinforced by a steady stream of research on the dangers of carer "burden" (Zarit, Reever, and Bach-Peterson 1980) is incomplete. What carers' stories give voice to is a vital space-between where the everyday ethical work of care is enacted and where selves are transformed. The stories carers tell about their lives reveal processes that, over time, generate meaning: a sense of human connection, the emergence of new sensitivities and desires to care, a profound humility in the face of dying, a deep embodied sense of the sorrow of love. Then there is everything carers struggle to make sense of: uncertainty, loneliness, frustration, and hopelessness—complex existential states and emotions that are too often flattened by measures of "burden" or discourses of crisis. These stories keep care close to the ground of experience, while simultaneously expanding horizons of possibility; they take us back to the path.

Building a theory of care from the path, from the twists and turns of individual stories and their dramas of resonance, from the dangers and discoveries of care, means recognizing the cultural ecosystem, teeming with life, that envelops the trail. At times, this provides clues to what comes next, like the way the air feels just before a storm, but often it presents itself, much like this book, as an unruly "thicket of difficulties" (Levinas [1961] 2003, 29). The narratives carers offer from deep within the forest of day-to-day caring all tell us something about how to survive in a world that depends on caring for each other. They reveal life stripped down to bare essentials, to the immediate encounter and spontaneous responsiveness to another person's embodied presence. Yet, the stories of carers like Tomomi and Russell, who introduced the book, also show us that the care ecosystem extends beyond the inter-subjective and inter-corporeal dyadic engagement between the carer and the cared-for; they also include histories and cultural symbols that provide a narrative scaffolding for carers to make sense of their experience.

Stories become embodied in lived experiences, just as feelings loop back into meaningful narratives.[4] Because the situations of the carer and cared-for are always changing, the iterative process of meaning-making is never finished, even after the care recipient dies. Instead, carers' stories recruit new resources, images, relationships, metaphors, and memories. As this collage is patched together, the act of meaning-making itself can become a moral project of self-reflection, gratitude, forgiveness, and transcendence. Carers enact care in ways that make sense to them culturally and aesthetically, that is, as a feeling for the good in their situation, their context. The contextual differences between life in Japan and life in England meant carers' feelings sometimes led to very different ethical decisions: Tomomi sought a more intimate, engrossing, sympathetic sense of being-with her mother, while Russell hoped that employing professional services would allow him to "be a son" again. This difference is more than a distinction between so-called "collectivist" and "individualist" notions of personhood, but rather, I suspect, it is the result of the historical and cultural shaping of the meaning of care itself.

Before exploring these differences further, let us begin by defining care in more general terms. While some anthropologists have argued for a simple definition of care as "providing for others" (Arnold and Aulino 2021), my approach has been inspired by the more elaborate yet widely cited definition used by care ethicist Joan Tronto (1993, 103), who writes that care is "everything that we do to maintain, continue and repair 'our world' so that we can live in it as well as possible. The world includes our bodies, our selves, and our environment, all of which seek to interweave in a complex life-sustaining web." Tronto's definition establishes a way for thinking of care beyond the limits of specific care institutions, and opens the possibility of care that arises out of the everyday, ordinary practices. More importantly, it allows us to pay better attention to variations in the *relationships* that constitute an ecological "life-sustaining web" of the world, reminding us that the way differences are constituted depends on historically and culturally situated "bodies, selves, and environment." Care might not always look as we expect it, as normative assumptions or intentions to enact ideal care do not always produce their intended results.[5] In every case, then, Tronto's definition must be accompanied by a rigorous questioning of what is meant by "life" and "the world" and how these might enhance or create friction with each other (Puig de la Bellacasa 2012, 2017).

Tronto's definition helps us to see the world as fragile, in need of careful handling, maintenance, and repair. What I observed, and what carers typically described as care, was not a perfect ideal of "good care," but an ongoing process that revealed the wisdom of "good enough" care (Mol, Moser, and Pols 2010, 13). Dr. Hayakawa, a ninety-year-old Japanese physician I spoke with, described the best care as "*ē kagen*," or "just the right amount" in the local dialect. But Dr. Hayakawa's choice of phrase also contained a sly wink. Colloquially, "*ē kagen*" is also used to describe actions that are overly casual, careless, or sloppy. To Dr. Hayakawa the best care is also, paradoxically, imperfect. Seeing my confusion when he used the term, Dr. Hayakawa explained that the skill of the physician lay in the messy (*ē kagen*) adjustment of "dosage" (*sashi kagen*), based not only on his expert knowledge of a medicine's chemical properties, but also on an intimate sense of each patient's individual history and lifestyle. Messy though it may be, the doctor understood that there was an art to caring that is easily lost in modern clinical interactions, an art that used the experienced physician's attention to *sympathy* as a valid form of knowledge about the suffering of another person and about the nature of illness (Soto-Rubio and Sinclair 2018, 1429). Such knowledge is not without faults, but nor for that matter are other forms of so-called evidence-based measurement and assessment approaches when applied to people's lived experiences. Despite the "evidence," in practice, rigid definitions of good or bad care can break down. Dr. Hayakawa's "*ē kagen*" is what Mol (2008, 12) calls a process of "tinkering": persevering through the process of making mistakes, recalibrating, and trying again and again. As carers tinker with solutions to care, they pull the weave of their stories tighter, making them less prone to unraveling when carrying the heavy weight of responsibility and commitment that ongoing care demands.

When Japanese and English carers spoke about the dangerous cliff edges and endless lonely shores of care, their stories revealed the weight of responsibility, endurance, grief, and love. The ways carers contemplated or enacted these ways of being-with-others were themes that ran throughout their stories, and something I try to convey through this book, by juxtaposing one story and another, finding points of resonance and divergence.[6] Since caring for older family members is such a fundamental part of our human story, it was easy for me to see the commonalities across cultures and societies as I began this research. Yet everywhere, carers and those they care for create worlds together that draw on cultural narratives in ways that make their experiences meaningful and moral and, as Steven Parish poetically observes in the epigraph, to "live, respond, go on." Differences between Japan and England emerged as I looked more closely at the ways individuals chose certain moments as meaningful or when a decision with moral implications had to be made. Whether carers chose to follow normative cultural patterns or find another way, their stories provided a glimpse into the influence of local cultural histories and environments. Through practice, carers became woven into more complex stories of personhood, relatedness, and the life-course rooted in culture. When it comes to this process, Japanese and English carers seemed to have different stories to tell.

Difference and Doing Good

In 2018, I spent some time living in Tokyo, where I volunteered each Saturday morning at the Catholic Missions of Charity in the middle of an area known as San'ya, in the northeast corner of the city. If there is one neighborhood in Tokyo where you are most likely to find an abundance of human suffering, it would be San'ya. For centuries, San'ya has been a refuge for outcasts (*eta*), criminals, foreigners, the destitute, and various categories of "nonpersons" (*hinin*) (Fowler 1996, 35–40). Today, the few young people one sees in San'ya are likely to be care workers employed by one of the many nonprofit charity organizations that have sprung up there in last few decades. Most of the once-thriving day-labor market has dried up, and former laborers—mostly single men with no assets, estranged from their families—now live off a small pension, disability allowance, or social security (*seikatsu hogo*).

Each Saturday, volunteers at the Missions of Charity cooked and distributed rice and curry to around 350 impoverished and unstably housed men, whom we all referred to as *ojisan* ("old-timers"). After volunteering at the charity for only a month, I was already becoming comfortable with the lively fellowship and hospitality among the volunteers. While peeling potatoes or packaging meals, we moved efficiently, but we also laughed and made small talk as we worked. Despite the friendliness among the volunteers, however, I was initially surprised at how few of these volunteers interacted with the *ojisan* in a similar way. When I asked the other volunteers about this, some explained that they didn't want to make the work too personal. Doing so, they felt, would take away from the larger spiritual purpose. As one volunteer put it, the satisfaction of charity was less about volunteers making the *ojisan* happy, and more about trying to "make God happy." To remind ourselves of this, we would intone Mother Teresa's prayer together each morning before departing for the food distribution point, reciting that if the Lord so wished, he would use our hands to reach out to the poor, and use our hearts to love them.

On one of my last weeks before returning to England, I invited a Japanese Buddhist friend of mine, Toshi, to volunteer with me for one of the Saturday morning meal distributions. Toshi was eager at first but quickly grew uncomfortable by the atmosphere of the charity, telling me, "We [Buddhists] do some similar work for the public good, but in our case, all of the preparation would be done silently, like a training practice [*shugyō*]. Then, when we distribute the food, we would want to try to touch the heart [*kokoro to fureai*] of the other person [by talking with them]—this is completely different!"

What Toshi referred to as "training practice" is a Buddhist tradition of self-cultivation through ascetic discipline (Schattschneider 2003, 2).[7] This could include a range of practices, from chanting, seated meditation, pilgrimage, or, in this case, the care of those in need. Although these practices are varied, what links all of them together is the subjugation of the ego through focused attention and openness in the present moment. The expression "touching their hearts" implies the realization of a kind of mutuality, or interdependence made possible through such discipline: touching collapses physical and emotional distance such that one cannot easily distinguish between touching the other and being touched by the other (Nozawa 2015, 383; Tahhan 2014, 15). Touching hearts, then, is a kind of sympathetic, affective resonance with another's feeling.

The difference between Buddhist and Catholic volunteers, according to Toshi, was not a difference in the moral value of giving food to those who were hungry. It was a difference in the way one thinks about how care ought to be embodied and the mood or atmosphere (*kūkan*) it should create (Böhme 2016; Miura 2017; Throop 2014). For Toshi, this included the feelings attended to during the careful preparation of the food, as well as the feelings of compassion that arose from the careful attention to the care recipient. The Catholic charity workers, in contrast, distanced their personal feelings from their acts of care. They considered this a form of humility before god, from whose grace this pure gift was passed. This is not to say that feelings of compassion did not motivate their charitable acts, but only that within a typically Buddhist cultural context, the moral value of giving is found most importantly in the cultivation of a compassionate self through ascetic practice and the intersubjective encounter with the care recipient.

What this anecdote suggested to me was that one axis by which we might distinguish care in Japan from that in England is that of *compassion* and *charity*.[8] In everyday vernacular, these two terms overlap so much as to be nearly interchangeable. Even in anthropological work, charity, at least in Christian contexts, is seen as the "implementation of compassion" (Elisha 2008, 156) or as something "underpinned by a utopian ethic of 'doing good,' . . . aimed at improvement, compassion, and intervention" (Trundle 2014, 15). Both compassion and charity usually entail a common palette of social and moral feelings and experiences: kindness, generosity, altruism, pity, empathy, tenderness, mercy, and love. Both might function to facilitate group identity, belonging, trust, and cohesion through sharing, commitment, and cooperation. Compassion and charity both imply a level of care that goes beyond normal boundaries of state- or kin-provisioned care, in ways that can make the difference between life and death for many isolated, frail, or disabled older men and women. However, I will argue that compassion and charity are examples of symbolically rich ecological configurations of care, which also guide experiences of carers looking after family. These different configurations bring together historical and cultural narratives, as well as the affective intensities and moral moods that afforded distinct resonances for different carers.

Compassion: Caring with Mutual Fragility

The English word "compassion" foregrounds the role of strong emotion: "-*passion*," which is derived from the Latin *pati* ("suffering") as well as the Greek *paschein* ("feeling"). This feeling is modified by "*com-*" ("together"). Compassion is therefore often defined first as "*emotions* of concern for the suffering of another" (Trundle 2014, 135, emphasis mine). In this way, compassion bears close association with empathy, sympathy, love, and pity (in the Aristotelian sense) (Nussbaum 1996; Snow 1991; Woodward 2002). Others have argued that it is not sufficient to end the definition there. Compassion also must be a sense of shared suffering that *motivates* one to alleviate the suffering of and/or provide well-being for another (Berlant 2004, 20; Gilbert 2017, 4; Schulz et al. 2007; Spikins 2015). Philosopher Steve Bein (2013, 88) refers to this two-part composition of compassion as a "moment of attentiveness and a moment of will."

The emotional aspect of compassion, the way of "co-feeling" with the suffering person, causes an unrest in our souls that can only be tended to by extending care. This suggests a close connection between our capacities for certain empathetic, affect-laden responses to others and our moral judgments that arise from this. Some have argued that compassion must also emerge from our uniquely acute human capacity for empathy and storytelling (De Waal 2011; Spikins 2015, 2017; Tomasello 2009). This emphasis on feeling and empathy is also common across the literature on the evolutionary biosocial basis for compassion (Goetz, Keltner, and Simon-Thomas 2010; Singer and Klimecki 2014) as well as psychological and philosophical work on the subject (Bein 2013; Gilson 2014; Nussbaum 1996; Porter 2006; Schloßberger 2019; Shulz et al. 2007; Soto-Rubio and Sinclair 2018). Many Euro-American psychologists and philosophers continue to debate the extent to which we can "share" feelings (Decetey and Svetlova 2012; Zahavi and Rochat 2015) or whether emotional empathy helps or hinders the ability to enact good care (Bloom 2017; De Zulueta 2015; Schloßberger 2019). Few researchers, however, have explicitly considered Buddhist perspectives on compassion, which emphasize not only the importance of suffering and concern, but also the dissolution of the boundaries of the self through acts of attention, affection, and somatic attunement to the other (Bein 2013; Lo 2014; H. Nakamura [1954] 2010).

When my Buddhist friend Toshi mentioned the way charity could be considered "training" (*shugyō*), he was referring to another aspect of Buddhist compassion that blurs the distinction between the compassionate feelings and compassionate acts. From a Buddhist perspective, compassion is always "interactive," without a subject or object (Halifax and Byock 2008, 40); compassion realizes this non-duality of being by cultivating "intimate spaces beyond consolation or assistance" (10). In other words, compassionate subjectivity produces and is produced in practice; carer and cared-for realize their mutuality of being such that there is no difference between caring for self and for others.[9] The practice of preparing food for the poor, then, could become a space of silent contemplation that transforms the sensory practice of peeling potatoes into an experience of mindful awareness of one's own experiences of corporeal vulnerability or dependence.[10] For the Buddhist, the heart must first be prepared for the act of care through practices of attention that heighten the openness to the care-recipient in ways that will produce embodied connection (*fureai*).

In Japanese, the term that best approximates the concept of "compassion" is *jihi*, a word formed by conjoining two ideographic characters that, taken separately, convey the virtues of "love" (*itsukushimi*) and "suffering" (*kanashimi*).[11] Steve Bein (2013, 89), who traces Buddhist compassion to the original Pāli language terms, describes the combination of these two characters as the "confluence of *karuna* with *metta*," sympathy (toward suffering) and loving-kindness (a motivation to remove suffering) respectively. To embody *jihi* is thus to have a disposition of openness and care toward a world rooted in suffering.[12] The ambivalence, or "shadow side" of care, already appears embedded in the term itself, which brings together seemingly contradictory feelings (love and suffering) and recognizes the ways they both entail a breakdown of the self, rendering it powerless, given over to the loved one. It may be slightly redundant, then, to refer to "dangerous compassion," since in Japanese, danger is already implied in the cultural context of the term.[13]

In everyday speech, however, Japanese people rarely used the Buddhist term *jihi*, unless it was to describe exceptional circumstances of extending care for more distant others (the destitute poor, sick animals, etc.). Instead, they were more likely to use the common expression "*omoiyari*." Anthropologist Takie Lebra (1976, 38) wrote that *omoiyari* was so important that she felt "tempted to call Japanese culture an "*omoiyari* culture." Lebra defined *omoiyari* as "the ability and willingness to feel what others are feeling, to vicariously experience the pleasure or pain they are undergoing, and to help them satisfy their wishes. Kindness or benevolence becomes *omoiyari* only if it is derived from such sensitivity to the recipient's feelings. The ideal in *omoiyari* is for Ego to enter into Alter's *kokoro*, 'heart' and to absorb all information about Alter's feelings without being told verbally" (38). The term *omoiyari* merges two verbal nouns—"thinking/considering" and "doing/giving"—not just thinking about doing something, but doing thoughtfully, carefully, in a state of concern. For example, one Japanese carer described caring as a process of "making an effort to really deeply attend to the other person. To see—not 'see,' but *coordinate* with the other person, guessing 'what should I do about this or that?' Trying to look into their heart [*kokoro mite miru*]. And you might get it all wrong, but as that experience accumulates, [that coordination] becomes more part of you." In carer narratives like this, *omoiyari* was not merely cognitive, but aesthetic, closely associated with the habituation of sensitivities that allow one to "become the feelings of the other" (*hito no kimochi ni naru*) or "become the body of the other" (*hito no mi ni naru*). Tahhan (2014, 16) notes that this "breaks down the binary opposition of subject *or* object and reveals a different ontology of subject *and* object."

Again, the overlap between *omoiyari* and compassion is hard to ignore, and is crucial for understanding the ways family carers oriented themselves toward the cared-for and made sense of care in a more pervasive cultural idiom. Carers who saw themselves as acting with compassion worked to develop the attentional and affective capacity to respond in a more spontaneous, sensitive way to the feelings and bodily ailments of the care recipient. Compassion, in this way, allows one to realize what Matsuoka (1995) terms "radical fragility," or a relational ontology of vulnerability that sets the scene for what I call dangerous compassion.

Attending to Buddhist formulations of compassion as a moral practice of empathic resonance aimed at realizing non-duality goes beyond its typical usage as merely a feeling or emotion in the West (Bein 2013). Lauren Berlant (2004), for example, has pointed out that the rhetoric of compassion enacts charity under the guise of a moral-emotional experience, or a kind of affective politics that reinforces liberal humanist models of personhood.[14] There is a problem if compassion becomes just another way to feel morally good without really doing good, especially in situations marked by serious inequality (Murphy 2015). Charity, by contrast, is understood as an *action*, typically though not necessarily motivated by feelings of love and kindness (Benthall 2012; Bornstein 2009; Itzhak 2020; Marett 1932; Scherz 2014; Trundle 2014). Rather, charity operates according to assumptions that human suffering is best attended to not by "a warm feeling in the gut" (Nussbaum 2003, 14), but through the disinterested gift, or the gift given in the name of God. While compassion was the dominant narrative among Japanese carers I spoke with, English notions of care were rooted in the value of charity.

Charity: Caring as the Gift

If compassionate caring generates an embodied connection between the carer and care recipient in ways that allow suffering to illuminate the world, charitable caring is a means toward a greater connection with the good/God, or its secular equivalent in the benevolent state. Ideally, charity aspires to be altruistic; it does not seek gain for the giver, nor does the specific identity of the recipient matter. It is also gratuitous; it goes beyond simply providing necessary care. The Good Samaritan does not ask whom he is helping before he provides first aid to the man he finds on the road, nor does he merely dress the wounds, but instead takes him to an inn and pays for his care (Zimmermann 2015, 299).[15] The Good

Samaritan does not stay and befriend the man, but goes on with his own life, leaving the one he helped in God's hands. To love gratuitously does not mean to love *more* than you love yourself, but to recognize one's limits.

A similar distinction between compassion and charity can be found in Max Weber's "Religious Rejections of the World and Their Directions" ([1920] 1946).[16] Weber outlines a typology of religious sociality that hinges on the distinction between two types of "abnegations of the world": "the active asceticism that is a God-willed action of the devout who are God's tools, and, on the other hand, the contemplative possession of the holy, as found in mysticism" (325). This bifurcation aligns closely with the distinction that I make here between charity (ascetic, God-willed action) and compassion (possession of the holy). Here I am concerned mostly with what Weber called "inner-worldly" varieties of these two religious forms, or those that remain active in the affairs of the world rather than retreating from it (as hermits, for example). According to his scheme, Japanese Buddhist notions of compassion would be exemplary of "inner-worldly mysticism," or of "broken humility," which embraces the aesthetic ("touching the heart") as ethics and its own kind of salvation from rationalism (1946, 341–42).

In contrast, Weber argues that modern notions of charity, or what he refers to as *caritas*, follow the route of "active asceticism," or religions of salvation, the archetypal form being Puritan Christianity. Weber ([1934] 2002) famously argued that the groundwork for the emergence of modern capitalism can be found in this ascetic religion, which entrenched an ethic of "vocation," routinized work, and thrift as a means of testing one's grace. Along these same lines, Weber characterized ascetic religions as bound by an ethic of "brotherly love-communism," upheld through generalized reciprocity and "an attitude of *caritas*," or charity: "love for the sufferer *per se*, for one's neighbor, for man, and finally for the enemy" (1946, 330). Charitable care was an expression of disinterested egalitarianism: since we are all equal and undeserving of grace, it could just as well be me who is poor or sick and in need of aid. But just as the Protestant ethic laid the ideological groundwork for capitalism, *caritas* laid the groundwork for modern philanthropy and other ways of giving that reproduced social hierarchies and notions of deservingness. Here I am trying to retrieve something of Weber's notion of *caritas* in order to understand the social and historical roots of carers' ethical lifeworlds.

The English word "charity" has its etymological root in *caritas*, which in turn is a translation for the Latin *agape*, a Christian love of one's fellow man, or the "unconditional love that constitutes the motivation for care" (Levy-Malmburg, Eriksson, and Lindholm 2008, 663). Popular author and Christian theologian C. S. Lewis (1960) wrote extensively on charity as the most perfect form of love, the undeserved grace of God that all other forms of love are subordinate to. "We are all receiving Charity," he writes, because

> there is something in each of us that cannot be naturally loved. It is no one's fault if they do not so love it. Only the loveable can be naturally loved. You might as well ask people to like the taste of rotten bread or the sound of a mechanical drill. We can be forgiven, and pitied, and loved in spite of it, with Charity; no other way. All who have good parents, wives, husbands, children, may be sure that at some times—and perhaps at all times in respect of some one particular trait or habit—they are receiving Charity, are not loved because they are loveable but because Love Himself is in those who love him. (1960, 121)

Since all are unlovable, Lewis reasons, "to love at all is to be vulnerable" (111). If compassion renders one vulnerable by opening our hearts and bodies to the world of suffering, charity renders us vulnerable to the heartbreaking imperfection of ourselves and the world. For Christians, like the San'ya volunteers, only God was truly worthy of this love, but all of us, Lewis adds, go beyond what is necessary when we are altruistically generous, hospitable, and forgiving of others. The goodness of charity comes not in the sympathetic cultivation of the giver's heart, as in Buddhist compassion, but in upholding the moral primacy of (God's) love.[17] As the volunteer in San'ya told me, charity was not about creating benefit for the giver or even for the receiver, but was a way to "make *God* happy."

While most of the English carers I spoke with were not regular churchgoers, many of them did have some spiritual faith that they drew on when coping with the difficult moments in care (more in chapter 5). But what was most striking to me was that English carers appeared much more occupied than the Japanese carers with their role in the management of paid care services. I did not make the connection between this focus on paid care and the ethic of charity at first, but looking at carer narratives in light of Weber's framework brought this distinction into stronger relief.

Weber was interested not only in religious practice in the church but also in the ways religious beliefs and values permeate and become hidden within the heart of modern secular institutions such as welfare. As I will describe later in this chapter, family care in England and the social welfare state were both historically constructed on the model of Christian charitable aid to the poor and destitute. Since charitable aid was seen as a means of supporting organic solidarity based on "brotherliness," rather than the affections of kinship, it is little wonder that family carers in England found it difficult to maintain both identities (carer and kin) at once.

While the religious ideal of brotherly love has shifted as care has become rationalized through state apparatuses that demand assessments, means testing, and other bureaucratic techniques for judging deservingness, the logic of charity is still evident in carers' attitudes toward social care. As family carers in England tried to find a meaningful role for themselves in the care ecology, they acted in ways that resonated with charitable organizations, providing financial and instrumental support while managing supplementary professional services. This does not mean that all English care was cold and heartless. Professional carers are still driven by the desire to do good, meaningful work for each individual, and charity, nonprofit, and volunteer organizations in both Japan and England have continued to provide vital care alongside basic state services. It might be the case that as the values of charity have been dampened, the rhetoric of compassion has grown, in part to deflect perceptions of coldness or anonymity.

This distinction between compassion and charity reflects the different themes that arose in my conversations with carers, and while each person's experience reflected a different shade or shape to these themes, they are, I believe, strongly tied to other specific cultural and historical differences between Japan and England that have developed over centuries. The same distinction between compassion and charity would not be as useful if I was looking, for example, at the practice of *seva* in Indian dementia care, as Bianca Brijnath (2014) has done. Brijnath's work shows the ways *seva*, or the "intellectual, emotional and physical care of elders based on respect" (2014, 5), entails the intimate, embodied, and aesthetic qualities of what I have termed compassion, alongside notions of duty and religious virtue that might be more strongly associated with charity. Filial piety rooted in Confucian worldviews and institutions across Asia often occupies a similar gray zone between compassion and charity (Ikels 2004; Shea, Moore, and Zhang 2020). As these examples demonstrate, the mode of care and the dominant value it embodies (its resonant frequency), be it compassion, charity, or something else, depend on the cultural and historical narratives and their affordances.

Care of elderly relatives is never performed uniformly across communities or families. Thus, on the level of lived experience, English carers and Japanese carers both practiced what I am calling compassion and charity over the course of caring for family members. However, when accounting for the ways they navigated the dangerous cliff-edges along the path (i.e., the different ways they ascribed meaning to care or made ethical decisions about care), Japanese and English carers were working from different moral maps.[18] Japanese carers, for example, often struggled with decisions to accept paid care or to transfer an older relative into a care home, in part because of the negative associations of such charitable caring. English carers voiced feelings of guilt if they moved an elderly relative they had been caring for into a care home, but they felt worse if they had to live with and attend to the intimate care of that relative themselves at home. After all of the interviews, support meetings, and home observations, I knew that compassion had an important role to play in *both* Japanese and English care settings, but it wasn't until I began to think about it alongside charity that I started to understand the motivations of carers and their relationships to socially and historically situated worlds.

Compassion and Welfare in Japan

These terms, compassion and charity, and the specific ways of being-with-the-other that they connote, became important during my time in the field, but they have much longer histories, and as Marxist-influenced scholars such as Michel Foucault have demonstrated, excavating those histories can provide a critical lens on the way subjectivity is constituted in the present. Jarrett Zigon (2007, 138) has argued that if we are to understand the moral experience of individuals like carers, we must first grasp how they came to be in situations that pose particular ethical demands and recognize the ways those situations also constrain how individuals can respond. While it is impossible to tell how much those histories have affected individual carers, they do help us to place observable differences into a broader narrative framework.

Buddhist ethics of compassion (*jihi*) was purportedly introduced to Japan in the early seventh century during the reign of Prince Shōtoku (574–622 CE). Shōtoku, who is often credited for both the spread of Buddhism and for devising the architecture of Japan's constitutional government, promoted the ethics of compassion as the basis of public-service projects, poverty relief, and care of the destitute and disabled elderly people. The Buddhist monk Gyōgi (688–753 CE) was an exemplar of this kind of politics of compassion during the early establishment of Japan's welfare state. A charismatic itinerant renunciate, Gyōgi achieved fame as he traveled the country, organizing his followers (many of them farmers dispossessed by a new taxation system) in the building of roads, bridges, shelters, and medical facilities for the poor and outcast (Quinter 2008; Sakuma 1994). Gyōgi and the heirs to his brand of Buddhism maintained their autonomy from the government, though they often cooperated with it, most notably on the construction of the Great Buddha statue in Nara.[19]

The cooperation between Buddhism and the early state continued with the development of welfare institutions for the sick, poor, disabled, and elderly, established in 757 CE with the "Retirement Order" (*yōrō-ritsuryō*). This order set the official age of retirement as sixty, at which time taxes would be reduced by half. The country would also provide a temporary care assistant (*jitei*) for those eighty to one hundred years old who could not be supported by family

or neighbors. State-supported welfare institutions were divided into four categories: *hiden-in* and *keiden-in* (primarily serving the poor, the orphaned, and
the abandoned elderly), and *yaku-in* and *ryōbyō-in* (mainly concerned with the
sick and diseased).[20] These institutions were directed toward the commoners and
established within Buddhist temples, radically departing from orthodox Shinto
belief that the sick and dying would bring dangerous pollution (*kegare*) to sacred
spaces. The Buddhist ethical system underlying social welfare was based on the
virtue of feelings of "love" and "deep sympathy" for the old and disabled (Toshimitsu 1958, 42–44).[21] Literary evidence into the medieval period (ca. 1155–1600)
shows that this ethic of compassion continued, with depictions of the frail and
suffering older person who becomes the subject of Buddhist salvation and
redemption (Drott 2015b).[22]

Life in premodern / early modern Japan (ca. 1601–1867) tends to be characterized as tightly organized and extensively regulated and monitored by the
Bakufu military government (R. Benedict 1946; Bellah 1957), yet although the
responsibility for the care of aging relatives remained in the family, arrangements for care provision were flexible. It was not until the late eighteenth and
nineteenth century, when increasing affluence and longer, healthier life spans
began to reshape kinship and inheritance structures, that the Confucian value
of filial piety long associated with social elites became more widespread (Berry
and Yonemoto 2019, 8–9). As Japan entered the modern period (1868–1945)
and established a constitution (1889), this Confucian-inspired system of household roles, structures, and values became formally established as the *ie*, or the
stem-family system. The *ie* was patrilineal and primogenitural, so younger sons
would branch out to establish separate families associate with the main line. The
ie system made the household head legally responsible for the continuity of the
household, including the care of elders, and for the perpetuation of the ancestors,
such as maintaining a grave (Tsuji 2002). This nationally standardized family
structure, maintained through a family registry and census system, facilitated
the rational management of citizens and reflected the ideal relationships between
the benevolent emperor and his children/subjects (Bellah 2003; Tamanoi 2010).
It also established a more rigid and gendered division of care labor, actively promoting the virtuous role of women as wives and mothers whose domain was
limited to the domestic sphere.

Modern Japanese welfare policy aimed to preserve the values of filial piety and
the responsibility of the family for the care of older relatives. However, increased
mobility, urbanization, and smaller families all contributed to an increase in
poor and isolated older people in need of care. The first legislation to tackle this
issue was the Relief Regulations (1874), based on European Poor Laws of "discre-
tionary and charitable assistance," but also "mutual care and support, driven by

compassion" (Hayashi 2015, 41). This law made public assistance available only to those without family, age "70 or older [and] who suffered from 'severe illnesses and decrepitude of old age'" (Garon 1987, 34). Bureaucratic efforts to cut costs of public assistance later added that even older people would have to "prove their inability to work" (35).[23] As modern hospitals, orphanages, and poorhouses became more prevalent, so too did new "charitable organizations" (*jizen jigyō*), most of which were run by middle-class Christians and, again, based on programs already functioning in Europe. In 1908, the Central Charity Association was established, and even the imperial household began making donations to Christian charities (Garon 1987, 47).

Family obligations under the *ie* system persisted as "traditional" norms even after the postwar constitution (1948) removed most legal obligations related to family care (Tsuji 2002). Most importantly, the traditional household continued to be embodied through rituals of care for the ancestors (Plath 1964; Smith 1974; Danely 2014), which Buddhist temples remained closely involved in. Japanese social welfare institutions also emphasized the collective unity and care of family, maintaining values of compassion even as charities proliferated. Even today, Japanese people are more likely to use a phonetic approximation of the word "charity" (*charitī*) rather than its translated equivalent (*jizen*), marking its foreignness and implying an incompatibility with traditional Japanese worldviews.

The first modern nursing home specifically for older people was the charity-run Anglican-Episcopal-affiliated Saint Hilda's Nursing Home, in Tokyo (1895). This was followed by several more Christian institutions across Japan.[24] Yet, because of the strong emphasis on family-provisioned care and the stigma associated with entrusting a family member to institutional care, charitable donations were slow in materializing, and the growth of nursing homes was slow.[25] In 1963, the Japanese government passed the "Act on Social Welfare for the Elderly," the world's first social welfare policy specifically for older people, even those who were not poor, alone, or living with severe disabilities. It established new welfare institutions such as senior citizen community centers and low-cost care homes that would be set up by local authorities to ensure that all older people could live with health, comfort, and a sense of purpose in life (*ikigai*). Care institutions were inadequate for the growing need, and they were quickly overwhelmed. Institutional conditions were also poor, reinforcing their image as a place of desolate abandonment known as *obasuteyama*, or the "granny-dumping mountain," after an ancient folktale about a son who leaves his mother alone to die (Bethel 1992; Danely 2014; Hayashi 2015, 39; Traphagan 2013).

It was no mistake that a key scene from a movie adaptation of the *obasuteyama* story was used during a presentation on care that I attended at a Presbyterian church in Kyoto during my fieldwork. In this scene, a poor farmer wearing ragged clothes, his world-weary face full of concern, carried his diminutive, gray-haired mother on his back as he trudged up the mountain where he will abandon her. "This is the future of the Age of Mass Eldercare [*Daikaigo Jidai*]," the presenter at the church announced with a grim, foreboding voice, "where each older person will be supported by only one working-age person!" He tapped a key to reveal another image on the same slide. This time he showed a bright and boisterous crowd of neighborhood festival participants, holding up the heavy gilded shrine of the local guardian deity. "Just after the war, things were like this," he said, a hum of understanding resonating in the audience, "with fifteen adults supporting each older person!" Again, the symbolic meaning of the festival, as a performance of sacred community solidarity (with the elder positioned as the deity residing in the shrine), now in decline, was not lost on the audience. Conjured alongside apocalyptic demographic charts, the specter of *obasuteyama* returned to us in the darkened room, no longer just an ancient story, nor even an image of the care homes of the past, but an image of the future of the family.

While a number of policies expanding the range and accessibility of health and welfare services for older people were enacted in the last decades of the twentieth century, hospitals, care homes, and care staff found it difficult to keep up with the demand, leaving the diminishing number of unpaid family carers to fill the gap. Japan's Long-Term Care Insurance Act (1999, hereafter LTCI) represented a radical shift away from the fully public system toward a hybrid one that incorporated private and nonprofit sectors funded by an even split between insurance premiums and taxes and administered by both (Campbell, Ikegami, and Gibson 2010; Hotta 2007; Tamiya et al. 2011, 1184). The new LTCI system was universal and mandatory, requiring everyone over the age of forty to contribute. Eligibility for coverage begins at age sixty-five, and the extent of coverage depends on results of a needs assessment (*yōkaigo-nintei*) largely based on "activities of daily living." The result is measured on a five-point scale (five being the highest care needs), and the insured could then choose the services needed from a variety of service providers, compliant with the LTCI guidelines. LTCI produced a boom in new service providers, increasing access while reducing overall care expenditures. However, Tamiya et al. (2011) found that despite the high rate of participation, LTCI had no positive effects on either care recipients or carers' subjective health status (1187). The authors speculate that carers' dissatisfaction arises from the persistent social norms regarding family care, particularly when the older family member remains in their home. They write, "Most [carers] feel burdened by their tasks but continue to care because of affection and a desire to help on the one hand, and a sense of duty and social pressures on the other. Effective long-term care policies alleviate but cannot obliterate these feelings" (1188). Short of obliterating feelings of affection and duty, then, any care policy that does not consider the strong resonance of cultural narratives is bound to prove inadequate. This is evident as well in the fact that employees rarely take paid care leave, preferring to dedicate themselves fully to either work or care.

Every major periodic revision of the system has resulted in greater restrictions on eligibility and higher premiums. The 2013 revision, for example, introduced means testing for the first time, doubling the copay contribution for older people earning over the income threshold (this was tripled to 30 percent in 2018).[26] At the same time, the eligibility threshold for nursing homes (*tokubetsu yōgo rōjin hōmu*, or *toku-yō*) was official raised to care level 3, an advanced level of care need that generally means the person is unable to live independently (nursing homes had already been prioritizing applicants who do not live with family and who have dementia or other complex care needs).[27] This policy change reduced the number of individuals on the national wait list for beds from 532,000 to fewer than 350,000 overnight. Changes such as these have made many skeptical as to whether the values of protecting universal rights to social care while providing individual options weren't being undermined by rationing of services and the shift to a more consumer-based approach. As one care worker I often spoke to bemoaned, "[before LTCI] we just thought of [older people] as people who needed support, and now they call them 'customers' [*kyaku-san*]! And even worse, the service providers are 'businesses,' and that means they are looking out for profit, right? Things have changed so much." Critics of LTCI sometimes point to the ways focusing on the individual insured/consumer rather than supporting families and communities have contributed to social disintegration. It is true that there is no provision in LTCI to offer care for carers, and it has weakened the dependence on informal ties in favor of more rationalized, bureaucratic formal systems. Unlike in the German hybrid care system, carers cannot opt for cash assistance if they choose to take on more responsibility for care (Campbell, Ikegami, and Gibson 2010; Makita 2010). But cash is not the same as compassion, and cash payments risk extending the sense of alienation that so many carers feel.

The historical legacy of compassion is difficult to see in most contemporary Japanese elderly care institutions (a point I return to in the final chapter), yet the familialist approach to care indicates a continuation of cultural assumptions about the importance of kin-provisioned care. As the carer narratives in the following chapters indicate, family carers reproduce a model of care that often resonates with and is sometimes directly inspired by Buddhist notions of compassion rather than charity. But just as the relationship between these two modes of care has been ambiguous across the historical development of Japanese social welfare, carers' experiences also reflect ambiguity and variation.

Charity and Welfare in England

I don't have to go much farther than the main streets near my Oxford home to find row after row of "charity shops," where volunteers resell donated goods to raise money for cancer research, hospice, Alzheimer's disease, and older people. Banks, supermarkets, and cafés usually have at least one collection vessel for donations of loose change to local and international causes, and claims of support for charity organizations are found on packaging for food products. Charity volunteers are a constant presence in shopping areas and rail stations, to the point where many people feel harassed by these aggressive "chuggers" (a portmanteau of the words "charity" and "muggers"). The biggest times for raising charity donations are Christmastime (where wearing garish Christmas jumpers is often a sign that one is raising money for a cause) and Red-Nose Day (March 14), which began in 1985 by the charity Comic Relief, initially to support those suffering from famine and displacement in Africa.

This sort of charitable activity is almost unheard of in Japan.[28] The same could be said for the numerous panhandlers and "rough sleepers" along the shopping arcades and parks across England. Even in the poorest areas of Tokyo, rough sleepers mostly avoid busy shopping areas during daytime, and even when they can be seen around areas like public parks and train stations, I have never seen anyone asking for money.[29]

There are hundreds of registered charity organizations in England that provide support for elderly people and their carers. Age UK, the Alzheimer's Society, and Carers UK are some of the largest charities, but other local charities are also scattered across the country. In addition, local authorities (provincial administrative bodies) commission charities, to fulfill their statutory obligation to uphold the 2014 Care Act. The Care Act was the largest single reform of social care since the 1948 National Assistance Act (which replaced the Poor Law). The most significant new provision in the 2014 Care Act has been the right of unpaid carers to their own care assessment. To date, no similar statutory obligation to care for carers exists in Japan.

The carer support organization that cooperated in parts of this study was a nonprofit partnered with other nonprofits and commissioned by its local authority, providing a range of services throughout the county while collecting information on the state of carers' well-being and the impact of policy changes on their lives.[30] The organization's website lists over one hundred carer support groups in its home county *alone*. In contrast, when conducting my fieldwork in Kyoto city (roughly twice the population of the county in England), there were only seven support group meetings for carers, two of which met only once every three months (most are once monthly). Much like the Comprehensive

Community Support centers (*chiiki hōkatsu shien sentā*) in Japan, carer support organizations in England act as a hub for a network of local groups and provide advice to carers on the phone or in-person, such as advice about how to access benefits or psychological counseling. In practice, the staff are often put in positions where they need to tend to clients in need of immediate assistance, which puts a strain on already insufficient resources. It is not easy to put a price tag on the value of the work that charities do, because while they must periodically bid for their contract, they must also spend resources collecting data, evaluating their activities, and making information publicly available in order to justify their cost to the local authority.

From the unpaid family carers' perspective, charities appear to be trusted and appreciated parts of the care ecology, more than simply a lifeline reserved for emergencies. Carers told me how they were put into contact with charity groups early on in their caring, sometimes immediately after receiving troubling news from a physician. These charity organizations, however, are only the latest manifestations of England's long history of reliance on charity for the care of elderly people. Evidence from medieval and early modern England suggests that older people were considered responsible for their own welfare in later life and in most cases could not rely on children or other relatives for care (Ben-Amos 2008, 17–18; Thane 2000, 73–74). The emphasis on raising children to be independent meant that older people held on to resources and continued to work when necessary to provide for themselves. In the fourteenth century, landowners were considered responsible for the prevention of "pauperism" on their land, and to that end would provide basic welfare or a retirement contract for older people who for some reason were unable to work. This contract did not necessarily result in transfers of land rights, but it did seek to honor the wishes of the older person.

Just as lords were responsible for assuring the basic welfare of dependent older tenants, in premodern England it was generally considered an obligation of the wealthy to provide for the poor and destitute (Thane 2000, 95). Religious charities played a large role in facilitating these transactions through fraternities, hospitals, and almshouses. Thane notes that "along with real compassion and a sense of Christian duty" many supported charities for other reasons, such as a fear of the poor, or as "a public expression of moral worth" and status (97). The decline of Catholic charities during the Reformation and the establishment of the Poor Law Act of 1601 did not see a decline in charitable contributions (especially testamentary bequests to charitable trusts and lifetime gifts or legacies to hospitals), but it did establish a statutory responsibility for local parishes to collect and distribute relief funds based on state criteria. This state rationalization of charity ran parallel to the ongoing support of children (particularly unmarried daughters), although there was no strong obligation to shelter or give significant emotional or financial support (Thane 2000, 145–46) as there was in Japan. Voluntary charity and philanthropy continued through the pre- and early modern periods in England, and since older people did not rely on family,[31] they made up a large proportion of beneficiaries.[32]

State and charitable poor relief organizations established various workhouses, almshouses, and settlement houses in the early modern period, ostensibly to shelter and rehabilitate the destitute of all ages, but in practice aiding a disproportionate number of older people. Older people who needed medical attention unavailable in workhouses were sometimes able to receive care and housing through Catholic charities, whose ethical stance on voluntary philanthropic support for the poor put them in conflict with the taxation-based provisions made as a result of the Poor Law (Mangion 2012, 518). The prevailing English cultural attitude of "self-help" and "independence" meant "destitution was seen as a personal failing or family responsibility" (Hayashi 2015, 16), so poor treatment continued. These institutions eventually became the basis for the modern nursing homes for older people in the twentieth century (Hayashi 2015).[33] From their beginnings, long-term care homes inherited the stigmatizing association of family neglect and poverty. While modern laws broke up the Poor Law to identify the special needs of older people and other groups, they largely reproduced assumptions about the structure of care since the medieval period, with independence and some family support (although not living together) as the preferred scenario, and formal care as the backup. As more English adult children today stay closer to home, the number of potentially available unpaid family carers has grown, but the care they offer is not only an expression of affection, but also functions as a kind of unregistered volunteering for the charity sector, rather than an act of filial piety or compassion.

In England today, individual financial dependence, regardless of family situation, is the basis for receiving financial assistance for care. Unlike their counterparts under Japan's national-insurance-based system, English care recipients are "self-funders," who are expected to pay for 100 percent of their care costs out-of-pocket until their savings and assets (including homes) are below the threshold of £23,250. While the national central government controls how local authorities can fund social care (that is, through local taxes and central government grants), defines their statutory duties, and as a result of the 2014 Care Act sets national needs and means tests, it is up to each local authority to determine spending, commission care providers, and make decisions about care delivery. Since 2009, these local authorities, however, have had to contend not only with rising numbers of older individuals needing care, but also staggering austerity cuts to their budgets for public services.[34] As a result, local authorities have been forced to reduce expenditures on social care, even as need has increased, leaving an estimated 1.5 million in England unable to receive the help they need.

As in Japan, local authorities have been forced to "ration" care by devising ways to reduce services or find less costly alternatives. Most care services, including 95 percent of all beds in residential care homes, are operated by for-profit and charitable independent providers (Competition and Markets Authority 2017). Adult day care centers, which are a critical component of respite care for unpaid carers in England (as they are in Japan), have been reduced by over 40 percent since 2010 (428 closures nationally between 2010 and 2018, according to a Freedom of Information request submitted by ITV News) (Robertson 2018). Kingston, Comas-Herrera, and Jagger (2018) report that the future will see even more burden on the state, since plans for raising the retirement age are likely to deplete the already shrinking reserves of available unpaid carers. About 20 percent of older care recipients need to "top up" their entitlement with additional paid care, either from small grants from the local authority or with money from other family members.

Returning to Weber's notion of *caritas* in light of this brief snapshot of English social care history, we can see how an early Christian moral worldview provided a "substructure" (Weber 1946, 338) for later frameworks of welfare, volunteers, and unpaid care. While we have seen the virtuous benefits of a universal unconditional love expressed in charity, Weber notes that when divorced from its religious significance, charity also becomes impersonal and "loveless" (Symonds and Pudsey 2006, 139). No doubt most of the carers I spoke to would agree with this evaluation of the current state of social care in England, and their own efforts show a dual role of providing the warm and affectionate care lacking in the system on the one hand, and aggressively advocating for formal support from local authorities on the other.

This "loveless" care was most evident when carers were faced with impersonal bureaucratic procedures like the online care self-assessment, used by some local authorities to identify "vulnerable" people in need of support. When I sat with two older carers—Pam and Doris—to go through such an assessment (printed out, it would amount to twenty-four pages), the trouble began immediately. I have transcribed their responses from my field notes to give a sense of the back and forth between the two carers as we looked at the survey on separate computers.

> PAM: These things are made by people far away who don't see the big picture.
> DORIS: I hate computers.
> PAM: I've done a computer course—in 1986!
> [*The registration screen requires a Captcha code to verify the person is "human."*]

PAM: "Are you human?" Why is it asking me that?

[*The code is sent to an email address, and it takes some time for Doris and Pam to find this and log in again. Finally, they begin to fill out the forms.*]

DORIS: [*Reading the screen*] "How many hours [do you care each week]?" That's the most annoying question. Some days it's two hours, some days ten! It's always different. I don't know what to put.

PAM: This writing is really small. We're supposed to rate from zero to five? What does that mean?

DORIS: It says, "How does it make you feel?" Oh, that makes me really cross!

[*A new question appears on the screen and allows a free comment answer.*]

DORIS: [*Reading the screen*] "Describe your caring role, what does it involve?"

[*She looks at the screen blankly, then types out "I don't know."*]

PAM: [*Looking at the question "How would you like the situation to improve?"*] I'd like a fairy godmother, please! [*She turns to me.*] What do I say? Weeks when I'm caring, I can't do the things I want. It's like I'm waiting for one of us to fall off the perch!

DORIS: [*To Pam:*] Sometimes you need to escape before you burst!

It took nearly two hours for the three of us to work our way through the document, but even when we had finished, none of us felt that the answers were an accurate appraisal of the situation. The questions seemed unnecessary, irrelevant, or alien to their experience. It was easy to see why people would give up on the idea of requesting assistance from the local authority if they had to complete this sort of assessment. Despite the good intentions of the makers of the survey, for Pam and Doris, the "anonymous care" (Stevenson 2014) of the digitized, quantified, and standardized assessment was another example of the failure of those in power to listen to and acknowledge the carers' stories.

Surprisingly, our failure to have a meaningful engagement with the care system gave us all a sense of resonance. We shared a few good laughs, as Pam and Doris shot one-liners back and forth at each other or pulled faces at the questions. They didn't bother with questions they found inane or off the mark; writing "I don't know" became a little act of resistance against being pinned down into a particular box. Offline, both women enjoyed talking with me and each other about their experiences as carers, and both were interested in trying to improve the system through a "proper conversation" rather than an online feedback form. The idea that the state-commissioned charities were ultimately the ones responsible to make sure carers were able to care was never in doubt, and so Pam and Doris ticked the boxes so that the state could have its data and continue funding carer support. The network of charities were places where carers could have that "proper conversation" with someone who could empathize, and despite the pressures and uncertainties in the sector, carer support staff were driven by a palpable sense of ethical responsibility and a desire to "make a difference." On the micro-level of these personal interactions, carers could often find "good enough" care to cope a day at a time, and it would be a mistake to underestimate how potent ordinary moments of resonance can be for carers, or to dismiss them as ineffective for confronting macro structures of power.

While unpaid Japanese carers often felt excluded from the formal care system, English carers were more integrated into the formal administrative apparatus through the distribution of direct aid (cash allowances, "carer's premium," National Insurance credits, etc.) as well as through the Care Act of 2014, which recognizes the rights of carers to their own assessment and support separately from the care recipient. If one provides at least thirty-five hours of care to an older relative each week and meets the income criteria, carers can receive a small cash allowance. Around a quarter of a million carers currently receive this carers' allowance, managed by the Department of Work and Pensions separately from local council respite benefits, carer support grants, or counseling and psychological support. While this legal recognition of carer rights has provided a formal means to contest unfair practices, all of the carer benefits in England are attached to specific targeted criteria meant to channel this recognition to the most "vulnerable" carers, such as those who may be socially isolated, poor, or under greater than usual psychological strain.

At a one-day conference for carers, I attended a session on benefits for carers, where many of attendees had applied or received this carer benefit but had run into problems. One man, with a clean-shaven head and wearing worn jeans and heavy work boots, said that he couldn't get the benefit because of his pension. "The system doesn't cope with variation," he shouted from the back of the room. "It's wrong!" A buzz of voices reverberated around the audience in agreement. Others joined in, each with a particular variation. Some were caring for more than one person but still got the same benefits as a person caring for one. Others found the income cutoff for eligibility (£110 per week) too strict. Faced with this barrage of complaints, the presenter remained calm. Rather than answer individuals, she addressed the audience as a whole: "It's playing the welfare game. Use the points provided on the form to prepare for the [application] interview."

A well-dressed middle-age woman in the front of the room agreed, adding her own advice in a more sympathetic tone: "It's one of the worst possible things to fill out one of those forms. You have to do it with the worst scenario, your worst day [caring] in mind." A woman on the far side of the room wearing a light pink turtleneck sweater raised her hand. "It's great if you're coping day to day, but that's not going to give you benefits." She added, "You have to remember what it was like *before*. If you say that you're 'coping,' it's going to change your level of need [lower]."

Although policies like the 2014 Care Act may be based on a spirit of carers' rights and a universal entitlement to support, the comments by the carers in this session illustrate the yawning gaps for carers to fall through the system. For these carers, life was complicated, unstable, and ambiguous. While Japanese carers found it exhausting to yield themselves to this volatile world, they also saw it as a chance to grow and mature, to become more compassionate. English carers (and care recipients) preferred to keep family and caregiving separate and believed the social care system should support that arrangement. Careful management, "playing the game" (with sometimes subtle resistance like that of Pam and Doris), or direct political action were all at times considered part of the English carer's responsibility.

Matei Candea (2018, 4) has argued that "the discipline of anthropology has been a natural experiment in comparativism." Rather than criticizing anthropology for its imprecision (though there are other things about anthropology worthy of critique), Candea celebrates the "impossible method" and its embrace of myriad "versions and visions" of comparison. In the same spirit, this chapter outlines an alternate comparative account of care in Japan and England, one that attempts to understand these systems not through differences in their demographics or social policies, but through the modes of care that resound deeply within each. I could not have felt these resonances had I not immersed myself in the stories and everyday lives of carers, working to develop my sense and sensitivity and attention before turning to the historical and cultural materials. This experiment in comparison, then, has resonance, or the openness to being affected and transformed at its heart. Following these lines of transformation meant that I could not approach comparison of care as if I were neatly measuring two objects on a scale, but instead, as if I were learning to appreciate two complex and dynamic ecosystems, both affecting and affected by a similar climate.

Juxtaposing Japan and England as distinctive ecologies of care does not mean that each is self-contained, coherent, or complete. As Duclos and Criado (2020) have argued, the complex and ambivalent nature of care must be situated within a more expansive, dynamic ecological approach that can "lift up and foster the creation of possible 'existential territories'" (155). This generative approach to ecologies of care recognizes the ways bodies and atmospheres might not only meet, but pass through each other in a process of mutual transformation, or aesthetic attunement to what Tronto (1993) calls "the world." Caring can make the world more habitable and hopeful, in the sense that it reorganizes sensibilities and relationships to resonate with meaning. But caring can also reveal fragility, not only in the encounter with the other, but also in the collapse into alienation on the one hand, or catastrophic excess on the other. The capacity for resonance is not evenly and equally distributed across care ecologies, and this variation is itself an important point of this research.

Ethnographic cases reveal the complexity, variation, and potentialities of care in ways that denaturalize, unbind, and trouble generic categories and definitions. Juxtaposing individual cases both *within* as well as *between* environmental contexts provides further insight about the roles of political institutions, histories, religions, language, gender, and culture in the shaping of lived experience of care. While I have characterized the culturally dominant mode of care in Japan as "compassion" and that of England as "charity," these should not be confused with reductive notions of homogenizing national character. Rather, they represent certain durable logics that have been taken up at different times and for different purposes as different domains of life have intersected and become entangled. On the level of specific relationships of care, these modes are broken down further, as carers find their way through a process of narrative attunement and resonance, but not to the point of complete dissolution. For most carers, compassion and charity became sources of meaning and satisfaction, but also brought their own challenges. While Japanese carers struggled to maintain distance between themselves and the cared-for, English carers were more likely to struggle with intimacy. In both cases, the cultural context did not always provide a robust and compelling narrative for overcoming these frustrations, leading carers to find alternative solutions, discovering new paths and finding new voices.

BECOMING A CARER

"I didn't realize how serious things had become."

Yoko, like many members of the postwar baby-boom generation, was in her early seventies and caring for her mother. As she was an only child and a full-time housewife who lived with her mother, who was now ninety-six, there had been little question in her mind that she would be the one to take responsibility for her mother's care in old age.[1] Despite this, or rather because this was so taken for granted, Yoko did not think of herself as her mother's carer for years, not until the symptoms of her mother's dementia became more disconcerting:

> YOKO: Gradually, gradually the dementia came out, but about twenty years ago my father died, and maybe from about fifteen years ago we lived together. We lived together for fifteen years, but she started saying strange things, and her forgetfulness was getting horrible. That continued for a while, and, well, there were more and more instances where I thought, "Are you really doing *that*?"
>
> DANELY: For example, can you remember some things she did?
>
> YOKO: Well, not very good things really. Like saliva.
>
> DANELY: Saliva?
>
> YOKO: Saliva. She started spitting here and there. And I think maybe she'd forget where the toilet was, so she'd open the door of the entranceway and she'd go outside. And so the symptoms got pretty serious.
>
> DANELY: And at that time, you lived together.

YOKO: Right. We were together the whole time. We were already living together. [The problems] didn't happen all the time. Normally, we'd just gossip [*seken banashi*] or just talk to each other normally, and she wasn't unusual at all, but then all of a sudden, she'd eat a whole banana and then she'd get into the fridge and eat and eat, and I'd feel like, are you okay? One time I peeled a potato and just put it in a bowl while I went out to pick up some shopping that I'd forgotten, and when I returned she'd eaten it.

DANELY: Oh, raw?

YOKO: Raw! And so I thought, "Oh my, my!" [*Arya-rya-rya*], and I put a rope on the fridge so she couldn't get into it and doing all sorts of things like that. But since we were parent and child, I didn't realize how serious things had become. But it was really, looking at it from the outside, it was a pretty serious situation. So I thought, well, for the time being I'll take her to a day service center, and since I had no idea about other people's [caregiving] situations, I decided to fill out the care assessment form.

Here, Yoko took a pause. The narrative of living together and talking "normally" as "parent and child" had started to break down in the face of her mother's uncanny behaviors. Yoko started to consider herself "from the outside." She would have to become more attentive of her mother, catching these unfamiliar urges that challenged her own capacity to safeguard. Looking at this situation from a third-person perspective initiated a process of identifying as a carer, a new relationship with the social world, where her role now included an external recognition of responsibility materialized in the form of the care needs assessment.

Filling out the assessment form renders the ambiguous role of "carer" into a concrete presence. For years, Yoko was reluctant to fill out the form, but when she did fill it out, it ended up marking a shift in her narrative identity: a movement from being just family to becoming a family carer. As an extension of LTCI, the form is designed as a care needs self-assessment of the insured person (the cared-for), but it is often not something manageable for someone like Yoko's mother who has advanced-care needs such as cognitive impairment or dementia. Yoko and other carers, therefore, become conduits, filling the gap, trying to gauge the capacities of the cared-for and answer each item in its place; the carer is unable to voice her own concerns or troubles through this device. The form brings a little sense of clarity, but like the English forms described in chapter 1, it also drastically reduced and sifted years of Yoko's experience as a provider of care into neat and tidy tick-boxes that obscured the lived experience. At the same time, the form presented a turning point for Yoko's ability to reflect on her positionality toward her mother; it might have been the first time she had ever shared these intimate details—feeding, bathing, toileting, sleeping patterns—with another person, let alone a stranger. As inconsequential as these marks may seem in themselves, they not only made their impression on Yoko's own subjective narrative, but they would also go on to influence what level of care her mother was eligible for under the LTCI provisions. As such, they would guide the decisions that Yoko would make about her mother's care and her relationship to that care as conditions progressed and became more demanding. Taking a step like filling out an official form is both the act a responsible carer is expected to make and, simultaneously, an act that hands over responsibility as a carer to the social system.

In this chapter, I begin to look more closely at narratives of becoming a carer in Japan and England. Interestingly, in both cultural contexts, carers described their entry into caring as a moment of assuming *responsibility*, whether codified in legal designations or as a matter of cultural norms. The shape of responsibility changed over the duration of care, structuring and restructuring the ethical reflections of the carer as well as the inter-subjective relationship with the cared-for and third parties. It was neither wholly a matter of individual virtue (developing one's character into the virtuous role of a responsible person), nor was it simply about following social norms and prescriptions. Already embedded within the notion of responsibility, then, was a notion of *responding* to something or someone who is "other" and who compels you to respond; to be response-able is, as Levinas ([1961] 2003) imagines, the act of "not turning away" as much as it is facing toward the other (Altez-Albela 2011).[2] Even when a carer is not acting as a primary carer, such as when Yoko placed her mother in a care facility, that sense of responsibility endured, but it was also called into question: what were the limits of responsibility? To whom are we responsible, and why?[3] Is there a point at which taking responsibility becomes irresponsible?

These are questions carers contend with daily as they cross the threshold of responsibility. Assuming responsibility as a carer entailed an ongoing commitment to the cared-for; practices of care were no longer merely situated or spontaneous reactions, but the fulfillment of a broader, socially inflected story. The role of a family carer, as opposed to a paid carer, is ambiguous, and the boundaries of responsibility and commitment were constantly renegotiated. Family history, the presences or absence of other available relatives, interactions with formal care services, and cultural expectations all come into complex interaction with each other in ways that rarely produced tidy solutions. It was in these interactions, however, that we begin to see the ways cultural differences might matter, and how they set a trajectory for future experiences. Becoming a responsible carer is a process that is ongoing and always unfinished, always in that mode of *becoming* (Danely 2021).

Caring Is Unexpected

Like Yoko, carers in England also felt becoming a carer began when they received some external recognition of their responsibility; but what caught my attention most was how this recognition was often registered with surprise.

Jill, an English carer close in age to Yoko, told me, "I never thought of myself as a carer until someone sort of said, "You can join the carer's association" and things like that. But even then, I didn't really think of myself as a carer. I just thought, if I can get a few benefits for Dad, then that's fine." Denise, another English woman, told me, "I didn't expect to become *a carer*," appearing shocked as she said the words, as if just realizing their strangeness. We sat around a table with four other carers, and all quickly agreed. "That's right, isn't it?" said one man. "Even if you know people who have done it, you don't expect that it'll happen to you until it happens!" Another spoke up, voice shaking: "I didn't know that I was a carer for a long time, then it was like I found out I was a caring daughter. I had to somehow become a carer in my head." I wrote in my notes: "caring is unexpected(?)" and underlined it.

In part, this feeling of surprise expresses the lack of preparation felt when becoming a carer. Japanese carers like Yoko often spoke of how they assumed they would take on some care tasks, but they too felt a lack of "mental/emotional preparation" (*kokoro no junbi*). *Kokoro* typically refers to one's mental and emotional state (as distinguished from a feeling in one's body).[4] Preparation of the *kokoro* would therefore refer not merely to acquiring knowledge and information about illness, care policy, insurance systems, and the like, but rather to the cultivation of a mental and emotional state able to respond to the other. Aneshensel et al. (1995, 22) observed that informal care was "unexpected," because "despite the fact that caregiving to older impaired relatives is becoming a common contingency of the life course, people typically do not see themselves as caregivers when they project themselves in the future." Carers were surprised that even when they knew what to do, they didn't know how to be.

Marilyn Strathern (2005) observed that "relatives are always a surprise," by which she meant that our taken-for-granted assumptions about individual, bounded personhood becomes challenged when we realize ourselves as deeply related to others: "The person as an individual turns out to be the person as a relative" (2005, 10). Strathern's observation, which she bases mainly on her analysis of the kinship relationships in Melanesia and Great Britain, also fits well with the kinds of care that I observed between people who care for older relatives. The notion that one was not a carer at one point and then in the next moment becomes a carer signals not only the inauguration of a new form of relatedness, but a revelation that one has been a relative all along to the cared-for, with little real sense of what that might mean.[5] Becoming a carer means opening up a more expansive notion of what it means to be a relative or to live up to one's responsibility as a relative, and this has implications for the unfolding of the future relationship as well as reflective work on the past.

In some cases, the surprise was understandable, as in situations where a sudden and unforeseeable event, like a stroke or a fall, resulted in a drastic change from a relatively healthy person to one with a major disability. But for others, like Yoko, realizing that one was a carer took some time—sometimes months or even years—to sink in. At some point, the gradual accumulation of small dependencies and odd changes in behaviors would reach a threshold of responsibility. When this happened, carers drifted into the new role, shifting their position toward the person they cared for, rearranging other responsibilities and commitments, and realizing that the care was bound to become more demanding in ways that were impossible to predict or prepare for. They might try to come to terms with this uncertainty by marking future horizons when care at home might no longer be possible, or by reflecting back on past horizons where difficult adjustments were dealt with (Hellström and Torres 2016). Since these horizons are never stable, but dependent on the interplay between the carer's sense of responsibility and the world the carer is responding to, the carer's identity is also perpetually rocked between moments of confidence and self-doubt.

As this suggests, disordered feelings cannot be the basis for identity without the carer riding out a sharp turn in the *narrative* of oneself and others. Certain events, certain ruptures of the everyday create spaces that need to be filled with something new. Sons, daughters, and spouses who take on care responsibilities might look back on the care they once received from the person they now care for, building a narrative of reciprocity and the life cycle. In this way, the sacrifices or commitments of the past take on an enhanced meaning for the carer, perhaps generating feelings of guilt and debt, but also making it possible to imagine a future narrative wherein the carer has the capacity to reciprocate for care received. This is a powerful narrative and one that counters the otherwise disorienting sense of surprise that comes with taking on the new role. By revaluating and connecting past events, however seemingly trivial they may have been at the time, to events in the present, the carer may find that the future course becomes both evident and logical.

But what if the relationship between the carer and the cared-for does not have this kind of narrative grounding? Families, after all, could be places where betrayal, abuse, resentment, or estrangement arise over the life course, and the persistence of these feelings casts dark shadows over the assumed responsibility of care. These feelings might be shared as well by the person needing care, who might decide it would be preferable living in a group care home or to rely instead on visits from care staff rather than accept family care. This does not necessarily result in an equitable solution, however, as family members may nonetheless feel obliged to care as a part of social expectations.[6]

The moral narrative of repaying one's debt, while stabilizing for some, never resolves the role ambiguity of family carers. The debt, after all, is never fully paid, and no matter how competent the carer, there is always a trace of guilt or inadequacy that lingers. As more professional services are brought in to assist in the care, this ambiguity, guilt, or inadequacy is revived; the rhythms and attunements that kept the carer afloat at home are disrupted once again. In Japan, it was common for carers who placed their older relatives in care institutions to "transfer the total responsibility" (Tamiya et al. 2011, 1188) to those professionals, rarely visiting or making inquiries. But for family caring at home while using a patchwork of community-based services, there was no sense of respite from responsibility. Despite turning over care to professionals, carers remained in an ambiguous role, figuring out what it meant to become a carer.

This was also the case for Yoko. After she had filled out the care assessment form, Yoko's narrative turned from the dyadic relationship of intimate care to one in which she mediated between her mother and an institution of care. In the first instance, the care assessment meant that she had to take her mother to the clinic for a health check.

> We went to our neighborhood clinic, and she put up such an awful fuss! [She was saying] "I won't go anywhere because there's nothing the matter with me!" But I managed to drag her there, but again, when we were to take off her clothing she started up again. It would be like that when we gave her a bath as well. When I would take her clothes off she would get hysterical, saying the most outrageous things like, "What are you doing to me?! If you do that I'll die!" Then we had to do an X-ray, and [I said] "Why don't we just take this top off a little," but again she had the same kind of fit. That was, well, I felt like things were really serious at that point. When they gave me the results, she was already *yōkaigo* 3 [assessed care needs level 3].

Until a couple of months before we met, Yoko had been caring for her mother at home, but about a year before she had started taking her to stay at a short-term overnight care home for about ten days each month, and day service a couple of days a week the rest of the time, for a brief respite. Short-term respite care is in high demand by family members caring for older relatives whose care needs were significant but still manageable without the need for nursing care or constant supervision. Like adult day care centers, respite care facilities lack flexibility (one cannot simply drop in for a few hours or days) and often must be booked well in advance. Yoko was unsure about this arrangement initially, but her care manager encouraged her to try it, recommending a slightly expensive facility across the city where she knew a spot would be available.

Like many older people living with dementia, Yoko's mother was often restless at night, and unlike full-time residential care, short-stay facilities typically have few nighttime staff on duty; after a few months, her mother had a bad fall one night and was subsequently hospitalized while she recovered. After she had reached her three-month limit in the hospital, it was suggested that she move to a large, nine-story geriatric nursing home (*rōjihoken shisetsu*) to continue her rehabilitation. If it wasn't for the recommendation of the hospital, Yoko probably would have taken her mother home and remained highly unsure about the quality of care at the nursing home. It was the only alternative that she could afford, however, and as her mother settled in there, Yoko began to slowly feel more at ease. She still made efforts to visit her there at least once a week, occasionally taking her out for a drive, but even this had started becoming difficult for her mother, and Yoko was thinking that she would have to stop even that.

For years, when Yoko was caring for her mother at home, she would take her mother on a ride in the car to see the cherry blossoms blooming. But this year it seemed things had changed: "I sat her in the car and got the wheelchair all folded up and packed and thought it would be so nice, but she just sort of sat there. I'd say 'the flowers are so pretty, aren't they?' but she wasn't paying attention. No matter how much I would ask, 'Weren't those flowers pretty?' she wouldn't look at them. My husband and son both asked, 'What's the point of driving her around if she's going to be like that?' Maybe she just doesn't even think of flowers and pretty anymore?"

I asked if perhaps her mother had come to think of the care home as her home now.

"Maybe." Yoko sighed, her hands slipping down the sides of her coffee cup as if being slowly drained of energy. I thought it best not to press further.

After Yoko had driven back to the group home to drop her mother off, she had taken a moment to talk to one of the care workers. Yoko has no siblings, and her family was not very receptive to her questions and complaints about her mother. The staff were the only people she felt she could be honest with regarding some of the difficult feelings about being a carer.

Although her mother became more accustomed to her new residence, she continued to get up at night, and fell and injured herself again on more than one occasion. Yoko told me she felt helpless; she felt both responsible as a carer and helplessly irresponsible for having placed her mother in the home. It has been an imperfect solution to an impossible problem.

"My Heart Can't Rest!"

Like Yoko, Hideki became a carer gradually, starting with a long period of amiable co-residence. Hideki's case was somewhat unusual among the male carers I spoke with, most of whom cared for their own parent or for a spouse. Although it was not surprising for women to care for in-laws, Hideki was the only male carer I met who was caring for the parent of a spouse: his mother-in-law.[7] Still, it would be a mistake to think of Hideki's case as somehow deviating from current trends in unpaid caregiving patterns in twenty-first-century Japan. With more families relying on dual incomes and the labor market becoming more fluid, men and women are taking on more care responsibilities without adhering to older notions of the *ie* and the duty of the eldest son and his wife. The proportion of male unpaid family carers in Japan is 35 percent, and in England, close to 40 percent.[8]

Hideki spent time in several different jobs before taking a position managing the reception counter at a high-end hotel in downtown Kyoto. His wife worked as a kindergarten teacher and gave private piano lessons in the afternoons. The couple never had children of their own. Hideki's real passion was ballroom dancing, for which he used to enter different national competitions several times a year until becoming a carer.

Since they were already living together in the same house, it felt natural to offer care when his mother-in-law became less independent. When she began to have trouble walking by herself, she refused to use a cane, complaining that it would make her look old. Gradually her muscles became so weak that she could no longer balance on her own and was even more sedentary. The rapid progression surprised Hideki, and it began to dawn on him that she was not going to recover. How long would she need care? How burdensome was it going to be? Who would do it? The surprise of becoming a carer came with questions no one could answer.

Between the cost and the time taken away from work, Hideki and his wife began to struggle. He was unable to concentrate at work and pleaded with his supervisor to allow him to reduce the number of nights he was required to work, even though he knew such a request would make it much more difficult for him to obtain a promotion. A few months after he had made this request, his mother-in-law was hospitalized, and Hideki took as much care leave as he could (the maximum three-month allowance for relatives with advanced care needs), staying in the four-bed hospital room with her while she recovered. After considering how this would affect his job and the impossibility of taking additional time off should another emergency arise, Hideki finally resolved to put in his resignation.

Hospitals are obliged to move patients who have stayed for two or three months, either to another institution like a care home or geriatric hospital, or to a family home. In Japan, live-in 24/7 care services are virtually unheard of. "If you have a family, they are particularly insistent that you go back home," Hideki explained. "They just say that as a hospital, they can't give any more help, and that's it." Since medical care and welfare services are separate in Japan, drawing on different sources of insurance and offering different benefits, leaving the hospital also opened up several possibilities for Hideki to make use of new paid services. When they returned from the hospital, Hideki's mother-in-law was at the highest level on her care needs assessment (5 out of 5) and for disability (1 out of 7). It took about two months to complete and approve the paperwork, but when that was finished, insurance would cover the cost of three daily one-hour visits from care workers (with a 10 percent copay). Hideki explained:

> Of course, she's in the house all the time, so we really can't go anywhere. So at night we feed her, and if she's sleepy we tried to give her a rest, then in the daytime, well in the morning there is a helper for breakfast and then another helper comes for lunch, and then once more in the evening. So those are the only times we can go out. Then once a week a visiting nurse comes. Thursdays, between morning and noon. And a visiting physical therapist also comes once a week. Then the doctor comes to visit once a month to check on the medication and all that.

Unable to work or to attend his dancing practice, Hideki became isolated at home, only able to leave the house for three hours a day when the helpers came or when his busy wife was able to give him a moment. "I wish there was more time to myself, but that's just the way things are [*shikata ga nai*]." He laughed nervously. He and his wife would still be responsible for preparing the food, keeping track of her condition and medications, making sure she had adequate hydration, and of course managing all the comings and goings of the paid care staff. I thought that Hideki might be especially good at managing all this, given his experience at the hotel, but he quickly corrected me. There was no going home at the end of the shift when he was caring for his mother.

For Hideki, becoming a carer for his mother-in-law was also impossible to disentangle from his sense of commitment, accountability, and responsibility to his wife. Taking this responsibility was not merely a matter of completing an assessment or signing a form; it meant a major restructuring of his lifestyle, his attention, and what it meant for him to be a husband.

> HIDEKI: If my wife keeled over—well that would be a huge problem, wouldn't it? [*laughs*]. If I dropped dead it wouldn't trouble anyone! [*laughs*].
>
> DANELY: [Your wife] didn't want to leave her job?

HIDEKI: She could have left, and then I could keep working, certainly that was one possible choice [*long pause*]. But I, well, if I kept working, you know, I didn't think I'd be promoted, and to be honest, I wasn't sure if I had the motivation to keep going at it [*sucks in breath*]. That was the most . . . well . . . [*long pause*] the thing I worried about the most. I couldn't say anything like she's *your* parent [so you take care of her] or something [*long pause*]. But it isn't easy, my heart can't rest [*kokoro ochitsukenai*].

Hideki was helped by his wife when she was home, but he was reluctant to place the responsibility onto his wife, even if it meant giving up his job, his passion, and his peace of mind. Still lacking confidence in his role as a carer, he relied on his role as a husband for a sense of resonance, but even this seemed to be emptied of meaning. Without resonance, Hideki literally became silenced, long pauses lingering throughout his responses.

HIDEKI: I'm probably what you'd call a mess when it comes to life [*iki-kata heta na hito*]. I'm clumsy [*bukiyo*] when it comes to life. It's my first time doing care. I had no idea what to do, to be honest. Even now I still feel that way.
DANELY: And for someone who is not your own parent—well, she is not a total stranger.
HIDEKI: Yes, you might think that but, um, well, it's difficult, you know?
DANELY: What part?
HIDEKI: Well, um, well, what part, I mean [*laugh*] I can only do what I can, of course she is a woman, so there are some ways I don't think she'd want a man to touch her body, but otherwise I want to do the best for her.[9] I do the cleaning and laundry, I do cooking too. Otherwise I try to support my wife. I think there's going to be a lot more ahead of us. From [this meeting] I have to go out to the ward office and the bank after this, so [my wife is] covering for me. It's like that, just packed in.

Hideki's struggles at reorganizing his identity and commitments and to become a carer were closely linked to his sense of a lack of self-efficacy (being "bad" or "clumsy" at life). This was compounded by the loss of a job and his inability to continue ballroom dancing (an area where he was the opposite of "clumsy"). The intersection of different forms of identity loss on the one hand, and the strained commitment to his role as husband on the other, made it difficult for Hideki to find a place of resonance with his new identity as a carer.

As the emotional and physical sacrifices of caring accumulated, Hideki could only endure in a constant state of uneasiness.

Warm Soup

One way carers crossed the threshold of responsibility was by moving in with or closer to the older relative.[10] Moving was a strategy employed most often when the older relative lived alone and was bereaved, lonely, or unable to live independently because of physical or cognitive frailty. For Kazuko, moving her mother from her hometown in northern Japan to Kyoto was something she had long thought about. Kazuko's mother had been living alone in a small rural village in Akita prefecture for about ten years, ever since her husband died. However, as many of her friends also died, she was becoming more isolated and uncomfortable in her old home. She had been experiencing more confusion and memory loss, and Kazuko and her sisters were worried by some of her uncharacteristic behaviors. One day, Kazuko's mother suffered a stroke when she was alone at home, but luckily she was soon discovered by a neighbor and rushed to the hospital. After her mother left the hospital, Kazuko convinced her to move.

> KAZUKO: While my mother was in the hospital I started preparing, just looking to see if there was a place in Kyoto that would take her. After that I went to Akita and looked after her for about a month, but I finally decided that it would be impossible for her to keep living on her own. My younger sister and I [both agreed]. While she'd been in the hospital, her dementia had progressed, so to go back to the way that she'd been living before was, well, she was already on the edge [*giri giri*], and that's why she was hospitalized to begin with. Because her body was destroyed. So of course she couldn't manage by herself, and especially since her dementia had become worse she was hospitalized. She kept saying that she could keep living on her own, but I explained to her that wasn't an option, so she'd have to choose between an institution in Akita or coming to Kyoto. It was really a life-and-death situation, I thought.
>
> DANELY: Really? That bad?
>
> KAZUKO: I think it was that bad because, of course, she could no longer manage her medications at all, you know? And her nutrition, she wasn't able to manage her diet either. [*Kazuko is getting agitated, looking worried.*]
>
> DANELY: You worried about her?

KAZUKO: I was worried. But she probably decided that it was impossible to live on her own. Mother was the one who had to choose whether it would be better to live in a familiar place where they spoke her dialect, or if it was better to live in a place where the environment was different but her daughter could get to her right away. Mother was the one who decided that.

Kazuko brought her mother to Kyoto, where she rented a small, single-occupancy apartment for older residents (*kōreisha jūtaku*). These living arrangements are becoming increasingly common, since waits of one or two years were typical for special nursing homes (*tokuyō*) covered by LTCI, and for-profit homes usually required large initial payments. Apartments, by comparison, not only provided privacy, but they did not require a large initial payment (typically ¥1–2 million) and required only a three-month notice before moving out. The one-room unit had an attached bathroom and toilet, a small laundry machine, and a kitchenette. Most of Kazuko's mother's belongings wouldn't fit in the small room, so she was only able to bring along a few books and some clothes. Rent and affiliated expenses amounted to about ¥180,000 per month (£1,200).[11]

After moving, Kazuko introduced me to her mother, and over the following months we were all impressed with how quickly she recuperated. Kazuko and her mother soon established a routine: a helper would come in each day for half an hour, and once a week her mother would spend the day at an adult day care center. These services were all covered by LTCI, so Kazuko would need to pay only 10 percent of the full cost. Kazuko checked in on her mother frequently, taking her for short strolls or to get a meal at a café. While there were no serious disabilities or illnesses to worry about, managing the busy daily schedule while working was hard, Kazuko said:

> There are people living there who are completely bed-bound [*netakiri*]. They have a hospice service [*mitori*] that comes in, they say. Well, I suppose it is easier for those who don't have any family, but since it is a normal rental contract, all the responsibility is on the individual and their family. Every day I go to check on her a little bit, do some shopping, for example, or bring her some tissues or detergent and so on. Also, I take her to the hospital to get her medicine, and I arrange things with another service for additional care. That's another few thousand yen on top of what is covered by insurance. It does get expensive when you figure everything in!

Kazuko's daily check-ins may not seem demanding, but once it was confirmed that her mother had stroke-related dementia, Kazuko began to worry and wait. She lived "close enough for the soup to stay warm," as carers some-times would say.[12] If her mother's dementia became more disruptive, she might be able to enter a group home. If she became frailer, perhaps a special nursing home. Kazuko woke each day unsure if something was suddenly going to change. Becoming a carer meant strengthening her friendships with those who have also cared: "It's really fun to be able to complain about my mother [with people who understand], like 'Can you believe this happened? Isn't mother just awful!'" Some of her friends included nurses and care workers, and Kazuko enjoyed learning from them about caring for someone with mild dementia. Bringing her mother to Kyoto and starting a routine where she felt she could support her and be sup-ported by her own friends have allowed Kazuko to make a smooth transition to the role of carer. After her mother settled in, her mood, dementia symptoms, and physical strength all improved, reinforcing Kazuko's sense that she had made the right decision and giving her confidence.

While in some respects, Kazuko's choices resemble what I have described as charity, her attention to these bodily signs and her interpretation of them as the result of the closer social proximity to her mother also reflected the beginnings of a compassionate disposition. In fact, Japanese and English carers resembled each other most during these first initial experiences of caring as they experimented with different ways to balance distance and proximity. In some instances, such as the next case I turn to, the responsibility of care was so sudden and intense that there was no time for this kind of muddling through. This case shows how vital an adjustment period can be for carers who are otherwise thrown into the world of a frail relative without the knowledge, emotional stability, or empathetic sensitivity to fulfill the responsibility they have taken on.

An Unexpected Phone Call

In the case of Paul, caring for his father gave him a last chance to connect after years of estrangement. Although these moments of connection were erratic, often torn down in a confused outburst as soon as they were built, for Paul they were traces of a relatedness that he longed for, to have a father-son relationship in a way he never had when he was younger.

Paul had a friendly, unassuming personality that didn't quite seem to fill his tall, squarely built frame. He lost his job around the age of sixty, and soon after, his wife filed for divorce, leaving him alone and making settlement payments from his pension. Paul was the eldest of his three siblings but never had a close relationship with his father, who he felt was always strict and emotionally distant when he and his siblings were growing up. His father served as a paratrooper in

World War II and returned to start work in the fire service, which offered a very secure pension and retirement at the age of fifty. After Paul's mother passed away, his father moved into a small bungalow and kept to himself. Paul made occasional visits to check in with his father, but these visits were never very pleasant, and he left feeling uneasy. Paul recalled that on one of these visits he told his father about the birth of his first great-grandchild (the child of Paul's son, who was not married at the time), at which his father replied cheerlessly, "He's a bastard then!" leaving Paul speechless. Paul's description of this disconnection and hurt was full of these sharp cuts, constant abrupt stops in his thoughts rather than long pauses, cuts that would return again as a wounded story of care. Paul was not the only one who was being "cut off," both physically and emotionally from his father, and the distance meant that no one realized how much his father's health had been deteriorating. Paul described the ambivalence he felt about being cut off *from* and cut *by* his father's behavior:

> He cut himself off further and further back, he cut himself off from his—he had a sister he hadn't seen for sixty years, who was taken away as a baby because his mother died in childbirth, and they had reconnected while my mum was still alive, and he even disconnected himself from her. He had his phone cut off and all this kind of thing, so anyway we go back and go back—and the only way that I could sort of tell how he was was because I contacted the local housing people and they used to make excuses to go and see him, and then they'd phone me back and say I popped down to see your dad and he's fine.

Although his father was reaching an advanced old age and living an isolated life a good distance away, he never voiced complaints about his health and seemed to be able to manage independently. Paul didn't consider that he might one day become his father's carer. Things suddenly changed, he told me, when he received a phone call from a hospital.

> They were confirming who I was and saying that "you're the next of kin," and I thought "Jesus Christ, he's died!" And so I thought, what's going on? "We can't tell you, I just need to confirm you're the next of kin." "What do you mean, you can't tell me? This is my dad in hospital?" "He's asked that we don't give out any information." "Well what do you mean?" And it kind of went on like this—eventually I thought, is there nobody down in the village left that I can contact? Because the only people that I did know, they had moved away or their business moved away. And I phoned another time and sort of said you know, there's only—they said, "well maybe you'd like to speak to a

social worker"—and I said, "well can they tell me anything?" and they said, "well no, but your dad has had a visitor." And I said, "well who might that be?" and they said, "we can't tell you," and I said, "well the only person I think might visit him"—and I mentioned this chap's name—and she said, "oh that's right, and do you know the second name? Yes, well he's been visiting your father," and I said, "you can give *him* information but you can't give *me* information?" And anyway, the upshot of it was I phoned this chap, and it turned out he'd moved back into the village and was popping down, and he'd discovered my dad frothing at the mouth and he'd stabbed [the neighbor] and various other things, completely flipped. And they'd taken my dad into hospital for his own protection more than anything, and it turned out he had attacked nurses and they had to get the police in—and in the end they wouldn't give me information. And so, it's taken a long time to get to this point, [he] eventually ended up in a hospital in [nearby town] that they told me about, but I still wouldn't have been allowed to see him or he wouldn't have wanted to see me because he didn't even know that I was getting information then. And then I got a phone call from him [from the hospital]. He said I've been a silly old bugger, "why don't you come down and see me?" You know, Christ. . . . so I got my brothers to come over—they only live thirty-odd miles away—and we went down and saw him. And he was as good as gold: "I don't know what I'm doing in this place, I don't know what's wrong with me, I forget things." So, the point was that I ultimately sort of spoke to them at the hospital and said look, they said he can't look after himself, and I said I've got a house and there's plenty of room for him, there's a toilet and shower and everything on the ground floor. And they agreed that I could take him.

Within the short span of a few weeks, Paul's life had completely changed. He was once again living with his father, whom he had spent most of his life keeping at a distance. Not only that, but he would soon be providing 24/7 care for him, trying to make some new connection. Not long after the move, however, his father's aggression and disorientation became more volatile.

Because of his father's generous pension and savings, he would be considered "self-funded" and therefore ineligible for most of the state entitlement benefits related to care. Paul wasn't worried about paying the bills, but each adult day care or residential care home that Paul took his father to refused to allow him to stay because of his violent outbursts. For Paul, unlike Kazuko, the transition to becoming a carer was chaotic and stressful, not because of his unwillingness to care, but because of the circumstances of his father's illness and sudden, unexpected proximity.

"I Committed My Life to Caring"

Emiko and I met for the first time at a crafting workshop run by the Pear Group, a neighborhood volunteer group for older men and women who live alone and have few social opportunities. I sat next to Emiko as she sorted out bits of precut felt on a small placemat in front of her. "These little pieces are so small!" she mumbled, as she glued the shapes onto a small ornament. Although the workshop was a social occasion, the room was library quiet as those present concentrated on their craft. One of the organizers had pulled me aside and whispered to me that Emiko's husband had died about six months earlier and that she would be a good person to talk to, so before we all went home, I made sure to ask her if I could drop in on her sometime to talk about my research. She looked up at me with a nervous smile, but as we were neighbors, it was difficult to refuse. I was nervous as well, since a conversation about care with someone so recently bereaved would inevitably bring up strong emotions.

A week later, as I took off my shoes in the entryway, just large enough for one person to turn around in, I looked up to see the ornaments from the Pear Group neatly displayed on top of a cabinet. Emiko led me to a chair at her small kitchen table, only a few steps away from the entrance. She poured water from the kettle into a small teapot, just big enough for the two of us, and before taking a seat I passed her a small bag of rice crackers that I had brought as a gift. "I'm glad you didn't bring anything too sweet. I'm diabetic, so I have to watch out for that," she said as she put the crackers in a bowl and joined me at the table. I took a sip of tea and took out my notebook, beginning by asking about how she and her husband met each other over sixty years ago.

> A friend introduced us. Just said, "How about meeting [this guy I know]?" I didn't like men who did the kind of work that women did. And he was a truck driver. He was a man and had a job, so I thought, that's nice. And there wouldn't be a mother-in-law [he was not an eldest son], so I thought, that's nice too! [laugh]. So we lived together for a while, against my parents' wishes. They were worried. "Why would you marry someone like that?" So for a while we didn't get married officially. It was about five years.

Eventually her husband was able to pass the exam to earn his taxi driver license, and with a little more financial security, they started a family. Emiko continued working, doing sewing jobs out of the house. While their respective jobs followed gendered occupational norms, the fact that they shared in contributing to the family income meant that there was a less pronounced sense of inequality in the house. Since her husband was not the eldest son and his family lived far away, there was little contact or support from his family; Emiko's natal family, who disapproved of the marriage, kept distant as well. Yet in some ways, their isolation allowed them the kind of freedom that many families did not enjoy at that time, and their affection for each other grew over the years. They made close ties in the community, although as the neighborhood changed over the years, she found it hard to keep up with the new neighbors.

After her husband turned eighty, he began to show more serious signs of decline: he lost his hearing, he would become cold easily because of poor circulation, and his body became weaker, so he ventured out less. Emiko thought some of his behaviors were a little uncharacteristic, but she didn't think it was anything more than the natural progression of getting older until his condition suddenly worsened considerably. She explained the lingering sense of guilt she had for not doing more to care for him at that time: "If I had called the ambulance [when I noticed the changes], it might have been better, but, well, it's not like it was too late or anything, since he was in the hospital for three months after that. I just keep trying to console myself, thinking if I'd only paid more attention to this or that. Maybe I should have done this or that."

When her husband returned from the hospital, he came with a rented hospital bed that occupied half of the largest room in the house. It was then that Emiko realized she was now his carer in addition to his wife. Over the year that she cared for him, his condition worsened, and Emiko constantly doubted herself, trying to make sure she didn't wait too long before calling the ambulance again when things changed. For her, becoming a carer disrupted the routines, habits, and rhythms of their married life, yet the "frayed everyday life" (Das 2006, 9) continued as she searched for a thread from which to reweave some new narrative of their relationship.

Bea, who was much younger than Emiko, followed a similar pattern in her progression from wife to carer, beginning when she noticed small but disconcerting changes in her husband Dave's personality:

> It was at the back of my mind that there's something not right—maybe it's depression? So we went to the doctors and said I think he's depressed because this is happening and that, and the GP picked up on it and said why do you think he's depressed? And I sort of said I can see the signs and this sort of thing, and she said I think it might be his memory more than depression, and at that point she sent us for an assessment, and

as soon as we got into the hospital I could see what he'd been hiding, sort of his own apprehensions all came to the fore, and I think he was a bit scared of the fact that he knew there was something wrong. He was able to talk about it at that stage, he can't really say it now, but he said to me, "I don't know what's wrong with me, I can't think straight." And it was then that I realized it is up here rather than just I-couldn't-care-less attitude.

Dave was Bea's second husband, a proud man, a man who made things, repaired things, worked with his hands, who understood tools. This makes his vulnerability ("I can't think straight") in the moment Bea describes visiting the memory clinic all the more heart-wrenching. He was only sixty-seven, so Bea did not imagine he could have something like dementia. The idea that she would become a carer for her husband and would see him through the progression of his illness terrified her.

The treatment, there was no treatment, the assessor said to me in the clinic that "you're just going to have to change your life because there is no treatments. Leave here today and get on with it." Wow, you know? What do I do? And because I had a husband saying what are they talking about, what's the matter with me, and I'm thinking, god . . . So I tried to explain to him very simply that your brain's like a circuit board, and in your case some of the connections are a bit dodgy, and while they work occasionally they don't work all the time. So you're going to remember one day but you might not remember the next, and you're going to start to forget how to do things. And he was just so angry! "That's ridiculous, there's nothing wrong with me," and he kept saying there was nothing wrong with him, and then he would do something really weird, and it was obvious that there was a problem.

Her fears had been realized, and she left the hospital in tears. Her narrative of spending their empty-nest years bonding with her husband was suddenly swept away, and her "big strong man," her "soulmate," was gone. The horizon of her life had tilted, giving her a feeling of vertigo. Becoming a carer in this way was a kind of bereavement, an initiation into a new everyday that would be punctuated by a gradual drip of losses with no way of knowing what would come next, when he would wake up and forget some cherished part of their life, or when he would no longer recognize her as anything other than his carer. She referred to this new phase as her "half life," as if something had detached and drifted away, lost in the fog. But like Emiko, what held her together and allowed her to move on in her new role was her commitment to their marriage. She told me, "Despite everything, he is still the person I married and the man I committed my life to caring for, and this will be the one thing, I am sure, that will sustain me when things get much worse and ultimately, when he no longer remembers who I am, that will bind me to him when all else has gone." For both Bea and Emiko, taking the responsibility for becoming a carer was already prefigured in the commitment of marriage, grounded in experiences of times "richer and poorer, in sickness and in health." Sudden and surprising as the revelation of becoming a carer was, life as a carer was not a matter of starting from scratch, but of retuning attentions to the fragile other, becoming their protector and security in a world where they could no longer securely dwell.

Care and Commitment

The process of becoming a carer is complicated by the ambiguity of the word itself. "Carer" (or *kaigosha* in Japanese) can be highly specific political category referring to a contractual or legal designation of guardianship and authority to make decisions about care and to liaise with care institutions. In both Japan and England, the term had a bureaucratic tone and is more closely associated with paid care workers rather than family. Echoing Weber's interpretation of "vocation" and the "calling," researchers like Aneshensel et al. (1995) adopt the construct of "career" (which they distinguish from formal, paid "occupation") to describe "the movement of an individual through a series of related stages" (18) defined by "a changing constellation of activities and functions" (19).[13] Carers wavered on whether their care was mainly an extension of the already existing relationship or a new "stage" in an unfolding career. The care that frail elderly family members required, from medical assistance to intimate personal care, exceeded both the typical support offered to adult kin and the kinds of instrumental support offered by paid carers. Caring for elderly relatives could entail anything from bathing them to managing their bank account to simply listening to them, and it was up to the carer and the care recipient to anticipate and attend to all these needs.

For family members, becoming a carer was more than just a rational process of tabulating needs, forming plans, and taking on new tasks. It was, in some ways, taking up a responsibility that had already been lying in wait but that had not yet emerged into one's narrative identity; becoming a carer was an ethical decision of turning toward the other, to reconfigure one's own world to better resonate with the other. Taking responsibility meant giving oneself over to the other, to the fragile open hand reaching out. In this gesture, the construct of the family, its ecology of care, is also shaken, as the relationship between carer and the cared-for becomes radically altered. Children become like parents, husbands become like wives, spouses like children. The resonance ripples out beyond the immediate dyadic encounter, affecting other relationships, recalling memories, altering the ways one moved in the space of the home, dismantling the narratives of hoped-for futures.

Becoming a carer involved an ongoing process of retrospectively considering the attachments, identities, and memories that formed the meaningful basis for one's commitment to the care, but as the narratives of unexpected responsibility suggest, the impulse to commit was made from within a web of already existing relationships and ongoing commitments. For Hideki, the care of his mother-in-law could not be separated from his committed relationship with his wife. Kazuko and Paul both cared for widowed parents, taking responsibility when their siblings refused. Spouses relied on commitments they had made in marriage before their partners became frail and disabled. Shifting into a role as carer made sense in these cases because it resonated with these past relational commitments. While honoring a commitment meant projecting oneself into a future, it did not make that future any more certain or knowable.

Most carers I spoke with could identify a moment when they felt they first became a "carer," when their narrative identity took a turn in a new direction, when slowly or suddenly the landscape became transformed. For some, it was a slow process of refiguring identity as a spouse or child (Yoko, Hideki), while for others, it was a response to sudden crisis (Kazuko, Paul, Emiko, Bea). Yet in each case, becoming a carer was unexpected; the surprise of relatedness was the threshold of responsibility to care. If responsibility is a threshold, what lies on the other side?

When we are called on to care for others, we realize our own embeddedness in and dependence on the world, those roles that only we can fill and from which we cannot easily slip away. Responsibility may empower and motivate carers to exert more control, but as these cases show us, even when the care recipient is placed in a nursing home, as in Yoko's mother's case, control escapes. This calls on a different kind of ethical configuration of responsibility, not as the exercise of reining in risk, but as something similar to what Jane Guyer called "durational ethics," a steadfast, patient endurance in the face of "*contingent* situations, within *concatenated interconnections*, with respect to possibly *obstreperous or vulnerable* other people and near futures when anything could happen" (Guyer 2014, 402, emphasis in original). This durational ethics of responsibility defines the role of family carers (as I discuss more in the next chapter) but also stands in contrast to the ethics of formal care institutions, which were viewed as transitory services rather than places of enduring connection, places that one moved through but did not stay with. In contrast, being a good family carer meant accompaniment, being there before, during, and after care has ended.

Finally, looking closely at the gesture of taking responsibility reveals it to be more than simply the fulfillment of one's duty or the burden one bears. True, there can be strong social pressures to care, but in the cases I introduced, carers were not hostages to care; it may even become a source of freedom. Guyer (2014, 400) and Zigon (2007, 138) have argued that a socially constituted ethics means that responsibility is a precondition for freedom, not as autonomy, but as shared life. A similar notion of freedom can be found in the work of Japanese philosopher Washida Kiyokazu (2015), who argued that caring should not be seen as "servitude," as it may be portrayed in the paradigm of social welfare services, but a "freedom" of following the "weak" (114). As an example of this freedom, Washida cites the case of Bethel House, a group home for people living with schizophrenia that was the focus of Karen Nakamura's (2013) ethnography *Disability of the Soul*. For the "vulnerable" residents of Bethel House, "freedom" was not so much a matter of self-determination as it was a cooperative experiment in mutual care that many thought would be impossible outside of restrictive institutions. Like residents of Bethel House, many unpaid family carers would realize freedom in their own "fragile subjectivity" (*moroi shutaisei*), "incomplete existence" (*fukanzen na sonzai*), and interdependent shared life with the cared-for and others. The freedom of following the weak, then, was freedom conceived of as care: mutual "liberality" rather than individual "liberty" (Washida 2015, 115). Is this the freedom that lies beyond the threshold of responsibility?

Washida reminds us that durability of care is constituted by and intertwined with human fragility (both the carer's and the cared-for's). In the next chapter I look at how carers experienced and endured fragility, vulnerability, and fatigue under the heavy weights of responsibility.

3

FATIGUE AND ENDURANCE

"Every day I was going, going!"

Having spent the afternoon with Sayuri, it was hard for me to visualize her early years caring for her mother-in-law. Sayuri seemed to move in slow motion, gracefully unrushed. Sometimes she would pause and gaze off to one side of the room, a look of faraway concentration on her face, then she would slowly come back to our conversation, holding my eyes intensely, yet beaming with a soft, beatific smile. Her voice was soothing; you could rock to sleep on its rise and fall. Sayuri even continued smiling when telling me about the hard times during her first experience of unpaid caring many years ago.

> SAYURI: I got married when I was twenty-one years old. It was pretty early, right? A month after I got married, my husband's mother was struck down [*taoreta*] with a bad stroke, and from then on, my life was caring [*kaigo*] for the next thirty years. I was changing my mother [in-law]'s diapers before I was changing my baby's diapers. I was just twenty-one years old, so it was really hard.
>
> DANELY: Well, you were healthy, though, only in your twenties.
>
> SAYURI: That's true.
>
> DANELY: You might say it is better than being an older carer.
>
> SAYURI: Yes, I was healthy. But I was still immature as a person. Mentally and emotionally, and [without] knowledge, I was more than anything immature as a person. A big turning point was when our second child was born with a mental handicap. Until then I had energy

and felt like I could handle everything, and I put a lot of effort into child raising, but I had no idea that raising my handicapped daughter would mean getting so much help from other people and how much public [welfare] support I would have to get to take care of her. All that that time I was just caring for my daughter and caring for my mother [in-law], and it was like, I'm not going to survive. I thought my daughter was going to need me to look after her all her life until I got old myself, and I just thought it was my destiny to live my life caring for my mother [in-law] and daughter.

Sayuri continued caring for both her mother-in-law and her children, then her own parents. Although it is unusual in Japan for someone to start caring so young, the growing number of smaller, more mobile families means that it was not unusual that the care for both parents and in-laws (then spouse) might all fall on the same person.[1] Initially, I was shocked when I heard carers tell me they had been caring for ten years or more, but as I spoke to more people, it became evident that it was more unusual to provide care for only a year or two. Like Sayuri, people who care for so many years tended to become more isolated and fatigued. Sayuri continued, her voice beginning to crack, and her smile melting away from her face.

It was like I was in another world. I would always be home, and we lived on the ninth floor of an eleven-story apartment building. One time my husband found me standing out on the veranda holding my child, and I guess it looked like I was about to jump off. I don't have any memory of it at all, but it might have been that at the time I was thinking [if I jumped] I could die. Every day I was just working my hardest, not really paying attention to other people. There was a time when my heart [kokoro] became a devil. I thought all kinds of, well, really horrible things. The evil-hearted Sayuri—black! When my heart would become the devil, I really, it was really like, "if only [my mother-in-law] would die," I would think horrible things like that. How could I have thought such a horrible thing? I would wonder afterward. But it was like at that point, I was backed into a corner, you know—I thought about just setting the house on fire and burning it all down. We would die together. I had times when I thought like that. And so now I really understand how a person feels when they say they wanted to die together [with their care recipient].

Sayuri wiped her tears away and regained her composure, even managing a little laugh at herself for getting so emotional recalling her past. Studies of daughter-in-law carers in Japan have consistently shown greater struggles with emotional well-being when compared to daughters caring for parents (Elliot and Campbell 1993; Long, Campbell, and Nishimura 2009; Nishi et al. 2010), and studies of dual carers (those caring for both the young and the old) show that they are some of the most at-risk groups (Yamashita and Soma 2016). One can look at statistics on topics like these and manage to feel very little. They more or less affirm what we might already assume but are presented in a way that is more abstract, impersonal, and dispassionate. Drinking tea with Sayuri while she opened up to me about this intensely traumatic time in her life, broken by the weight of care responsibilities, was something entirely different. I felt both deeply moved and disturbed by the images she conjured. How could someone who had spent years lovingly committed to her responsibility of care turn to such dark and violent fantasies? How does someone endure through the remaining months or years of care after having had such thoughts?

As Sayuri noted when we spoke, she was not alone in the pain of caring. When Japanese family carers spoke about times when they contemplated suicide, homicide, or both, they also referred to the experience as being almost automatic and disembodied, as if possessed by the thought, suddenly feeling their heart become a demon (*oni*) or devil (*akuma*) that was agonizing to resist. Among health care professionals, this might be considered a symptom of "compassion fatigue," or the "stress, strain, and weariness of caring for others who are suffering" (Shulz et al. 2007, 6).[2] This term was first used to describe job strain among nurses and other paid care professionals who were responsible not only for keeping patients alive (or seeing them through their last days) but also for responding to them with empathy and affection (Coetzee and Klopper 2010; Figley 1995; Mason et al. 2014; Melvin 2015). Research examining compassion fatigue among informal, unpaid family carers of older relatives is extremely rare compared to that examining paid care staff (important exceptions are Day and Anderson 2011; Day, Anderson, and Davis 2014). Part of the reason for this gap is the prioritization of a certain kind of data for use in managing staff and running institutions. But unpaid family carers are just as susceptible to exhaustion, and as Sayuri's case shows, this can place both the carer and the care recipient in extremely unstable conditions where fantasies of violence or abandonment begin to resonate with the pain, hopelessness, and invisibility of long-term care.

In Japan, compassion fatigue was typically known simply as "care fatigue" (*kaigo tsukare*), a potentially dangerous though not uncommon experience of anyone providing long-term care, whether paid or unpaid.[3] Like Sayuri, other Japanese carers also found ways to ascribe meaning to *kaigo tsukare*, associating it with the transformative beginnings and emergent sense of vulnerability that attuned them to the cared-for (Danely 2017b). This held not only practical value (i.e., made them more responsive carers), but it also provided a means of attributing virtue to endurance. English carers also experienced care fatigue, but rather than seeing it as a part of the experience of caring, as something that drew them closer to the experience of the cared-for by rendering them more vulnerable and open, they tended to cope through emotional detachment: "stiff upper-lip," or "just getting on with it." When this attitude became unsustainable, English carers found relief through using formal respite care or by hiring someone to take over the care so they could spend some time alone.

In this chapter, I want to consider how fatigue may be considered part of care rather than something that hinders it. If taking responsibility was at the core of *identifying* oneself as a carer (chapter 2), fatigue was the beginning of *embodying* this identity. Enduring, persevering, and surviving fatigue enhanced sympathetic responsiveness in ways that would open up possibilities for being-with the cared-for and for reencountering them with vulnerability and compassion.

No Fatigue Like Care Fatigue

As I pedaled up the long gradual slope following the Kamo river, which runs south through Kyoto city, I began to feel our big green bicycle becoming slower and less steady. My daughter was riding in the front-mounted child seat, just behind the handlebars, while my son took the larger backseat. I was seven months into my fieldwork, and he was already insisting on speaking to me in Japanese: "Keep at it, Papa!" I redoubled my efforts, raising off the seat with each pedal push, the children cheering me on. I felt as if their voices were harnessing my last reserves of power to finish the agonizing climb. When I think of metaphors for the long road of caring, gradually becoming more brutal, heavy, and exhausting, I think of this road up to the park. The difference was that I could endure my fatigue because I knew my ultimate goal. Carers rarely have that assurance.

Finally, drenched in sweat, I reached the park. The children ran off to explore the playground while I collapsed, heavy with fatigue, under a large blue tentlike shade structure. Unfolding a paper fan and catching my breath, I glanced around me at all the other families enjoying the glorious spring day. There were a few older people, but most were young families, laying out picnic spreads or lazily reading books. My eye caught a young girl who looked about the same age as my own daughter (three), sitting on a short wall playing a game with her mother. Again and again, the mother would press her half-clenched fingers against the girl's knee, slowly pushing them into the knee more and more so they would spread out, sending an electric twinge through the girl's body. All the while, the mother would say "Gaaaaman, gamaaaan,

gamaaaan!" (Endure, endure, endure!), drawing out the words as if she were pulling elastic.[4]

Tickling is a form of touch that can be pleasurable or painful, relying as it does on the activation of the same nerve fibers responsible for both sensations. Perhaps this young girl was learning to exert her mind over matter, retraining her body's impulse to twist away from the wave of sensations rippling through her. Or maybe, just like the voices of my kids on the ride up the hill, the game was just as much about the power of that word, "Gaman!" and the playful submission to the demands of her mother. This was not a prelude to an inevitable explosion of giggles but went on for several rounds while the girl kept her lips determinedly clenched tight. I couldn't imagine my own daughter would last through even five seconds of this excruciating delight. It was such a simple game, yet it expressed so much about the everyday manner in which touch carried with it the particular values and ways of being-with-others so important for social life in Japan: vulnerability, restraint, endurance, pleasure.

The game of endurance reminded me of a time, years earlier, when I had lived in a part of Kyoto not far from the park. Nearing the end of fieldwork, I joined the other men in the neighborhood for the festival of the local *kami* (Shinto deity). I had participated in other festivals, but owing to a shortage of able-bodied young men, the portable shrine, traditionally carried through the streets on the men's shoulders, was now usually instead lifted onto a cart and rolled like a parade float. But this neighborhood was still relatively young, so on the day of the festival, we managed to merge our collective energy to carry it the whole way, squeezed in tightly around it, about fifteen of us on each side, bearing its massive sacred cargo. The shrine was about the size and weight of a small car, and as we walked, others would tap in to quickly swap places and give others a rest. I remember several moments of panic when I felt my arms and shoulders shaking and spasming in exhaustion, and I pictured them crumpling as we lifted the massive structure up over our heads at each crossroads, again and again, the great bells jangling on its wooden sides. I was amazed and relieved when it was over that I hadn't let it fall on anyone. Of course, with so many of us, I doubt the shrine would have fallen even if my strength did give out, but the feeling of danger motivated me to try just a little harder. *Gaman!* We endured. We survived. Bodies pressed next to each other, synchronized, unable to think about ourselves as separate from others or from the sacred load we carried. I was stiff and sore for a full week afterward.

Dramatic ritual performances (and neighborhood playgrounds) are not the only places where one can observe the celebration of perseverance in Japan. Effort and self-sacrifice, especially when they are in the name of a collective, be it the family, school, or workplace, are not only encouraged but expected (R. Benedict 1946; DeVos 1973; Kondo 1990). While the tireless fighting spirit has long been associated with male figures, from the samurai to the solider to the salaryman (Roberson 2005), a more fundamental prototype for the power of endurance is the mother, who stakes her life and her moral purpose on the love she devotes to her children (Borovoy 2005, 503; Ozawa-de Silva 2006).[5] Mothers are not only carers, but they endure in their responsibility, often to the detriment of other work or personal dreams, not to mention health and well-being. In Japan, care is defined as much by what carers endure as what they give.

Like mother and child, this bond of caring endurance means putting one's own body on the line. In caring for a frail older relative, the body of the carer and cared-for again come into frequent intimate contact, generating a practical embodied moral knowledge of the other (Chattoo and Ahmad 2008, 551; Twigg 2000). With some practice, carers learn ways to lift and move an immobile body, using the weight of both bodies to shift position together. They learn how to be careful of sensitive skin or joints, how to read subtle movements of the eyes, grunts, or half-formed sentences. This attunement to the feelings of the cared-for can help the carer respond to the constant adjustments and disruptions to routines, but it also means entering into the world of someone who is often confused and suffering, opening up to the fluidity between the broken bodies of the carer and the cared-for.

"There's no fatigue like care fatigue!" Makiko told me later at the monthly meeting of the Apricot Group. She wasn't joking. She looked me straight in the eye, holding me in that gaze as she said this. Makiko had cared for her mother-in-law for years, but now she was caring for her husband. She was rarely able to leave her house over the last year, as the care was full time. "It isn't like taking care of children. At least with them, you know they'll learn and grow up. With older people, well, there's just one way they're going."

Even listening to the stories of carers like Makiko, I felt exhausted. The work they described, both currently and sometimes over past periods of several years, was relentless. "I take care of my mother all day," Makiko continued. "I feel like I am doing fine now, since I've been doing it so long, but there have been times, especially at the end of the day, when I would sit at my kitchen table and feel everything get dark, and just cry." Makiko would convince herself that she was just in that mood because she was exhausted, and she would try to go to sleep, lonely and worried, dreading being awoken again in the dead of the night, as she usually was.

In contrast to the shock of initially becoming a carer (or realizing that one had been a carer without knowing it), fatigue was something that accumulated over time, due to the increasing needs of the cared-for and the diminishing time away from caring that helped carers recover and catch their breath. The slower pace of fatigue didn't mean it was any less dangerous, but only that it became more difficult to mitigate, since there was no single catastrophic event precipitating the fatigue but only a long string of events that, looked at individually, did not compel a clear and decisive response.[6] Fatigue cannot be located in a singular, catastrophic event but accumulated through a series of what Elizabeth Povinelli (2011, 13) describes as "quasi-events," or moments in everyday life that "never quite achieve the status of having occurred or taken place" and thus pose a different kind of ethical demand than that of the crisis. This confounding aspect of fatigue makes it especially hard to grasp except through imperfect formulas like psychosocial scales or self-assessment surveys. But how does one calculate or operationalize the feeling when your father has fallen on the bathroom floor, as one carer described to me, when all you can do is sit there next to him, knowing that you won't be able to pick him up alone? What potentials or capacities might such moments of exhaustion and despair disclose?

Fatigue is both a falling back into the body and an alienation from it. The body refuses to move, to speak, or to think clearly. There is a numbness, and yet a sense of weight.[7] For carers like Makiko, this feeling would come after she had put her mother to bed, rather than during the caring itself. It was as if, in being with her mother, she was able to turn her attention away from herself, acting only with compassionate attention to her mother, enduring. But it was when she was alone that the sense of hopelessness would descend, not as something to endure, nor as a form of resistance, but something in between (Wilkinson and Ortega-Alcázar 2019). Endure, endure, endure. Until the subject-object distinction blurs. "I wondered if I'd ever have my own feelings again," Makiko confessed to me, "but then [Mother] would call me, and I would just say, 'OK, here I go!'"

Perseverance and Mutuality

For Japanese carers, fatigue and endurance were associated with deeply held values of discipline and selfless compassion. Just as fatigue manifests in the body, so too does this sense of compassion. In some cases, carers, weary and wounded from the tasks of caring, found their attunement to the body of the person they cared for to be so heightened that they no longer felt entirely separate, but rather an extension of the other. In one instance, for example, I met a friendly middle-aged male carer at a small support group meeting in Kyoto who described a similar perspective. He had just been to visit his mother, whom he has been caring for at a distance (*enkyōri kaigo*). "My brother lives right there in the same city," he explained, "but he doesn't even go to visit my mom. So, I end up driving three hours to go see her, clean up her house, take care of all the arrangements. If I didn't do it, who would?" This sounded similar to the sentiment of English carers, but the man continued:

"[My mother and I] are the same life [*inochi*]. If one part is weaker, the other has to make up for it, just like the organs in your body."

Tomomi, who, like this man, also went back and forth from her home in Kyoto to her mother's home for several months before deciding to move in, described her experience of fatigue, endurance, and inter-corporeality with her mother in almost the same terms:[8]

> It was so much more complicated than I ever could have imagined it would be. I wasn't thinking that someone could change that way, becoming so aggressive and saying such awful things—I guess she's been starting to get confused these days, but I still feel like, "how could you say those kinds of things to your daughter!?" But then I have to remember, Mother's sick. So I *endure* all that while I hold her hand, or take her to the toilet. That feeling is just—well, how should I respond to it? I just think, she's not well . . . she's sick, and I'm healthy. And health is such a precious thing, so when I am healthy, then I can help her. If I keep *persevering*, things will turn out okay.

For Tomomi, the empathetic impulse manifested first in touch, then in a sense of responsibility as one body to another. Tomomi felt responsible not only as a daughter, but as a healthy body responding to one that is sick. Such "feeling along with others" meant that healthy and sick could be contained within the same relational body, a body of mutuality and resonance rather than difference and incommensurability.

But while she was growing closer to her mother, she also felt herself becoming more distant in other intimate relationships:

> When I was taking care of mother I didn't even want to speak to anyone. I was so tired. I had no desire to speak to other people. I would sometimes speak with [my husband], but I wouldn't speak much. Just be in the house and watching TV that I didn't want to watch. It was too tiring to talk to others. When I went back to my mother I actually felt relieved. I was more at ease. I knew I had to pay attention to someone else, and it felt easier.

Tomomi's relief at returning to her place of resonance registered as the relief of moral self-displacement ("paying attention to someone else"). But she no longer resonated with her prior home and husband; her voice had left her. After Tomomi's mother died, she moved back to Kyoto, and we caught up with each other at a small, dimly lit café near the Kamo river. She would be returning to her family home in a few days for the forty-ninth-day anniversary of her mother's death, when, some believe, the spirit of the deceased is pacified and able to move on to the "other world" (*ano yo*). Tomomi was still a little unsteady since the care ended, but she wanted to tell me about the way things were in the last few weeks of taking care of her mother:

> I couldn't sleep. My mother was next to me, and I would always be hearing her [saying] "Ooo! Ooo!" and it really felt just like I was hearing the devil's voice. It was excruciating. I would say, "What's wrong, Mum?" but all she'd do was moan. And when she couldn't eat food, [I'd say] "What's wrong?" and all I could do was just rest my hand on her body, or hold her hand. I'd be like, "What should I do for her?" But it was like that every day, when I was caring. It felt like I wasn't sleeping even when I was sleeping. When I'd wake up I would see how she is doing, and when the helper came, the helper would take care of her for a little while, and I would get a little time to do something for myself. In the evening a nurse would come and ask, "Is she okay going to the toilet?" "She doesn't have a temperature?" "Shall I take her blood pressure?" and once a week, on Sunday, my older brother would come over for three hours. I'd go to this *gyoza* restaurant that I love, and eat, then have cup of coffee and go back home and switch places with my brother. That Sunday, once a week, that rest was so important. And then once again when Monday began, it would be the same thing all over again.

The "devil" appears again in Tomomi's story, along with its haunting, unhomely voice, and again Tomomi would wait out the uncertainty, holding her mother's hand as if it were an anchor to resonance. The helper would only come for an hour at most, and Tomomi would use this time to do tasks associated with care: "I could maybe do half an hour of shopping, but I couldn't go very far. Sometimes I would have a little longer so I could go do some errands at the hospital and so on, but as far as time to do something fun, there was none of that!"

Although her brother lived in the same city, his own work and family responsibilities limited the amount of time he was able to care. After Tomomi told him that she was losing sleep and scared of getting totally exhausted, he agreed to take one evening, three hours on Sundays, so Tomomi had a few moments to catch her breath. It wasn't a lot, but it was time when she could take some small refuge from the relentless demands and return again to her own body (through food and coffee). Tomomi learned to hold presence with her mother, to accompany her, trying and failing repeatedly to read her feelings, but continuing to try again each day. Enduring her exhaustion, Tomomi didn't appear anxious or worried. Perhaps the numbness of fatigue provided an escape from thinking too much, a chance to be present.

Exhaustion and Excess

"Sorry I'm treating you like a psychiatrist. You know, you just—there are so many things, and you can't escape from it!" The corner of the room where Paul and I talked was a little like a psychiatrist's office, except I was the one on the couch and Paul had chosen a bright-red chair close to the wall. I had chosen the room out of a concern for privacy. Carers came to speak to me, taking precious time away from the person they cared for, and I didn't want to struggle in a noisy café or other public spot. Carers often wanted desperately to get out of their homes and to talk to someone about their experience. Paul felt isolated since taking responsibility for the care of his father, whom he had never been close to, and who was now living with serious physical and cognitive impairment, including aggressive behaviors that prevented him from being able to stay in a care home. Paul found little comfort from family and friends, and he felt his own mental state becoming dangerously shaken. Unable to escape and yet unable to find a rhythm, Paul was becoming desperate. I listened:

> A friend of mine said you ought to go to the doctors and they'll help you with some pills—and I said I don't bloody want pills. You'll get some sleep and this sort of thing, and I know there would have been a few occasions when I would have taken the lot. Too much. In these meetings you hear people say they'd go for a walk if they could, but they can't. Just do something to get away from it. I can imagine people heading to the bottle, or something stronger. It's just so—you lose your independence. You completely have to give yourself over to caring for this person who doesn't appreciate it in any way. You become this sort of automaton. You don't even get into a rut, because everything is always changing. A rut can be comforting in a way, like having a regular job, a shit job you know, you've got a job and you're nine-to-five or whatever. But yeah, there's no consistency to anything. You know? Every day is a new experience, and frequently not a good one.

Paul's casual comment that he might have "taken the lot" of pills was the sort of "dark humor" frequently employed by current carers in England, like a soft landing when they've inevitably reached the rock bottom of their fatigue. Here, Paul's efforts to get help from a professional paradoxically leads him a step closer to the edge of the cliff; the pills are the punch line, an absurdity delivered deadpan from a character in a lab coat. Paul wasn't the type who would take this experience as a basis for judging what works for other carers who get by with the help of sleeping aids, antidepressants, and the like. Every carer is caught in a different set of circumstances and composes his or her own narrative, and whether they take medications or walks in the woods hardly matters.

Paul wanted me to chuckle along to his story, and I did, but I didn't let that be the signal to shift the conversation. By the time we had sat down to talk with each other, I'd talked to enough carers to trust his gesture was a way letting me in on the joke and into his world, through a side door. Paul's fatigue had somehow made suicide an attractive possibility, at least when he was at his lowest. In his state of mind, even the help of a well-intentioned doctor was like handing him a loaded gun. Out of one trap and into another. I know that explaining the joke is a sure way to kill it, but when I think about this conversation now I still smile, picturing Paul's stunned expression as the doctor offered his best support, and the doctor's face when Paul regained his composure enough to tell him "I don't bloody want pills!"

Paul struggled to articulate his experience of being caught by care. He had not told his story to anyone, not in full, and he gave the impression that he was still trying to make sense of it as we spoke. On the one hand, Paul states that he felt like an "automaton," unable to act independently according to his own will; yet, on the other hand, he had to be constantly vigilant, sensitive, sharp. Caring did not allow for the steady tedium of a "shit job"; it was never "consistent," always "new," and "changing." Care fatigue does not look like the "rut" of factory work; it was a weariness of "affective labor": always demanding attention, intensity, performance, and authenticity, response and responsibility (Hardt and Negri 1990; Hochschild 2012). In most instances, Paul's father's confusion only led to relatively small incidents, but nonetheless, these kept Paul constantly on watch.

> You'd be sat there and hear something clonking around—what are you doing? "I'm making tea." But you know, there are only two of us in the house, and he's made six cups of tea. And all the milk will have gone so I'd have to sort of, I don't know, do you need to go to the toilet? "Yes I think I do." Okay—so I'd sit him on the bog while I nip around to the little shop to get another pint of milk, this kind of thing, because you just couldn't leave him. And then you add to that the things like having to wash him five times a day, and I can tell you, wiping your ninety-four-year-old dad's arse isn't as much fun as you'd think!

The mess of his father's "leaky body," its pungency and disorderliness, were inescapable. Paul felt himself coming apart at the seams:

> And basically, I've got quite a large room upstairs where I sort of just, it's like a living room, but I've got a room in there and the computer's in there and this kind of thing, and you just sort of—I'd go up there and

just burst into tears sometimes. Just in anticipation for what's next. And as I say, I thought that I could deal with things, you know. But it rips you apart, it really does.

It is little wonder that Paul felt ripped apart. He had slept only a few hours over the last few days and was slightly delirious, but was excited about being part of the research project. I was starting to feel tired, too, trying to mentally hold on to all of Paul's expressive gestures and turns of phrase, his dark humor. It was clear that he cared deeply about his father but was overwhelmed by the demands, both physical and ethical, that strained his capacity to form a coherent narrative. Paul's sense of being ripped apart is reflected in his narrative, which splits and frays from monologue to dialogue (with narration), as if he were watching the scene rather than within it; he not only experiences his father's delusions as "othering," but Paul himself becomes "othered" as a carer, as someone who must somehow respond to an unhomely and disordered world that stands apart from him.[9] The following dialogue is actually a monologue, where the voices crash over each other, Paul's identity ripped apart rather than resonating.

Ultimately to get him into the home, you have things like all of a sudden there's CLONK-CLONK-CLONK!
"What in god's name now?"
"Paul! Paul!"
"Yes, mate?" I'd look down and he'd be fully dressed.
"Come on, you've got to get out."
"What's up?"
"Gas cloud."
"What? Gas cloud? Who said?"
"It's on the news."
"What news?"
"Well I've heard it's on the news."
I mean I don't have a television, well I do, but it never goes on.
"Where did you hear it?"
"I just heard it, there's gas we've got to get out we've got to get out it could ignite any time!"—and he'd go into details about this gas, and you know this would be five o'clock in the morning. "Of course there bloody is, they wouldn't warn us otherwise!"
And Jesus Christ . . . I'd get him calmed down. "They'd phone everyone, there'd be announcements, an automatic phone thing if there was a problem." [I] talk him out of it, talk him out of it. Then try and get him back to bed. And then another time: What the hell's that? And he's sat on the bottom step of the stairs, and I thought I'd hidden all the knives,

but he's found a little serrated-edge knife, the kind of thing you use for cutting up fruit or something, you know what I mean. And he's cutting through the stair carpet.

"What are you doing, Dad?"

"Um, doing what you should be bloody doing!"

And I said, "Come on, stop it!"

"Call yourself a bloody soldier? You should be trying to get out of this bloody place!"

And I said, "Come on, blah-blah-blah," and then he tries to stab you and all this kind of thing. "Bloody traitor! Bloody traitor, no wonder we're in here!"

He was in a prisoner-of-war camp—he actually wasn't, but that was where he felt he was. But it was, you know, trying to get the knife off him and this kind of thing, and he'd be kicking and spitting and this sort of thing—come on, you need to get back to bed, more to the point I need to get back to bed! But there were so many episodes like that.

Beyond the harrowing content of Paul's story, it was the vivid and visceral form of its retelling that struck me most. Paul's voice changed completely when he "played" his father in these exchanges. It became low and curt, like the bark of an old dog. His acting brought the scene to life, but Paul wasn't sure what to do with it. The voices Paul used to perform his fatigue, not unlike the voices of the "devil" heard by Sayuri and Tomomi, had an uncanny quality of excess (Ivy 1995, 85, 149), of the embodiment of something not fully absorbed by the self, yet returning tenaciously, even haunting. His care didn't seem to help; he didn't feel like he was learning or growing or becoming more resilient from this. Pulling him to opposite extremes of exhaustion and excess, loss and overload, Paul's grief was tearing him apart. Judith Butler ([2004] 2020) writes that in grief, "one does not always stay intact. One may want to, or manage to for a while, but despite one's best efforts, *one is undone*, in the face of the other, by the touch, by the scent, by the feel, by the prospect of the touch, by the memory of the feel" (23–24). A tall, physically strong man, Paul was undone by the responsibility of care, by its repetition and unpredictability, which together removed the possibility of preparing or managing his life. Even sleep, the most basic routine element structuring his day, had become violently disrupted.

Paul's references to the "shadow side of care" were not always cushioned with humor. During one of our "psychiatry" sessions, which ran nearly three hours, Paul depicted the situation with his father as worse than I had imagined. I suggested that we take a walk, and for a while we talked about other topics aside from care. It was nice to just see him chatting casually, relaxing a bit more. I switched the recorder on again, and we stopped in the corridor, speaking in low voices like conspirators.

> I don't know—I don't know—you run out of knowing where to, where it should go, apart from doling out suicide pills. Because again people I talk to, you might not have heard it but I've heard it, and you say if it was a dog—you know, it's a wicked thing to say, but it's true—or it's a difficult thing to say or to admit that you've thought that, but it's true. . . . It's such a *moral*—I don't know if moral's the right word—you know, I could be completely frank about it and say for everybody I think who has a relative in the same situation, to be honest if they passed away it would be better, because there's no more, that's it.

Paul's last confession to the "psychiatrist" is, aptly, his grasping toward the future, only to be confronted by the endless fatigue of slow death. He has not only "run out" of options, but even the ability to know where to go. He is completely in the dark, and in the dark, death becomes easier to imagine. Death is not only an escape from his burden, but it is an event, a finality, some stopping point. But here, his role as a son and a carer sits uneasily with his wish for his father's death. There's no easy solution to Paul's dilemma, so he is left with depletion: "There's no more, that's it."

Paul had transferred his father to a care home that specialized in dementia care, and there hadn't yet been any issues with aggression. Instead, his father mostly sat on his bed, unable to read and uninterested in TV or socializing. I walked Paul out toward the bus stop.

Vulnerability

Fatigue, as Paul's story attests, can turn affectionate care into a baffling and torturous ordeal. While researchers have widely recognized the negative physical and mental health effects of carer "fatigue," the stories of carers vividly attest to its complex resonances and ambivalences. Fatigue, especially as an affective response to empathetic relational work, both produces and is produced by cultural narratives. What I noticed was that for Japanese carers like Sayuri and Tomomi, even experiences of severe fatigue resonated with a moral narrative of compassionate attunement, while for English carers, fatigue was perceived as a sign to back off and seek more formal care support. When Tomomi says that she endures her fatigue holding her mother's hand, she is not merely repeating a script of Japanese compassion and concern for others (*omoiyari*), but rather she is communicating something about the ways she has come to resonate with the stories of fatigue and the forms of moral relationality it affords. For those like Paul, who have a stronger orientation toward individual autonomy, this breakdown of the border between the worlds of the carer and the cared-for is perceived as dangerous. While fatigue was sensitizing Paul affectively to his father's condition, the unpredictability and violence of his father's symptoms (themselves the product of certain lifelong history of emotional distance) meant that this new sensitivity only deepened Paul's difficulty adjusting. Transferring some of the care responsibilities to paid carers or institutions, on the other hand, allows carers to continue relating to the cared-for as a separate person, allowing them to continue acting according to an ethic of charity.

Another way of approaching the notion of fatigue that might better capture this distinction is to understand it as vulnerability. Vulnerability, like fatigue, renders one more exposed to the world and to the possibility of harm. Yet at the same time, vulnerability is an essential part of our ability to care openly for others, to build trust and to form ethical commitments (Brown, Danely, and Rosenow 2021). Judith Butler, who has been one of the most prolific writers on the subject of vulnerability and its relationship to care, precarity, and politics, argues that as fragile, socially constituted bodies, we are vulnerable, "attached to others, at risk of losing those attachments, exposed to others, at risk of violence by virtue of that exposure" ([2004] 2020, chap. 2). It is no wonder, then, that the fatigue/exhaustion felt by carers is more profound than that of a mere laborer, since it entails these grief-laden relational exchanges. At the same time, it is vulnerability, with the way it enables us to resonate and empathetically connect with one another (even under conditions of fatigue), that is fundamental to good care. Vulnerability, in situations of care, cannot be seen as wholly good or bad, nor should it be the basis of a politics of care, in the ways health and social care providers might label certain people "vulnerable" or "at risk" in order to target them for interventions. Rather, again after Butler, vulnerability, for the exhausted carer, is a function of the ties we have to each other. Butler (2021, 37) continues:

> Those ties indicate a form of relationality that not only implies a way of thinking about the body, embodied cohabitation, but also the co-production of modes of life. . . . It is already and from the start a relational problem, presupposing a relational predicament that is to some extent incalculable. If I feel that I can be hurt, that says something about the kind of being that I am—it also says that I am open to a world and to others that act on me in ways that cannot be fully predicted or controlled in advance, and that something about that openness is not, strictly speaking, under my control. . . . The body is given over to others in order to persist.

Butler's notion of an "embodied cohabitation" in a world where I have limited control or ability to predict means that I am not only vulnerable toward the demands of other people, but even vulnerable to my own ambivalent "emotional and bodily responses" (Gilson 2014, 103–4) to those others. Not surprisingly, then, vulnerability is also an openness to different cultural narratives that might provide meaning to those spaces of cohabitation. In other words, vulnerability cannot be understood merely as a subjective state or feeling, nor is it merely the universal ontological condition of social life, since it is always relational and situated within particular histories and symbolic environments. The kinds of vulnerability that Japanese carers value will not necessarily be the same ones that English carers do, and this will affect the ways fatigue comes to matter.

The vulnerability of older, frail, and disabled care recipients has been largely described in terms of "contingent vulnerabilities" and ways to remedy them through social and health policy (Laceulle 2017, 2). In England, not only are care recipients assessed as "vulnerable," but since the 2014 Care Act, carers too have become categorized according to vulnerability. Paul and four other carers I spoke with were all contacted because they fit this category according to the answers they gave on just four items of the local authority's self-assessment. Three of the four questions used to assess "vulnerable" carers were concerned not with physical, but social vulnerability. Most telling, perhaps, was one question about how much "control you have over your life." The assumption that carers are well when they feel "in control" reveals the cultural assumptions around categories of vulnerability and their inadequacies in capturing the lifeworlds of carers, for whom attempts to "control life" can quickly lead to even more frustration, fatigue, and even violence.

While these contingent vulnerabilities align with states of "precariousness" (Allison 2013; Grenier and Phillipson 2018; Han 2018), the kind of vulnerability that those like Butler and Gilson are pointing to goes further. By starting from a different set of assumptions, a different story of care, one that presumes a shared human fragility and relationality, these theorists help us to begin understanding care as a condition of existential and epistemological vulnerability (Laceulle 2017; Gilson 2013), one that opens up the carer to other ways of being-in-the-world with others and to other ways of feeling and knowing. Japanese notions of compassion, with their emphasis on the capacity for embodied empathetic attunement with the cared-for, more closely resemble this notion of vulnerability, providing a culturally meaningful narrative into which carers can organize their experiences, both positive and negative. For English carers, however, openness had to be carefully managed through distance and the use of paid care; fatigue may have brought feelings of vulnerability, but this had little role to play in the tasks of care.

Managing Fatigue

For those who, like Paul, cared for a family member in their home, fatigue was often managed through "respite services," where a paid care worker would stay overnight or when the care recipient would stay for a few days in a short-term care home. Japanese carers often made use of weekly day service or even longer one- or two-week "short-stay" respite services, but overnight care would be unavailable for all but the very wealthy, who could pay for this out of pocket. In England, however, carers found respite care much more accessible, sometimes paying for it using the carer's allowance. For Charli, who lived with her father while she provided care, doing without respite was "unimaginable." When I asked Charli about fatigue, she described it as a "feeling that there is no end in sight. That you're just kind of plowing on through this fog of tasks that give you no sense of—hope is the wrong word—of being totally immersed and having no space to think." While Charli hoped to continue providing some care, she expected that she would come to rely more and more on support.

For older English people, living independently was considered a sign of dignity and vitality (Miller 2017), which could be preserved through offering practical support or through visiting-care-assistant services.[10] While carers remained somewhat constrained by this arrangement, making regular visits or remaining on-call in case of a sudden crisis, they were also able to protect their own sense of emotional distance, and for them this meant being a more effective care manager. Compared to Japanese carers, English carers found providing physical care, including feeding and dressing, degrading for the person they cared for, and they spoke often about the mental discomfort and stress of having to pay constant attention to the cared-for, especially when signs of rapid decline became more obvious. By living apart, unpaid carers often exchange these physical and affective tasks for the more rational, bureaucratic tasks of managing services.

Simon, for example, lived separately from his mother, but according to him, this meant that "all the time you are in shock, 'oh, this person can't do this anymore, can't do that—it is *constant* adjusting.'" Finally, things had come to the point where he brought his mother to live with him; but even while there was closer physical proximity, Simon still erected a mental barrier between himself and his mother: "I had to do the bathing and the sort of personal stuff, and I dreaded it! I eventually just did it, and I would have to take myself out of it, put a kind of wall up. I would just pretend it was someone else I was caring for, not my mother." Like Russell, whom I described in the introduction to this book, Simon found it emotionally distressing to perform personal care for his mother. The sensuality of physical touch was discomforting (for both carer and cared-for). Again, Butler's words rang out in my head: "One is undone by the face of the other, by the touch, by the scent, by the feel." The bond that Simon felt with his mother couldn't transcend the dread of the touch that threatened to blur the border between bodies, so instead he erected his own wall, the only way he felt he could preserve his mother's dignity and his own. To care for her in such an intimate way was for him, as a son, a form of violence. Yet if he could imagine himself as a paid carer, it was a form of charity.

Amy, who also lived separately while caring, also mentioned the importance of "adjustment" as she and her husband cared for her mother-in-law. Small moments of adjustments were ongoing, but these never led to the big change that everyone seemed to sense right around the corner, when they would move her to a residential care home. Amy's mother-in-law lived alone but was either unable or unconcerned with cleaning the house, so Amy surreptitiously did her best to clear piles of trash, clean dishes, and scrub toilets. "If it wasn't working for me, if it was really, really stressful and unendurable for me, I would be making it clear I was unhappy. I suppose with somebody who's that old and I've known for so long, and that you can see it coming, um, there are 'adjustment points.' But we really did ask ourselves, you do, you just see this person declining and think what's going to happen? And when do we have to intervene?"

Since her mother-in-law rejected the idea of having a visiting care assistant, Amy and her husband had thought about placing her in a care home, especially since it seemed there could have been potentially life-threatening problems if she continued to live on her own. While the current form of care helped maintain the semblance of independence, Amy and her husband were both confident that it was not something they wanted to maintain for much longer, and a bigger "adjustment point was in order":

> That was the real existential question for us before she broke her hip: at what point, how does, how far do we let it go? Because it was clear that she was desperately unhappy and lonely and bored out of her skull, and it was so sad to go over and see her in her house, you know. She'd be there, and the television would be flickering. Either it would be blaring loud and we just felt so apologetic for the poor neighbor, or, you know, and the subtitles would be showing and it would just be this flickering thing in the background and she'd be wrapped up in a little blanket and she might not have moved or eaten anything or seen anybody—and she never remembered the carers came. Tablets, medication? Do I take tablets? You know. Is there someone that—and part of this I think was her preference for denying, she has a superb capacity for ignoring unpleasantness and things. Ignorance has served her very well in her life, so I think she has decided—which was her attitude to dirt, you know, she

denied its existence. And if you really can convince yourself of that, it's admirable. It bears no relation to other people's reality, but . . . but it's very, very sad, and I'm glad that she fell and broke her hip and this was precipitated, because it could turn into something that was good.

Falls are common "adjustment points" for care recipients and carers alike (Boyles 2017), and while this can be very painful and frightening for a frail older person, as Amy admits, it can also bring the relief of instigating a new stage of care, a move closer to the ideal form of charitable care. Interestingly, Amy does not simply think of this as a straightforward, rational decision, but an "existential question" that prompted reflections not only on her mother-in-law's safety (nutrition, medication) but also on the quality of her life (the "flickering thing" her only company, the festering ignorance of dirt). Although she does not ask for charity, Amy and her husband finally deem it the right time and, in the end, the best moral solution.

After the hospital, Amy decided they would see about moving her mother-in-law to a residential care home. One of the responses that made her feel much more at ease with this decision was the thoughtful, caring nature of the care home staff, who were aware that the timing of the transfer would be key:

> I had conversations with the brilliant lady who manages the care home, and said god, shouldn't we have done this years earlier? And she's said if you do it too early they don't settle, and even with what she—she visited [my mother-in-law] when [she] was still in hospital to see if she was a fit, and this was after we had said we would like her to come here—and she said well, you know, I think this is good, but I want to do my own evaluation because they don't trust what the NHS tells them because the NHS wants to get rid of the "bed blockers," as they're called, so she did and she said we will accept your mother but on a month's probation.

Amy's mother-in-law did end up moving into the care home, leaving Amy and her husband to sort through her financial affairs and her house, cluttered with decades of accumulated possessions. Although Amy was very proud of having kept her mother-in-law in the village, she was also aware of the limits of that arrangement and felt the burden of having to do so much for her mother-in-law without ever really giving her the comfort of companionship. The transfer to the care center meant that Amy no longer needed to be concerned that her mother-in-law would be lonely and neglected; it was the best solution for everyone:

> Going into a care home can be the best thing that can happen to someone, and that is a wonderful thing to know, that is a wonderful thing to have witnessed. . . . My mother-in-law every time she wakes up from her

dozes there's a smiling face offering her a cup of tea and a piece of cake, and I think, well, it could be worse! And actually, there are people with twinkles in their eye in her care home, that I think they have Scrabble afternoons and whatnot, and you know, it's not so completely dire.

Amy's description of the care home is a direct contrast to the solitary room lit by the haunting flicker of the television, and shores up her narrative of having made the best moral choice as a carer. It also reflects the kind of potential for a redemptive narrative of institutional care, saving both the cared-for and the carer from the burden of fatigue and social isolation. In a study of community care of older hospice patients, anthropologist Daniel Miller (2015) argued that contrary to those who feel social life has been diminished by institutions, for English carers, "community exists only to the degree that it is created by the institution" (351). This was certainly true for Amy's mother-in-law, but also for Paul's father, who declined in isolation before coming to live with Paul.

Another carer, Jane, described her engagement with formal care institutions as a central part of her responsibility as a carer, one that would help to preserve the dignity of her parents by saving them the embarrassment of being cared for by Jane (Miller 2015, 352). She explained that her parents moved into a small flat that she had had built for them after they became less independent. The flat allowed her and her parents to live next to each other, but in separate, independent quarters. Living together already involved considerations of privacy and autonomy, and with greater dependence, help was needed.

> I don't think anyone anticipated them getting this elderly and decrepit really. I mean they certainly didn't. And then of course once mother couldn't walk we had to have carers come in. . . . They have three-quarters of an hour each in the morning to get them up and washed and dressed, showered or whatever. And then they have an hour after lunch to take them to the bathroom, an hour around tea time to take them to the bathroom again and what have you, and then they come at nine o'clock to put them to bed. . . . Sometimes it can be a bit of a battle!

Jane's narrative orders times and tasks into a schedule that is busy but orderly. The formal carers allow ordinary moments, in what is often an unpredictable and exhausting schedule, to become discrete items, a translation of quasi-events into proper events. But what struck me most here was her use of the "battle" metaphor, which I hadn't run across in over a year of talking with Japanese carers.

Variations on the "battle" metaphor, however, were common in carers' narratives of managing the less-than-glamorous task of mediating between the care workers and care recipient. Some English carers like Jane told me that they saw care management as a task that required more skill and sensitivity (and therefore more care) than what they considered more menial "physical" tasks:

> I'm the one who would kind of gather information and make the phone calls, [like] when can I upgrade her attendance allowance to the higher level? what kind of thing should I watch out for in the form when I upgrade to the higher level? and then trot around and get the signatures and, you know—it's that kind of managing the bureaucracy of a sophisticated social-welfare-providing government that kind of was my remit as a carer, rather than the kind of physical "here's your breakfast," "here's your medication," "I'm going to help you change your clothes now." I didn't really do that.

Descriptions such as these help complicate the binary opposition of family care versus institutional care, allowing us to see the ways carers leverage institutional resources to enact moral agency in ways they couldn't if they were burdened by fatigue. What might be seen in the Japanese context as irresponsible or even neglectful was, on the contrary, heroic.

The Potentiality of Endurance

Fatigue was perhaps the single most defining characteristic of unpaid carer stories in both Japan and England. In cases where the carer must constantly attend to the cared-for, or when there were erratic and aggressive behaviors or nighttime wakings, the exhaustion of family carers was profound. Yet to reduce fatigue to merely depletion (of energy, sleep, will, or "resilience," for example) produced as a consequence of the labor of caring fails to see its *generative* quality as an embodied state of transformative potential (Wilkinson and Ortega-Alcázar 2019). This is so often the problem with the gerontological literature on "compassion fatigue" or "carer burden," which operates from a basic assumption that carer resilience stands apart from and in contrast to existential vulnerability and fragility. Yet vulnerability can open carers up to more complex assemblages of the "ugly feelings" (Ngai 2005) of care: irritation and pity, boredom and awe. I have argued here that fatigue and endurance are repetitively enacted by carers in ways that make ethical action possible. Caring demands entrance into the world of the sick and suffering, only to be thrown back onto oneself in a state of fatigue, until one is called again, and again. Enduring this, whether through cultivating mutuality or "battling" for respite, fused moral imagination to embodied states.

Likewise, enduring this oscillation between engagement and despondency, present-moment attentiveness and floating adriftness, does not mean merely keeping the course, as if one could remain unchanged by the experience of care. Fatigue is the shadow of endurance, hope, and thus of a care that must bring these into the world. For Japanese carers, endurance also meant engrossment, or the feeling that "the reality of the other [is] a possibility for himself [sic]" (Noddings 1984, 15). Sustaining this engrossment, allowing it to manifest as subjectivity rather than slip back into fatigue, is the ethical task of caring, which can only be accomplished by finding narrative anchors, sources of meaning that tie the carer to the world. Just as Tomomi reminds herself, holding her mother's hand and imagining their mutuality of being, her fatigue is transformed into care. It is in displacing rather than reasserting herself that endurance becomes effortless; she is responding without resistance.[11]

English carers tried to avoid co-residing or providing close personal care, but even at a distance they too were weighed down by the "endless fog of tasks" of care. While Paul had to endure some of the most intense episodes of fatigue, all those who lived apart from the person they cared for also identified times when they felt emotionally and spiritually worn out. In contrast to the Japanese carers, who saw fatigue as a sign of empathetic resonance with the pain of the cared-for (a step toward a more compassionate relationship), the English carers were more likely to maintain a distance and to "knuckle down" while waiting for a key "adjustment point" to seek out relief in the form of paid care. Paul and Amy both shifted their perspective away from the cared-for and onto the institutional structures of formal social care. As extensions of these charitable care institutions, they developed a sense of when to adopt an attitude of patient endurance, and when to "fight" for the care. One English carer told me that she had to develop a "terrier attitude," saying "you have to keep on and on and on. Like a little terrier dog, just keep on going. There's no quick fixes."

These different cultural responses to fatigue reveal the extent to which notions of bodily integrity and vulnerability, fatigue, and endurance guide ethical decisions regarding care. These decisions, in turn, provide an important scaffolding for the development and adjustment of individual narratives as the care continues, bringing with them further challenges as well as chances for carers to build relationships with the cared-for and with others, particularly fellow carers (chapters 4 and 5). For Japanese carers, fatigue and endurance came with the risk of enduring (*gaman*) too much, "waiting," as one care manager told me, "until they were almost at the very end" (*giri giri made*) before they called for help.

English carers, on the other hand, tended to become more strongly entrenched between their battles with the social care bureaucracy and their attention to the person they cared for. They continued to grieve and to love, even when it threatened to rip them apart, but they took the responsibility to "cope" or find emotional "resilience" in their struggles. At the same time, they kept one eye always looking toward the horizon, listening for the gallop of social care to appear, anxious that it would not come in time. In this way, their selflessness was less a giving over of oneself to the cared-for, as a mode of compassion would have it, than to the social care system and its ethic of charitable care.

In either case, carers' narratives demand that we see fatigue, vulnerability, and endurance as intertwining threads in the broader project of reorganizing subjectivity. Like the small girl in the park playing the game of endurance with her mother, can we start to see perseverance as play, risk, and self-experimentation? Where does the tickle become pain? And where does the feeling go next? Caring, which began with the commitment to responsibility for the other, extends through the transformation of the body and its attunements, reshaping practices of attention and an emotional feel for the world. These changes propel new questions about capacities for endurance as a form of being-with, one that perhaps requires a different sense of chronicity and futurity that does not presume it is only a transient state to be overcome, but one that repeats, each time with a difference.[12]

DANGEROUS COMPASSION

Taking the safe roads through life, avoiding risk for the sake of a past one feels beholden to or a future still under construction, is rarely tenable in the context of caring. Pasts seem less real or relevant as relationships change or memories become confused. Futures become murky and uncertain even as finitude haunts every moment. It feels like too much to hope—one must act, beyond the hope of hope. In times of exhaustion, the horizon of possibilities feels diminished, and life becomes narrowed to survival in the present. Just being present, however, doesn't afford many assurances; it means being present to and empathizing with someone experiencing confusion, pain, or the agony of a slow death. This is not easy to accomplish unscathed. Resonance has its risks.[1]

In this chapter, I describe the ways carers inhabit what I call *dangerous compassion*. As described in chapter 1, compassion entails a relationship based on the resonance of empathetic imagination and attunement between the carer and the cared-for. Dangerous compassion describes the fragility of this encounter, the ways it sometimes calls for what Rev. Martin Luther King Jr. called a "radical selflessness" that shifts the inter-subjective experience of caring for another. While care fatigue sinks the soul into "violent, dark revolts of being" (Kristeva 1982, 1), even carers who have endured through the abject darkness know that potential dangers are always lurking in the daily ethical decisions that lie ahead.[2] For the carers I spoke with, responsibility, endurance, and danger came to settle into common territory, even reaching what

Arthur Kleinman (2019) described as a kind of "balance and harmony" (153). Kleinman reflects,

> These became, as the horizon of what was possible narrowed, the best of days. Nothing special happened. Joan didn't somehow get better. The decline continued. But periodically we arrived at moments, important moments, when the caregiving and care receiving seemed to reach an equipoise. This was simply the way it was. The pain didn't disappear. The tasks didn't dwindle. Yet we were happy within the severely diminished limits set by this most troubling disease. Together, we felt at such times that we could handle it. (2019, 153)

Dangerous compassion entails reaching a place where the carer and cared-for have developed enough capacity to live with the potential dangers of physical, emotional, and existential fragility, so that they are able to continue the work of care. In both England and Japan, this shift in the ways care was felt and experienced had long-lasting effects on the carer, but it was also a kind of fork in the path. While English carers tended to turn toward paid care options to mitigate the risk of the "not yet" (Hellström and Torres 2014), Japanese carers more often took on a task of self-transformation, cultivating a new form of embodied compassionate subjectivity. That is, they became more open to adopting sensitivities, attentions, and emotions that would allow them to continue to care.

What I have noticed in carers' stories in both Japanese and English contexts was that one rarely arrives at this point of dangerous compassion without first experiencing some narrowing of horizons, whether this is due to fatigue or some other circumstances. Dangerous compassion is balanced on a knife's edge. This is a kind of care that works at the limits of the safe ground of the self, that tries to mind the gaps between self and other with a heightened sense of responsivity and responsibility, without succumbing to the vertigo of displacement, fatigue, indifference, or grief. In order to become responsible and responsive to the other, compassion must entail both the vicarious experience of another's suffering and the openness to being changed by that experience. Sudden disruptions to care can plunge carers and care recipients back into exhaustion and anxiety. Dangerous compassion speaks to the uncompromising challenge of finding meaning and purpose beyond the banality of comfortable life, but it also situates this challenge within relationships of care. The role of personal and cultural narratives, then, is to provide ways of anchoring the carer to other points of resonance beyond the empathic work of caring.

Dangerous compassion is not only compassion that takes risks with the self, at times radically and abruptly shifting the narrative around care, but it also prompts revaluations and critical responses to social relations more generally.

A window is opened to the possibility for being-with, for resonating with others and with ethical narratives and meanings. It is a new way of sensing and making sense of the world.

The Compassionate Body

Kyoto can be glorious in the autumn, attracting photo-hungry visitors from around the world to its temples, shrines, and gardens. The gingko trees lining the streets in my neighborhood had turned a dazzling gold and were beginning to join the other trees in shedding their broad, fan-shaped leaves along the streets and sidewalks, where the wind scooped them up in rustling pools of color. After Tomomi and I caught up with each other, I brought up the memory of her helping her mother to stand (introduction, 1–2), remarking on how good she was about understanding her mother's feelings. Tomomi smiled and recalled the exhaustion of that time, before adding, "When my mother was in pain—well, there were times when I couldn't tell if she was in pain, but I always imagine that she was. I would think things like, 'If I do this or that now, it might be a little painful for her,' and so on. So, for myself, me, Tomomi—it is about more than what *I* want. Well, I can't *become* my mother, but I *tried* to become her."

At the time, the remark didn't catch my attention. Perhaps, only a few months in the field had already made me so accustomed to these sorts of descriptions that I was already taking them for granted. Reading it later, though, I wonder how I could have missed it. Tomomi eloquently described both the empathy and the opacity that renders her vulnerable in that face-to-face encounter with her mother. She described this transformation later in that conversation as being of "one heart and body" (*isshindōtai*), resonating with her mother. Tomomi's efforts to try to become her mother, to become "vulnerable for the Other's vulnerability" (Nortvedt 2003, 227) beautifully conveyed the embodied experience of dangerous compassion.

Touch and other forms of close attention to the body became a routine part of everyday care for Tomomi, especially after her mother lost her speech; and with her own fatigue, this empathetic resonance became even more fragile and acute. Gradually she noticed the sense of hypervigilance (*hoshin-jōtai*) that made her sensitive both to her mother's pain and to changes in mood: "Because I was [caring] everyday, my attention just naturally, well, my body—" Tomomi took a moment and began again:

> When you are caring every day, when you're always looking at the other person's state, you notice all the subtle changes. Something like they only

eat a little of something that they ate all of the day before, so you think about what other kind of thing you might give her. Maybe I just became much more aware of things. Even when it's other people, I might think, I wonder if that person's having some trouble? It was because of looking after my mom when she couldn't speak. I didn't know if she felt good or not, but I would think to myself, I think she'll be happy if I do this or that, she'll be happy. When you do that every day, it's like it gets recorded on your body. Carers have that kind of body, it is supersensitive.

Tomomi's body was transformed, or reinscribed by care. Rather than becoming numb from the repetition of touch, she came to inhabit a "supersensitive" body, and I wondered if this sense of fragility was limited to the care of her mother, or whether it affected the way she responded to life more broadly. After thinking about it, she told me about an experience she had the previous week, seeing another carer struggle. Perhaps because of her own experience of caring, what she saw continued to disturb her, lingering in her mind:

> Someone I know is taking care of her mother, and [the mother] does the same things, always repeating herself and getting confused. When I watch her, she's always scolding her, saying "*I already told you! Why do you have to ask me so many times?*" and being really harsh with her. I see that and I think, now, wouldn't it be better if you just went with the flow of things? [Carers] just get so upset. For me, watching that is really hard. I wish she could just relax a bit. Because even if you're sick, you can hear, so it's really painful if they feel like they are being scolded. I feel so terrible for her mother.

Tomomi told me this story not out of a sense of self-righteous obedience to a moral principle or ideology, but because she was surprised at its visceral impact, which made her reflect on how her own relationship to the world had become transformed. She endured and adapted and cultivated affective sensibilities that allowed her to "face" others. With this carer's body of compassion came a sense of moral responsibility, first toward her mother, then toward others. This narrative resonates with broader cultural patterns of self-cultivation (Kavedžija 2019) and intense physical and mental training meant to incorporate values of humility, gratitude, and empathy (*omoiyari*), be it as a religious devotee (Schattshneider 2003) or a new employee (Kondo 1990). It reflected the cultural narratives that enable certain kinds of experiences to be meaningful and memorable not as contained events but as embodied responses to the world.

Tomomi and I kept in touch over the years since her mother's death, during which she traveled the length of Japan, moved to a new city, and dedicated herself to her work. She had even taken up the Japanese martial art of aikido, which can be translated literally as "the way of unifying life energy." Like caring, aikido can be seen as a spiritual and philosophical practice premised on the flows of life energy (*ki*) that move, pass through, and connect us to each other and to the environment. Not knowing much about aikido myself, I asked if Tomomi felt it might have something to teach carers about how to use the body and mind. She took a moment but responded confidently, "Caring for my mother was like *ukemi*"—a term that generally means a passive or nonresistant body. However, in Tomomi's case, there was much more to it. The *ukemi* in aikido was the training partner who received the blows and throws of the other active partner during practice. To the untrained eye, *ukemi* is just a matter of falling to the ground, sometimes after being tossed through the air like a lifeless bundle of cloth. In actuality, Tomomi explained, *ukemi* was a serious technique that took years of practice to master, since the *ukemi* who does not fall properly is at much greater risk of injury than the active partner. Not only that, but falling properly is not about simply being prone, but collapsing in such a way that the body can quickly get back up. Caring was also about the long, painful process of learning to fall without getting hurt, learning that only in actively receiving the other could harmony emerge from what often felt like chaos. I kept asking questions, fascinated by how naturally Tomomi had found a way to continue developing her compassionate resonance by adopting a culturally elaborated, embodied ritual practice. Tomomi's case reminded me how much we can learn by paying attention to the ways carers describe their worlds beyond the immediate tasks of care: from the flows of life energy in aikido, to subtle remarks about the flow of seasons in everyday talk of the weather, the aesthetic sensibilities of care permeated the atmosphere and the senses (Saito 2010).

Ordinary Adventures

The first time I heard a carer in Japan mention the word "compassion" (*jihi*) in the context of care was about two months into my fieldwork. I was sitting in the kitchen of Chie, an eighty-year-old woman, and her husband, Seiichi (ninety), whom she had been caring for at home for the last three years. Chie's posture and manners were graceful and elegant, her short, bobbed hair was always neat, and her makeup subtle and delicate. I had met her at the day-service center where I volunteered, and hearing about my interest in carers, she invited me to her home after my shift for a cup of tea. Following the hand-drawn map she gave me, I arrived on my bicycle, just as Seiichi was being helped out of the day-service van by one of the staff.

Moments later, the three of us were sitting at the kitchen table, a small pot of tea and a plate of soft orange persimmon slices in front of us. Seiichi, who was seated on my left, slowly swiveled toward me in his seat, mustering his breath before finally belting out, "She's the best mommy in the world [*kaka tenka*]!" Chie cast her stare across the table at Seiichi's gentle smile. "He always calls me 'mama,'" she sighed, finally smiling a little herself. "Isn't that silly?"

Chie and Seiichi were moderately wealthy, compared to most of the carers I interviewed, but although their house was spacious and opulently decorated with ornate furniture and fine art, it also felt eerily abandoned. Their three children had all attended elite universities, and two now lived abroad. The third child lived in Tokyo but visited even less often than the other two, according to Chie. Over the last few years, Chie explained, they used only four small adjoining rooms: the kitchen, a small room used for her husband's physical therapy, the bathroom, and the bedroom. When he wasn't resting, Seiichi sat in his usual chair, which was covered by a large baby-blue absorbent cushion. "I have to keep the cushion there because sometimes, well, there's a 'murmuring,'" Chie says when she notices me glancing at it. She uses her words carefully, poetically, avoiding the cold clinicality of "urination" in favor of the gentle image of a flowing brook.

At Chie's side, resting on the edge of the table, was a dark purple metal cane, decorated with gently weaving vines of yellow and pink flowers. About three months earlier, Chie had injured her back straining to lift her husband. While she was recovering, she reflexively shifted her weight to one side, rather than use a cane to support herself, and this led eventually to even worse pain and debility. Still moving slowly, she would do her best to use the cane, but Seiichi still needed assistance transferring out of bed or chairs, and that was a two-handed job. It was easy to see how, for both of them, with age and repetition even minor injuries could quickly become dangerous. Chie seemed frustrated when talking about how long it had taken her own health problems to improve.

Chie would sometimes feign that she was not a "real carer," saying that she didn't really do much, and that others had it far worse than she did. But most days it was up to her to look after her husband, morning to night. Despite a regular schedule of visits from professional helpers, health staff, physical therapists, and her husband's attendance at day service twice a week, she still felt she had almost no time left to care for herself. Even on the days when Seiichi was at the day service, she had to meticulously plan her errands to fit everything in. Like the grand home that had become reduced to a few small rooms, Chie's life was whittled down to the necessities of getting through the days, but she did her best to make life livable within the diminished field of possibility.

Seiichi quickly finished his tea and sat quietly with his hands in his lap. When Chie spoke about care, she tended to leave out personal examples, perhaps because it would be too embarrassing to discuss in front of Seiichi, so I thought it best to let the conversation wander for a while, coming back to the topic of care if she steered us in that direction. Then Chie surprised me with a different kind of story, one that, like the moment of Augustine's inspiration, began with a momentary impulse to "take up and read," and led quickly to a remarkable self-transformation:

> One day, I just took a random book off the shelf and started reading. It was an old book I had when I was in university and had an interest in Buddhism. I feel like the information just went in and out of my head [at the time], but I read another and another, and that's how I found out about Nakamura Hajime. His book was a little too difficult, I couldn't get through it, but it was interesting. Then I got a recording of his lectures and just listened to them at night. Sometimes I would fall asleep before the end of the talk!

The lectures, she went on to explain, were about the work of the early thirteenth-century Buddhist reformer Shinran Shonin (1173–1263), a revolutionary religious figure who in many ways invites comparisons to Martin Luther in Europe (Ingram 1971). Like Luther, Shinran rejected the strict and secretive authority of institutional religion and preached a form of Buddhist practice accessible to all by virtue of the compassion of Amida Buddha ("the Buddha of Infinite Light"). Nakamura Hajime was a scholar of Shinran's Buddhist thought and the author of another well-known book titled *Compassion* (*Jihi*) (H. Nakamura [1954] 2010). It was this work in particular that sparked something for Chie: "I hadn't really thought much about Buddhism before; it felt like I was looking at it in a new way. And my outlook on everything changed, like the clouds parted! I felt like I had been ignoring other people, just thinking about myself. But now, if someone needed some help, like an old man getting into a taxicab, I would just help without a thought. I guess you could call that compassion [*jihi*]?" She laughed. "Maybe a Buddhist would say that!"

Chie had hesitated slightly when using the word *jihi*, as if she were trying to figure out how to pack something wild into a box that seemed large enough but was not quite the right shape. There was a resonance, however, between what she understood as compassion and the kind of spontaneous impulse to help others that had grown out of her habituated practice of care. This impulse was not proceeding from a sense of duty or obligation, but because of a new sensibility of the world. This resonance had a particular aesthetic and affective mood to it, and an openness: "like the clouds parted."

I was surprised that Chie would even venture to use the term "compassion" to describe something so seemingly ordinary as intuitively responding to a frail older person straining to get into a taxicab. Perhaps her quiet, self-conscious laugh meant she was a little surprised herself. But the ordinariness of Chie's daily life shouldn't diminish what to her was a moment of epiphany; the things she did, the ways she responded to the world, suddenly mattered differently from before. It was not that her actions had changed substantially—she was not responding to an immediate and particular crisis or "moral breakdown" per se (Zigon 2007)—but rather, her relationship to the world and to others in it had shifted, such that she no longer experienced caring as an externally imposed ethical obligation or duty impinging on her personal freedom, but rather as something that emerged from the cultural ordering of embodied experience. "It's funny," she continued, "I'd never told this story to anyone else." She smiled, shaking her head. Then, another thought came to mind.

> CHIE: Maybe it's the environment I grew up in? My father [a doctor] was a person who loved pleasing other people. He looked after so many people. And my mother [*pauses*], my mother was a woman with an extremely compassionate heart. Yes, my mother really had an amazingly compassionate heart. I still can't imitate the way that my mother was. My older sister and I would say this to each other all the time—we can't imitate Mother!
>
> DANELY: In what way?
>
> CHIE: Well, you know, to cast aside your ego to make the other person happy. To not care if you become a sacrifice [*gisei*]. That kind of person. She put her children's happiness first. You hear all these stories today about families with problems in the home and everything—I never knew anything like that. Our mother was amazing. I will never be able to do what she did. She was a very quiet person, but had an amazing personality. So, I can't be like her, but maybe there's been some influence on who I am today. Maybe.

Chie's qualification that she couldn't be like her mother but would still seek to imitate and carry on her mother's example closely resembled the closeness Tomomi described about spending the days with her mother.

As I paused to take notes, I noticed Seiichi shifting in his seat next to me. Chie was already standing up when Seiichi looked over to her and softly said, "Toilet." She excused herself politely, leaving her cane on the table and slowly walking behind my chair, still shuffling slightly, to where her husband sat waiting. When she reached him, I watched as she stepped in and pressed herself against him, one hand reaching around his back to grab the waist of his trousers. Their postures and bodily rhythms were matched, her husband making an effort as well, and like partners in a well-rehearsed dance, the couple moved up to standing in a quick, fluid movement. She did not seem to lift him so much as move his body in such a way that Seiichi could stand himself. He paused and steadied himself quietly, holding on to his wife's arms as she slid her hands down to grasp his forearms. When he was steady, he began shuffling forward; still in synch, she looked around behind her, moving backward out of the kitchen doorway toward the toilet. Seiichi let go of her arms when they were there, and found the security of the familiar walls and grip handles installed there. Chie bent down and helped him take his elastic-waisted trousers down. He lowered himself onto the seat, and she closed the door, waiting outside, leaning against the wall.

Watching Chie and Seiichi navigate the procedure of a simple trip to the toilet was transfixing. In the context of the home, this procedure, which I would regularly perform for Seiichi and others at the day center, felt more intimate. There was no cheerful small talk as the care recipient was paraded through the large, brightly lit room to the toilet. The pace of Chie and Seiichi's movements was slower as well, giving them a feeling of quiet purpose, almost like a dance. She sensed what he was capable of, and therefore how much she would have to lean and pull to support him. The small rooms and narrow corridor gave a sense of security that wrapped around to protect the vulnerability of the two dancers.

When her husband needed her, she responded, performing that empathetic resonance in the slow choreography of supportive yet fragile embrace. They held this moment between them in a silent synchronicity, but it was also a moment that would repeat itself again and again, and would not get easier. At the same time, Chie was strengthening the narrative resonance she found in Buddhist teachings. Sandra Laugier (2009, 9–10), after novelist Henry James, described the transcendental quality of care in ordinary life as "the scene of adventure and improvisation"; "a development of sensitivity" and "relation and appreciation." Such adventures, and the vulnerability or danger that they entail, can be subtle, ordinary and quiet. Care often looks like this. Laugier's understanding "adventure" also reminds us of the creative potential for "moral experiments" (Mattingly 2014b) that bring about something new and sometimes transformative. In many ways, Chie's role and her world had become smaller, but the word "compassion" seemed to open her up in ways that allowed for the ordinary, adventurous moments that made up her world.

Dancing with Danger

The Buddhist notion of compassion that resonated so strongly with Chie was not merely an idea but was embodied in the careful attunement she demonstrated in her relationship with Seiichi. Other Japanese carers rarely used the word "compassion" but instead described this attunement using idioms of bodily merging (see chapter 1) such as "one heart, same body" (*isshin dōtai*), becoming the other's feeling/body (*hito no kimochi/karada ni naru*), or having "coordinated breath" (*iki awase*). Other phrases that were used most often to describe care were "facing" (*mukiau*) the cared-for or "snuggling up" (*yorisou*) to them. These corporeal metaphors expressed the sense that care was something that entered and was expressed through the fragile and fleshy body, prior to other cognitive and reflective appraisals and in ways that were more valuable.[3] Moreover, these metaphors were relational. They described bodies that were directed toward each other, pressed together, vulnerable and resonating to the point of almost merging with each other. Doing care while aesthetically attuned to the cared-for meant being able to respond to a body as a body, corporeality itself as a mode of responsibility and responsivity.[4]

One carer who helped me understand the ways the aesthetic and the ethical (responsivity and responsibility) were expressed in Japanese idioms of care was Naomi. A tall, long-limbed woman in her mid-fifties, Naomi was trained as a professional dancer.[5] She had been caring for her father for several years and, for a short time, worked as a paid carer as well. When I asked Naomi about her experience as a carer for her father, she immediately compared it to dance:

> Maybe since I was a dancer, I understand. [I think to myself,] "maybe I should do it this way? Maybe this other way would feel better?" I have to adjust because I am not always feeling great. . . . If your own mood is going up and down all the time, it isn't good at all. It's incredibly offensive to the [other] person [you dance with]. . . . Even on the stage you think, I want my body to go this way, but then from the audience perspective it might not appear that way at all. So, it is the same when I provide care.

Naomi not only paid attention to the ways her own body coordinated with her father's, the way Chie and Seiichi moved around together, but in doing so, she displaced this attention onto an imagined "audience perspective." This audience intrigued me, so I suggested to Naomi that perhaps this kind of staging or performative aspect of care might have helped her avoid letting her emotions get the better of her. Naomi thought about it for a moment and agreed that there was always a danger of losing emotional composure, but she told me that she was always aware that her father and other people she had cared for were highly sensitive to her emotional state, so she would have to be careful about managing her feelings. Here again was another way that Naomi saw care as a kind of dance:

When I started working as a carer, I remembered the way I had danced in a pair [in the dance company]. I thought, how shall I dance [as a carer]? The person being cared for, the disabled person, and the care helper get into a kind of coordination, they do everything like one, two, three [*she makes lifting motions in a kind of rhythm*]. If everything is too prescribed, you get this distance in the relationship. So, there are times when it doesn't work out. I thought, this is just like dancing. But I didn't know how difficult it was going to be. It was so difficult! I thought it was going to be easy, but it is serious. And the [cared-for] is so sensitive! Of course, you need to have skills and technique to care, but that's not all there is to it! Because [the cared-for] is so hypersensitive [*binkan*]. So even when I am just entering a room, they can tell exactly what I am feeling on that day as soon as I come in. People who aren't able to even move are really hypersensitive [to feelings]. If I'm kind of annoyed or something, they know. They are aware of the littlest thing, like [*she motions awkwardly*] if I move my hands this way when I touch someone, or the way I would hold a spoon to feed [my father], there are ways to do it right, but if you're a little off, they know. They know if it's rough or feels a bit sloppy, or whether it is careful. They sense this better than I can! Sometimes you'd get upset. A lot goes on between two people [*futari no aida*].

For Naomi, the hardest part of caring, whether it was for her father or for other disabled people, was this work of modulating feelings, smoothing them out so the body would be able to perform the techniques of care in a responsive way. Learning to dance the "duet" of care was an eye-opening experience, but the physical and emotional fatigue it brought on (combined with strict working conditions and high staff turnover) led her to quit her job as a carer after only two years.

Naomi was no longer able to dance professionally as she used to, but she still wanted to use her understanding of bodily awareness and attention with other carers like herself, so she began organizing workshops focusing on sensations of physical contact with the older person's body. Her workshops included simple meditative mindfulness work, as well as pair work, such as using only touch to slowly "read" each other's faces while keeping the eyes closed. Some workshops involved more improvisational movement-based exercises. These workshops were not the kind of training practicums that care aides might take to learn safe techniques for transporting or changing an immobile client. Rather, they focused on opening up the body as a sensory organ through which relationships with others could form. Before such a relationship was possible, Naomi explained, participants would have to take time to build awareness of their own body's capacities for responding to sensation and the environment:

> [In the workshop] first we put aside the whole idea of care and really just [pay attention to] what is going on with your own body. Of course, everyone has back pain, headaches, stomach pains, or you're unwell or feeling sick and so on. There are lots of things causing bodily discomfort. It's not like, "if you do this, you'll be cured," but first of all, it was a time to turn toward one's own body [*jibun no karada ni mukiau*]. So we get the carers together in lots of different pairs and do some things, and then, well, you return to the body [*karada wo torimodosu*]. Then in the later half we focus on memories—something nostalgic, for example, like a memory of touching something with one's hand . . . like there was a grandma, and you know, older people's hands don't have much moisture, so you know, if you go like this [pulls skin on the back of her hand] it is like one, two, three, four, it doesn't go back the way it was right away. So there was someone who used to think that was fun to play with grandma's hand like that.

Again, the idea behind these aesthetic, sensory experiments and their narrative connections was not to reinforce the bounded body/self as the central locus of acting in the world, but to carve out a performative space from which one could attend to one's own body through the encounter with the other's body.[6] This same technique was applied to sensory memories. Participants realized that the sensory memory is embedded in their body, so that recalling and performing it allows the participant to experience it again from a distance; the familiar has become strange and the strange familiar, as anthropologists like to say.[7]

Naomi explained that this experiment in bodily aesthetics allowed for a more "objective" view of oneself, a sense of how one might feel to the other whom one is touching, from empathetic imagination: "[By doing the exercises] you start to look at movements 'objectively.' Not the way you want it to go, but the way the other person sees it. . . . What is it like for the other [*aite*]. What kind of voice, facial expression, touch. . . . So, although you may not be old yourself, of course, you will be, and you can start to get a feeling that there is a common sensibility [*kyōtsū kankaku*]." This process moves attention from one's own body to the other's body, then back to one's own body as felt by or with the other's body. The loop creates what she calls the "common sensibility," a kind of inter-corporeality (Al-Mohammad 2010, 52; Csordas 2008) or a sense of the mutually responsive and responsible, resonant "we."[8]

Naomi and her father did not always dance their duet in step. Their closeness lent itself to regrettable reactions as well. "I might raise my voice [to scold him]," she admitted, "but after, I'd regret it. [I'd say] 'Damn, I did it again!'" At ninety, her father lived alone, without friends or connections to the community, and he rejected the idea of moving to residential care if he became frailer. Naomi said that she would figure some way of continuing to care for him, but she knew he could be "neurotic," and she worried if she would be able to handle it.

The ability to imagine oneself from the other's perspective, the way Naomi explained her duet with her father, provides an opening for the development of compassion. She trained carers in her workshops to understand compassion as an inter-subjective and inter-corporeal aesthetic as well as an ethical and creative project. Creativity, whether in care or other contexts, takes a risk, but it is because of this risk that it is so valuable to moral projects of compassion (Wall 2005). Carers dance creatively, carefully, often on the edge of a cliff of dangerous compassion. While bodily exhaustion can pull both the carer and cared-for closer to the edge, there is something in this creativity and its infinite capacity for crafting relationships that keeps carers anchored to the ground.

Eating Intimacy

The attunement of bodies, feelings, and moods demonstrated by Chie and Naomi was also apparent in the relationship between Japanese carers and food. For carers, feeding was one of the most important barometers of the everyday ethics of caring. From the preparation to the spooning, to the cleaning up, feeding not only involved intimate bodily practices, but usually took place in an atmosphere of almost silent meditative concentration. Carers used their intuition and attention to the nonverbal expressions of satisfaction or disgust, adjusting flavors and portion sizes to strike just the right balance. Like the movements of the dance, feeding hinged on sensory resonances that were ephemeral yet repetitive, as much about fleeting presence as they were about the recurrence of absence.

Whenever I visited Chie, we sat around the familiar kitchen table. On one afternoon, I had arrived just as the paid care worker who helped with cooking had left, and the savory aromas still hung in the air of the small kitchen and dining room. Chie told me that she was grateful for this service, but it didn't last through the week, so she would buy small, individually portioned microwavable meals from the convenience store. "These meals are wonderful," she told me, handing me one of the soft, bulbous sachets pinched shut at the top with a stiff seal. The picture on the front showed a plump brown lump of hamburger glistening dreamily in a demi-glace sauce. I handed it back to her as she explained, "I wouldn't be able to make them on my own, and even now, he'll eat a whole hamburger if I make it [from the package]. I am just grateful for that. He still jokes that I'm the best 'mommy'!"

The importance of careful feeding as a means of developing empathetic resonance was understood by both men and women I spoke to, but there was no doubt that feeding was associated with the comfort, nurturance, and protection of the mother.⁹ During my fieldwork, the Family Mart convenience store chain was even marketing microwavable meals like the one Chie showed me under the label "Mother Cafeteria" (*Okāsan shokudō*). The television commercials cleverly poked fun at their own nostalgic, "home-cooked" image by re-creating the atmosphere of a typical family melodrama where a young man returns from the city to his hometown in the country because "all of a sudden [he] wanted to eat [his] mother's cooking." He blissfully savors the nostalgic tastes, sitting at the kitchen table of his rural childhood home, back to back with his mother, who faces the stove, stirring a steaming pot (actually just boiling a ready-made sachet). The next scene shows the young man catching his mother, still wearing her apron, in the aisle of the convenience store, filling a basket with the "Mother Cafeteria" meals. Most important for this joke to work is the fact that mother does not *eat* at "Mother Cafeteria" but remains at the stove while the food is enjoyed, her feminine labor and sacrifice performed by her shadowlike presence in the background of the other's experience (Lock 1993, 172). The notion of food as a form of intimate communication of love, care, and sacrifice between family members (one that enacts empathy but avoids the certainty and directness of words and touch) is a theme frequently employed in Japanese family stories.¹⁰ Despite the curious absences of older eaters at "Mother Cafeteria," these dramas were reenacted by carers like Chie every day, with the help of aesthetically appropriate props.

The vicarious enjoyment felt by the carers when the care recipients eat all of their meal was matched only by the sense of failure and despair felt when care recipients refused food or became unable to chew or swallow.¹¹ When I first met Ando-san, a small but fiery woman in her late sixties who cared for her in-laws at home for five years, her first words to me were "making food was the hardest part!" Ando-san went on to explain that after several hospital stays, her mother-in-law's food intake had decreased dramatically. The change had been due to the stress of moving back and forth as well as the lack of good food in the hospital. "Since mother could hardly eat anything after, I had to really think about how to present food that she would enjoy—the way the colors went together, or the textures and so forth," she said. Ando-san, who prided herself on her cooking, felt challenged both physically and emotionally by this task in a way that she had never felt before. The stakes of this aesthetic care were life and death. "The hardest thing" she told me, "was when they would leave some food on the plate.

If they don't eat, they can't live! So if I am not feeding them something, I am killing them. When you can't eat anymore, that's the end."

Another carer, Hanako, told me that she feared her mother wasn't going to
live much longer, so she didn't mind letting her eat whatever she wanted, even
though it wasn't healthy:

> When she stopped eating—when someone just can't eat anymore,
> well, you're getting close to the end. It is one of the most fundamen-
> tal things—walking or moving, and eating. Near the end—my mother
> loves potato chips, you see. To the point where you'd be thinking, "Are
> you really eating potato chips again?" Every day she'd buy a bag. And
> I would say, "Eat whatever you like," and she'd eat so much. She'd even
> hide it from other people when she ate them! "Today you said you'd eat
> something else, and now what are you doing!" I'd say over and over.
> But when I thought about it, well, what does it matter if she eats what
> she likes? It doesn't really cost that much, so I'd just work it out with
> our budget. But when she'd eat them, you could see in her face that she
> really enjoyed them, and I would be happy too. That feeling that she was
> happy would just suddenly appear like that.

To be responsible for preparing food and feeding an older family member was
to live in anticipation of the grace of a satisfied smile, one that could melt away
the emotional weight of the day or week, but that would have to be repeated day
after day. Carers of people living with cognitive impairment sometimes spoke
of the worry they felt when the person being cared for lost memory or speech,
spending days and nights in discomfort and confusion. But the familiar joy and
recognition of commensality remained despite everything else. The sensation of
being-with-others, attuned to the fundamental joy of food, endured. In this context—and particularly if the care recipient could not speak—chewing, salivating,
and swallowing all became interlocutory acts that restored this vital connection
to the world of others. Eating reassured those cared for that they were worthy of
desires, pleasures, and love. Isn't this the meaning of care?[12]

From the inter-corporeality of care emerges the ethics of the dance, the rhythm
of shared life, the air currents of shared breath. In the Japanese case, eating was
much more than merely a means of survival; it was a means of communicating
the liveliness of life, the hunger and enjoyment of eating and feeding. No one put
it more poignantly than Emiko, who accompanied her husband during his last
days in the hospital when problems swallowing had led to him being fed through
a PEG tube (percutaneous endoscopic gastronomy).[13]

Emiko turned away from me when she began telling me about feeding her
husband during his last days in the hospital, only a few months earlier. "At the

very end, he wanted to eat eel!" she said, starting to giggle. "I wanted to give him even a little bit of eel, but . . . well, [the nurses] were worried that food would get into his trachea, so he always had to spit it back out. But I felt so bad for him, so I would give him little bits of food secretly. I'm glad I was able to do that for him." Emiko looked away again, saying, half to herself, "I never did give him that eel." She then gazed again at the empty corner of the living room where her late husband had lain in the rented hospital bed during the months that she looked after him. She is not a large woman, but her skin was pulled taut over her swollen hands, which anxiously rubbed the sleeve of her black sweater. While the memory of the forbidden food tickled her, the regret about not being able to feed her husband eel lingered on. The food he was unable to swallow gave him only sustenance of the soul, just the sweetness of another's presence.

When I left Emiko's house, I felt aware again of the fundamental joy of eating, of incorporating acts of care through the smells, tastes, and visual beauty and bounty of food. But I was reminded as well of hunger as a lack not only of food, but of connection to the world. Among the most pitiful beings in the lower realms of Buddhist cosmology are the "hungry ghosts" (*gaki*) who live on without a place to dwell, abandoned, their huge distended abdomens and thin necks transforming them into a grotesque metaphor for human loneliness.

At a seminar intended for family carers that I attended at the Kyoto city hall, participants were taught not only how to feed an older care recipient ("using chopsticks will stimulate the brain and stave off dementia!"), they were also shown how to clean the teeth and mouth with a variety of brushes and how to massage the mouth and jaw. For the older person, we were told, breathing and eating become more difficult to coordinate, and while both are essential functions, they also posed risks to each other, especially if food becomes lodged in the trachea or becomes a source of infection in the mouth. The instructor led us in exercises that we could do to learn how to breathe in a manner that would allow the cared-for to eat orally as long as possible.

"Care of the mouth is essential!" declared the instructor. "It doesn't matter if you have lost some teeth or your muscles are not working perfectly, but *enjoying* eating is vital if you want to remain a part of the *community*." The instructor then asked the audience of about fifteen men and women, "What is the opposite of community?" There was a hushed chatter among the group, and the speaker smiled, finally hearing something she liked in the murmur.

> Right! The hospital. The hospital is *not* a place for community, but a place for medicine. Usually older people who are admitted to the hospital come there gaunt and malnourished and thin. They don't eat well. The food there, well, there are all sorts of staff coming in and going

all the time, and so there are all these things that they just don't think about, and then the food that they give you is all the same, you know? Hospital food is not so tasty [*laughs*]. Soft food, tasteless stuff. So I try to think about getting enough salts and making food that would actually be appetizing. Otherwise they just give you rice porridge instead of real rice. Just stuff that you only eat if you are a sick person. The appetite just goes away.

For the act of feeding and eating to be a form of care, it must be something that inspires desire and pleasure of the senses and stomach; there must be appetite for life. Though aimed at practical skills for dealing with the often messy, private work of feeding, all of us followed directions with the seriousness of a sacred ritual (at one point the speaker did recommend religious chanting as a way of strengthening one's breathing). "In order to live better lives together, we must [not forget] 'care for the mouth. It is support for living!'" as the last slide exclaimed.

When I spoke to some of the audience members after the talk, I was not able to find any unpaid carers. Most, it turned out, had come to the seminar that day to learn about caring for themselves. "I want to start some good habits now so I can keep eating well even when I'm old!" one woman in her forties told me afterward. The message for these carers, or care-recipients-in-waiting, was that food was not merely nutrition, but it was appetite, enjoyment, and most of all a way of being with and for others, resonating with them in a most fundamental sense of community.[14]

Facing the Other

Izumi cared for both her own parents and her husband's parents in overlapping succession over the course of just over twenty years. Three of the four people she cared for lived with dementia in their last years. Like Naomi, the dancer, Izumi was well aware of how people living with dementia were incredibly perceptive, and so for her, caring was most of all a matter of keeping a pleasant expression on her face and maintaining her composure. "I would absolutely never say anything if something upset me," she explained. "Even sad things too. Anyway, whatever the case was, if I didn't [discipline] myself, and approach her with a bright and smiling face, [there would be trouble]."

This wasn't easy for Izumi, whose husband lost his job while she was in the midst of caring for her mother. As a result, their family had to move to a smaller house and make do with less. After the move, her mother's condition deteriorated, and she was hospitalized. Despite all these hardships, not to mention the grief and worry over her mother, Izumi had to maintain her careful "bright" face: "Even when I opened up the door, I would first put on a smile, check it in the mirror, and *then* I would open the door." She continued,

> IZUMI: It was mentally, emotionally [*seishinteki*] taxing. . . . First of all, the other person [*aite*] doesn't see [everything]. Only the *face*, that's what she sees. She only looks at my face, and wonders what kind of expression is on that face. So that was the hardest of all, making sure that she didn't see through me.
>
> TAKI: [*A friend sitting at the table*] You are outstanding!
>
> IZUMI: No, it isn't praiseworthy! It's *experience*. Experience. I am grateful that I was able to see off both of my parents. They have really allowed me to study [*benkyō*] so much.
>
> DANELY: Study?
>
> IZUMI: Right. Mental/emotional learning [*seishinteki benkyō*].[15]

For Izumi, learning to control her face, to care through a form of ego-displacing dissemblance or creative masking, was an experience that cultivated her to learn and embody spirit (*seishin*). Like Chie, Izumi said that this had helped her to better appreciate the spiritual value of Buddhism. Izumi's parents were devoted adherents of Buddhism, but Izumi had not been particularly interested in it before she began caring. From a Buddhist perspective, she explained, you have to act unselfishly, to try to "snuggle up [*yorisou*] to the other's suffering."

Carers of frail older relatives, especially those living with dementia or other cognitive impairment who may be unable to speak or express themselves clearly, are well acquainted with the importance of the face—both their own and that of the cared-for—as the most important means of nonverbal connection. Not only did carers constantly search the face of the cared-for, looking for the faintest clues of recognition, but they made their own face visible to the cared-for, bending down or moving in close, eye to eye when they spoke, in an effort to comfort and respond.

After a month of initial interviews, I realized that most of my questions were about the negative effects of caring on health and relationships, but that I hadn't included any questions on what carers learned. This was a problem. Not everyone could answer confidently when I asked about what they had learned, but Tomomi did not hesitate: "The biggest thing that I have learned was *how to face the other* [*aite ni mukiau*]. I think I've become stronger now because I can understand other people's feelings better." As if to underline the point, she leaned her head forward slightly to come eye to eye with me and held my gaze for a moment.

Apart from corporeal metaphors listed in the previous section, the most frequent expression that Japanese carers used to describe their experiences of close intimate care was "facing" or "turning to meet [the other]."[16] In Japanese, "turning to meet [the other]" (*mukiau*) is a phrase used in everyday speech that might apply to various contexts in which one turns attention away from one's own thoughts, feelings, or desires in order to attend and become open to someone or something else, often with the purpose of cooperation or conciliation. The fact that Tomomi and other Japanese carers used this phrase also suggests a special significance that goes beyond everyday fluctuations of attention to touch on a deeper kind of resonance and responsibility. For Tomomi, caring for her mother produced a presence or posture of what Tahhan (2014, 119) calls "mutual deepening," a kind of touching without physical contact, where the exposure and openness of one person meets the other with empathy and care (*omoiyari*).

As Tomomi remarked, "facing" not only allows one to "understand other people's feelings," but it is a posture that implies a kind of selfless responsiveness—facing disrupts the normal boundaries of individual selves in ways that afford the potential for compassionate encounter. This resonant proximity also implies an ethical decision to resist turning away from the cared-for, allowing carers to deepen their understanding of themselves, to face and accept their own limitations and vulnerabilities. "A face offers itself, gives itself, and calls me out of myself" writes psychologist James Hillman (1999, 102), but in doing so, does it not, by virtue of its responsiveness, also inaugurate a new possible way of being-with and being-for-the-other? When Tomomi mentions learning to face the other, is this different from Chie's embodied ethics of compassion?

This question was also a central concern of the philosopher Emmanuel Levinas, whose phenomenological approach to ethics is encapsulated in the notion of the fragile encounter with the "face" of the other, a face that "exceeds the idea of the Other in me" (Levinas [1961] 2003, 50) or that is irreducible to "the self-sameness of [my] own being" (Throop 2012a, 163).[17] What was important to Levinas, and what seems to resonate with carers' expressions of "facing," was the way the face penetrated its opacity and mystery through the ethical demand. "The face speaks," writes Levinas, and "to speak to me is at each moment to surmount what is necessarily plastic in manifestation" (Levinas 2003, 200). Hartmut Rosa (2019) calls this the "silent call" of the face, which can only be treated with indifference by "suppressing resonance" (70). Just as resonance involves both connection and autonomy of the agents involved (Susen 2020, 312), and touch demonstrates the ability of the skin to both separate and communicate (Tahhan 2010, 2014), Pinchevski (2016) argues that for Levinas, the face "both connects and separates—connects by virtue of separating—producing commonality while maintaining its in-betweenness."[18] This "in-betweenness," or what in Japanese relational aesthetics is referred to as *ma* or *aida* (Crapanzano 2003, 51; Danely 2014, 23–24; Kavedžija 2019, 65; Tahhan 2014, 45), is presence that is characterized by openness, or a loss of the self in order to welcome the other (what Levinas called "sacrifice") (Altez-Albela 2011, 42–43). For both Izumi and Tomomi, then, we might say that "facing the other" meant giving one's face over to the other as an act of care.

While Japanese carers held a close association between the face of the ethical encounter and the fleshy face of intimate inter-corporeal sensibility, the English face was more difficult to decipher. Differences across class and region were impossible to discern from the small sample for this research, yet some English carers echoed the stoic line that caring was something you "just get on with," a sentiment that brings to mind the face that wears a "stiff upper lip." For these carers, the care was something one had to "cope" with or "manage" by placing some distance between the carer and the cared-for. Caring in the English context was less about developing compassion than it was about extending charity, protecting the dignity and autonomy of the cared-for and oneself. Yet for each individual, there were moments when feelings of love and deep connection troubled their sense of self and led them to develop new sensitivities and confront moral choices. This dangerous compassion, however, rarely coalesced into a stable sense of identity that resonated with broader cultural narratives or practices of care, as it did with Tomomi and other Japanese carers. Instead, as the following example illustrates, the English carers found themselves caught in a tense dissonance between empathetic resonance and narrative resonance.

Compassion and Charity in Tension

Russell, in his mid-fifties, lived near his childhood home, where his mother and his younger brother still lived. Russell's mother had been growing increasingly frail and cognitively impaired over the years, to the point where she could no longer make herself a cup of tea, and after she had a bad fall on the stairs (her bedroom and bathroom were on the second floor), Russell and his brother decided she would need constant supervision. Russell would spend most days with his mother at her home while his brother was at work. When I arrived at the house, his laptop was open alongside an array of papers and folders spread out across the length of the dining room table. The chair faced the living room, so that he could keep an eye on his mother.

Russell has a kind of awkward manner that very intelligent people often have, as well as a particularly English habit of self-effacement and hesitance with his words. When he first agreed to an interview with me, he seemed flustered trying to grasp at the right way to phrase his thoughts: "I think, um, I think I quite like [caring]. . . . I think, I think I'm not terrible at it. . . . I'm not . . . I think I've learnt that I am capable of doing it."

Yet despite this sense of capability, Russell also had concerns. Like other carers, for him care had stirred up a mix of emotions, none of which seemed to have a clear and certain resolution. "You know, because there are all kinds of challenges where you're a bit embarrassed really, and, uh, I think a son caring for a mother is kind of quite a hard dynamic because it's a female—it's been traditionally a female role, so I think it's difficult. But I do find it a privilege to look after Mum really, but a worry and a strain as well. Um, you know I think it's very important that we all have the opportunity to go away and do other things, because it's confining."

What I found most interesting about this conversation with Russell was his admission that he coped with his ambivalent feelings not by trying to become closer to his mother, but by widening the distance, escaping from intimacy's confinement as a way of preserving his mother's independence and dignity (as well as his own well-being).

Russell put a kettle on, and the two of us chatted casually in the kitchen of the large, two-story home. Russell's mother soon appeared in the doorway, a petite woman with a friendly face, whose well-dressed appearance was only slightly disheveled by a missed button on her navy cardigan. She looked to her son, as if to ask who I was, still smiling pleasantly and going through the familiar motions of welcoming a guest. Russell explained, slowing his speech and repeating some details as he watched her expression. She looked at me again, started to say something, then lost the thought, looking away and mumbling a long train of words that I could not make out. I kept my attention on her, hoping this would be reassuring, while Russell tried to piece together what she might be saying, checking in with her to see if he had got it right. She paid attention to him intently but didn't respond, then she quietly walked back into the other room and sat in her usual armchair, and Russell and I followed with tea and biscuits.

"She knows she wants to say something," Russell explained as we followed her into the other room. "She just can't quite connect that with her speech. I usually have to kind of prompt her over and over to make sense of it." It was a cold day, and the garden, visible through the large glass sliding doors, was still blanketed in the previous week's snow. Russell sat a cup of tea on a small table beside his mother's armchair and bent down to meet her face to face. "Careful, it's very full." As we sat down, he continued where he'd left off:

> Prompting. Prompting. I mean, yeah, I think that we could reach a point where that would be a concern because it's—I'm forever looking at

things through Mum's eyes and through Mum's skill set, and so through our skill set and through our eyes this house doesn't look like it's fraught with danger—but for Mum it is fraught with danger. She doesn't see it that way either because in her mind it's her home, so—and we occasionally have little battles about should that piece of furniture be put into storage because it's another thing—you know, this living room was less cluttered than it was a while ago. There was more, and it's gone.

Again, Russell draws a sharp distinction between the world of his mother and the one that he (and I) inhabit, showing a carer's concern for the "dangers" that she is oblivious to. He sees this work as safeguarding and protecting her, which comes from a certain empathetic awareness of her limitations and concern for her safety.

Russell's eyes were fixed on his mother as she slowly lifted the tea to her lips, her hand trembling slightly. Turning to me, he tells me that he wouldn't really be able to say everything he wanted to say, given the situation, making a quick glance back in his mother's direction. Some things would have to wait until another time.

As we continued our conversation, Russell noted how difficult it was for him to really understand what it must be like to be an older person but that his feelings have started to evolve toward an acceptance of this, as well as an acceptance of his own limits.

I think as a family it is very difficult though. It's challenging. And I can't think of any way that it wouldn't be. It's impossible for it not to be challenging. I think you kind of learn what you're capable of, what your boundaries are, and where your limits are. You are—I think as we get older we look at life as a journey with a hill up and a hill down, and I think you—I think now I'm much more likely to hear somebody who's very young and hasn't got any experience of what we've been through say something. Say, I'm going to be a racing driver when I'm seventy, and you think, yeah, well good luck with that one! You know, because you've kind of got no idea, have you—and to be honest with you, with Mum, as much as I understand I don't understand, because I can't understand.

Each day was another reminder that he cannot understand. Yet, implicit in Russell's statement was his strong commitment to care, despite this unknowability. This moral decision was possible only because he first acknowledges his separation from his mother as well as his own boundaries and limits. While the interview continued, I watched the way Russell attended to his mother, from getting up to steady her hand with the teacup to simply asking her questions from time to time to keep her involved. There was an easiness and familiarity to their relationship, a real feeling of compassion as Russell watched his mother, giving her space but also ready to spring up if she were to tip her cup over or try to get up.

Synchronizing to this tense but slow tempo was one of the most difficult adjustments for Russell:

> RUSSELL: It's tiring in a strange way because you can look at a day and think I didn't do much today, because everything—[*turning to his mother and raising his voice slightly*] Mum, this is a frustration, isn't it? Because everything takes quite a long time.
> MOTHER: Oh yes, and I'm sick and tired of it!

Russell and I both started, a little surprised at how clearly she spoke (very differently from the incoherent words earlier), and the timing of her interjection was so spot-on that all three of us ended up laughing. As Russell began speaking again, however, his mother continued to try making her point, suggesting that she had no intention of making a joke.

> RUSSELL: So, you know—going upstairs takes a long time, getting something, getting dressed, having a meal takes a long time. Tidying up takes a long time. Writing Christmas cards . . . and that, I think I— I think I've learnt that I'm human, that I'm not—there's a part of it that's hard, that it's work. It's not that it's physically terribly tough, it's just—it's dealing with change and also finding space for yourself. I think that's the hardest balance of all. I was talking to [my friend] about it, and I was saying—I don't know, it's uh . . .
> MOTHER: [*Trying to get our attention*] Sometimes I wish I'd never been born.
> RUSSELL: Oh Mum! No, she doesn't mean that. What do you mean you wish you'd never been born? No, you can't mean that. Oh Mum, I think what she's saying is—Mum . . . no she doesn't mean that, that's her choosing the wrong language. Mum, what do you mean? Do you mean—I don't wish to prompt you, but—you don't wish you'd never been born, do you, Mum? You've had a great life, yeah? And you still enjoy your life! I am going to interpret for you. You mean—do you worry sometimes that you're a burden?
> MOTHER: Yes . . . yes.

Russell and his mother prompted each other here, getting back in synch. Just as he was beginning to talk about his own sense of human fragility that has come from following the pace of his mother, she interjected with "I wish I'd never been born." Russell's response showed that he genuinely admired his mother, and as he told me more about her life as a devoted Catholic who gave generously to charities, I could understand why it was painful for both of them to be in the situation they were in.

"I'll walk you to the corner," Russell called to me as we ended the interview. He quickly threw on a puffy navy-colored down coat and stepped into his boots. We had only walked two steps from the door before he became visibly more relaxed, rolling his head as if his neck was just released from a vice. "After the fall, she couldn't dress herself," he said in a slow, dry monotone.

"I had to dress her. I had to put her *bra* on. It was hard. *For her.* There really is a point where you think you have reached your limits. You can't relate anymore. The end of your tolerance."

We start walking down the street between cars parked over the pavement, past a building site, trying to avoid the slippery, packed-down snow.

"There have been times when I've said [to her], if you keep doing some of these things, you're going to go into a home. I don't want to think about it," he says, under his breath. "Going up the stairs ten times a day, changing nappies that come in these great big packages. . . . There's going to be a time when she can't do that anymore. Then what? Get a home aide to come in to wipe her bum? Or I'll wipe her? I think that would do it. She would be floored. It would kill her."

His breath came out in puffs that disappeared against the gray sky. We walked close, talking in low voices like conspirators in the silent street. When we reached the end, he turned to me, serious again.

"She's never said that before, you know, about wanting never to have been born—" He stopped. It was time to go back to her.

Although Russell appeared to be in a comfortable rhythm with his mother's care while we were in the house, the post-interview walk outside showed that he was struggling to hold on. He resonated with his mother, feeling her discomfort with the indignity of being changed or doing everything slowly, but the relationship seemed to fight against this resonance, reinforcing separation, autonomy, and distance. The attentive, responsive care that he wanted to give her did not have a resonant cultural narrative to anchor it, and it was constantly slipping out of his hand.

A Quiet Liberation

The nature of resonance, whether it is resonance with others' suffering or their enduring life, resonance with the positively valanced cultural stories or the darker tales that haunt cultural corners, is to pull one into attunement to others and to the world. Attunement enhances feelings of connection, a rhythm or synchronicity of embodied habits of attention and movement. Tomomi, Chie, Naomi all demonstrated how this attunement results in a heightened aesthetic sensitization to suffering and a repeated practice of decentering the self to respond. I have called this "dangerous compassion" to emphasize the fragility of caring when pain and uncertainty persist alongside resilience and responsibility. Compassion, in the sense in which my Japanese interlocutors understood the concept, entailed not only empathetic imagination and the habituated impulse to care, but also an openness to the ethical encounter such that selves are transformed and transcended. Cultural models and practices of cultivating and embodying compassion through persistent physical and emotional exertion in everyday nonverbal acts of touching, feeding, and facing provided a familiar reference for Japanese carers, but this was still dangerous work.

I found that in contrast to the Japanese cases, English carers like Russell, whose general orientation toward care emphasized the maintenance of autonomy, independence, and bodily separateness, were more hesitant about the possibility of resonance. This did not mean, however, that empathetic imagination, love, or concern were absent in their care. Russell patiently, gently accompanied his mother, anticipating her words, her hunger, her discomfort. Yet I could also see in his narrative an effort to protect the distance between himself and his mother in ways he felt offered her more dignity. This orientation makes the choice to use paid care services not only logical, but moral from the perspective of charitable care. However, Russell's feelings of guilt and shame for pursuing more paid care support indicated that for each individual, care remains a fraught and complex matter.

"Seeing the world as dangerous and uncertain," Arthur Kleinman writes, "may lead to a kind of quiet liberation, preparing us for new ways of being ourselves, living in the world, and making a difference in the lives of others" (2006, 7). Dangerous compassion may offer this same liberation, but it is still a precarious and imperfect solution. We must not forget that one of the most iconic images of resonance is the shattered glass. Resonance exposes our fragility, particularly when we are trying to face the other. The closer we are to resonance, the more dangerous things become. It raises the question, how can a carer be responsive, vulnerable, and yet endure without breaking? For a carer who is physically and emotionally exhausted by the unremitting call to responsiveness that care often demands, compassion may further erode the tenuous infrastructure of the world—what Rosa (2019, 65) calls "catastrophic resonance"—or it might be the durable ethical lifeline to anchor oneself to others and to find transcendence.[19] In the next chapter, I look more closely at the ways narrative resonance shapes carers' stories, making experience meaningful, lasting, and the basis for building relationships of cosmic resonance with other carers.

COUNTER-WORLDS OF CARE

SAYURI: I never had a strong faith in anything particular, but my mother and father were strong believers in Buddhism, so when I was little I was always brought in front of the *butsudan* to put my hands together, expressing gratitude—I was brought up to respect this kind of faith. Education [like this] is so important, isn't it?

DANELY: [Respect for] something bigger than yourself?

SAYURI: That's it! Right! That's the thing, a kind of spiritual something. It can be a kind of weapon, I think.

DANELY: So going to the *butsudan* and expressing gratitude was a kind of education?

SAYURI: Yes. It's really important, I think. To cultivate the heart [*kokoro*]. There are so many carers who feel lost, and they need someone to guide them.

DANELY: And that is something that society as a whole [*seken*] has to cooperate in?

SAYURI: That's right. [*Small laugh*] I'm fine being just a small lighthouse. If I can just keep shining a little light to say "I'm here" [*koko da yo*], my life will be worth something.

DANELY: Like hope?

SAYURI: Just a little, a tiny, tiny light of hope. Jason, *you'll* have to be big lighthouse! Light up across the *world*! [*Laughs*]

Sayuri's encouragement hit me like a hopeful spotlight and a heavy weight. Would I be able to live up to her expectation? What responsibility did I bear to those carers whom I spoke to every day? How could my words possibly make their labors light? I envied the sense of smallness that Sayuri held on to. It seemed better suited to the humble task of "cultivating the heart." I come back to this moment when I think about all the carers whose life had become dim or dangerous, those who felt their grip on the world faltering. I come back to Sayuri's "tiny, tiny light" as a gesture of connection and generosity and love.

What does it mean to be "a small lighthouse"? For Sayuri, it meant taking the compassion she had cultivated and transforming it into a "weapon" of hope, a beacon cutting through the dark to guide other carers. Sayuri expressed this in the simple yet powerful expression of care: "I'm here." Before one can be a lighthouse, before there can be any light to guide those who feel adrift on the waves of dangerous compassion, there must first be a sense of "I'm here," a way of being-with, of comforting presence, accompaniment, watching, listening, touch.[1]

As I discussed in the previous chapter, being fully present and open to the feelings of the care recipient generated modes of emotional and bodily attunement for Japanese carers, enabling the kind of compassionate care they felt was expected of family, even as it risked danger to their physical and mental autonomy. Compassion was dangerous not only because it decentered the self, but because the infinite responsibility and uncertainty of care sometimes led to such a deep state of hopelessness that violence could appear merciful (Kato 2010; Mainichi Shinbun 2016; NHK 2017). Here I discuss how carers, like Sayuri, not only emerged from the turbulent storms of dangerous compassion, but also found a sense of meaning, or what I have been calling "narrative resonance." While up to this point I have concentrated on the "ordinary" repetitive habituated life of carers, in this chapter I heed Robbins's (2016) observation that ordinary ethics has a blind spot when it comes to matters of religion and transcendence and the ways these interact with and come to shape everyday ethics. Following phenomenologist Alfred Schutz, Robbins sees transcendence first of all as "that which is outside of our immediate perceptual existence" yet which is "inescapable in human life" within which "we are entangled" (772). While the transcendental must involve a "leaping away" from the ordinary, and in the case of religion, a sense of the extraordinary, it may still have profound effects on everyday transactions. For carers, embracing the transcendent gave them a stronger desire to connect with and to help others—to be a lighthouse. I argue that what was critical for these carers was the capacity for narrative resonance—be it in religion, ritual, or peer support groups—to bridge their experiences with the shores of emergent worlds and utopian projects.

While English carers also experienced vulnerability, sympathy, and compassionate feelings, the disposition toward practicing care as charity also meant that they made efforts to keep these dangerous feelings away from the care encounter, to depersonalize the care in ways that would make it easier to transition later to paid professional care. But with practical and financial concerns about the cost of paid care, English carers felt little choice but to "knuckle down" and "get on with it" until some subjective threshold was crossed. In the meantime, "coping" with care often meant escapes to be alone ("respite"). For others, love and faith helped them imagine meaningful counter-worlds that could encompass both the pleasures and the hardships of everyday care. Charity was part of the scaffolding on which these plans could hang, a logic that helped English carers to maintain a distance without backing away from their commitment and duty of care.

As carers integrated the cultural raw materials at hand with their personal narrative identity, they inhabited what I refer to as "counter-worlds," other possible worlds or transcendent visions of possibility and aspiration. Interacting with fellow carers in a peer support group or with one's faith community allowed certain lines of narrative to flow easily and others to change direction or fade to the background. Rather than providing a complete set of answers to life's challenges, counter-worlds preserve a creative fragility that allowed carers to reflect on their experiences in a wider frame, the edges of which lay beyond immediate reach. Recalling Tronto's (1993) definition of care (chapter 1, 20), counter-worlds reveal the transformative effects of "everything we do to maintain, continue and repair 'our world'" (103), the ways in which trajectories of change and ways of thinking otherwise produce changes in the ways we care. This chapter describes how carers produce and maintain these counter-worlds and their implications for mediating the dangers of isolation and the grieving process (described in more detail in chapter 6).

The Vastness of the Moment

"My body is wrecked."

Akemi winced as she said this, but her wounds, to me, were invisible, hidden by a modest, feminine blouse buttoned tightly around the neck, a cornflower blue cardigan, a small blue handbag, and a dainty pair of oval wire-rimmed glasses. I met Akemi by chance one afternoon as I was leaving the temple of the new religious group Sūkyō Mahikari, translated literally as "True-Light Supra-Religion" (Swift 2012, 275; Matsunaga 2000; McVeigh 1991). I had just taken part in a ceremony there at the request of a friend I had met at a carer support group, and as soon as I was outside I began scribbling descriptions of it in my notepad.

When I finally looked up, I noticed Akemi standing just a few feet away from me. I realized that she must have been watching my curious note taking, so I greeted her cheerfully, trying not to appear suspicious.[2] I showed her the notebook and explained that I was in Japan because I was interested in learning from carers, and when she heard this, she suddenly stopped still and looked at me intently through her glasses.

"I think we must have some connection [en], you and I!" she told me, finally smiling. After asking me a few more questions, as if to confirm her intuition, we found that we had recently lived close to each other in the United States, just prior to her moving back to Kyoto to care for her mother. It was as if the universe had spoken; she quickly agreed to meet with me again. As we parted, she motioned over her shoulder to the temple and smiled again. "I wouldn't be able to survive if it wasn't for this [faith]."

While both Japan and the UK are often characterized as secular, or nonreligious societies (Engelke 2014; Reader 2012), many of the carers I spoke with in both countries told me either that they felt a deepening sense of spirituality or a stronger conviction toward a faith they held before they started caring. Akemi would fit into the latter category. Since her student days, long before she became a carer for her mother, Akemi had begun following the teachings of Sūkyō Mahikari. Having no children of her own, Akemi, by her own admission, did not have a good sense of the responsibility of care until her mother had a serious stroke. Since then, her faith has taken on a new significance for understanding herself, her mother, and the meaning of care.

For three years, Akemi had been the primary carer for her mother, who was bedridden and living with dementia following her stroke. At first, Akemi would spend a few months in Japan before returning to the US, where she lived with her husband. But as her mother's condition progressed, she decided to move back to Japan long-term. Over the year previous to our meeting, there had been frequent hospitalizations, so Akemi had essentially been living at the hospital, helping her mother with personal care such as feeding, changing, and toileting. While the Japanese national medical insurance covers the cost of treatment and rehabilitation, it does not cover the cost of the room, which runs about ¥90,000 per month.

As we talked, Akemi's tone remained serious, even urgent. While some carers use humor to soften their stories, Akemi's journey had been one of earnest commitment and hard-won transformation. Her story was also one of estrangement and of return. Her revelation at the edge state of compassion inaugurated a deep resonance with a counter-world, one that merged her faith with her care. This counter-world was one in which her care afforded her an intensified experience of communication with a spiritual consciousness.

"The world we can sense is only a very small portion of what exists," she explained as a slight smile began to spread across her face.

> There is a whole world that we cannot see, cannot touch, but it is there. The universe is a stage, and we are all just acting out our parts, but the props, the costumes, the set, all that's been created by someone, and when I see it like that, I can see its beauty. So if I play the role that has been given to me, and I see that all this has been made by god [kami],[3] then I know that god's consciousness is within it. So care is not just about human relationships, but about a communication [kōryū] with that consciousness.

Akemi's initial conversion to Mahikari occurred when she was studying art at university. In a pattern similar to that of other lay-religious groups in Japan, Mahikari practitioners advance in levels of attainment, in their case by using their bodies as mediums through which the divine light can pass to others. This light animates the act of care, but unlike possession, it does not displace but heightens the embodied consciousness of the carer. When Akemi began to receive the light from others, she was skeptical at first, but her skepticism was soon replaced with wonder; she began to experience changes in perception and sensation, the ways she saw colors and the feelings expressed in her artwork.

Her parents, who did not follow this religion, became gradually estranged from her, and not long after she had left school, Akemi moved to the US and continued to practice there. When she moved back to Japan, she was unsure how her spiritual beliefs would be received by her mother, and was ready to leave if things became too difficult. But a few months became a year, then two years, then three. When we spoke, she still remained uncertain about how much longer her situation would last. Or, perhaps, how much longer she would last.

> Caring for my mother has been really hard. If I didn't have Mahikari, I'm sure I would have been useless. I don't sleep at night. Every ten minutes she's calling my name. In the afternoon I fix food, shop, do laundry, everything. I realized how much humans need their sleep. I start thinking strange things. They do that sort of thing to people in jail, right? Depriving people of sleep for days and then, even if they haven't committed any crime, they still confess! That's what it was like. When I was working or painting I could do an all-nighter no problem. That was because I was having fun and doing what I wanted—but this was too much. And I spent a year like that. My physical energy was depleted. Emotionally, I was depressed. But when I would go to Mahikari and

receive purification [through the light] I would emotionally reset. Just by hearing other people's stories, like a kind of alcoholic's therapy session, is fine, but you really don't change at your core. If you don't have that change you cannot overcome that kind of hardship.

Akemi's experience in her religious practice and that of being with her mother were complete opposites. For her, the deprivation of sleep, the monotony, and the emotional fatigue of constant attention to her mother bound her like a prisoner, draining her energy. Receiving the light from Mahikari practitioners restored that energy and connected her to the invisible world and transcendent purpose. Though counterposed in her narrative, fatigue and recovery were dialectically related, and Akemi's empathetic attunement of spiritual powers was a result of this; her experiences of caring and being cared for were in constant, circular co-narration. Care was at once the practical materialization of her religion's narrative of meaningful suffering, and a pathway to achieving a more compassionate subjectivity. For Akemi, the world that she described as lying beyond our own, the counter-world full of color and light and yet invisible to people like me, was a world that, for her, held the possibility of survival and transcendence.

Counter-worlds are more than merely distillations of utopic aspirations or transcendent dreamworlds; they are any "reality that manifests a distinction between present conditions and possible states of affairs" (Thomas 2017). As Akemi noted forcefully in her narrative, these counter-worlds offer the possibility of fundamental transformation in a way that merely sharing one's story cannot. Akemi's counter-world was not only envisioned, but embodied and aesthetic, something that linked it once again to embodied practices of compassion described in the previous chapter. Like Buddhist carers, Akemi believed that the effectiveness of care—the light—was contingent on the state of one's heart (*kokoro*), and the practice of care was the means of cultivating this pure and open vulnerability:

> AKEMI: If your heart is open, it will change in a good direction. That's why the most important thing about care is the humanity of it. Even if you have an incredible care facility, it won't be any good without good people.
>
> DANELY: What kind of people do you mean?
>
> AKEMI: People who just lost their temper [*kireru*] or are always annoyed. It's a matter of the state of their heart [*kokoro*].
>
> DANELY: And how has your *kokoro* changed?

AKEMI: I still have a lot in myself that I don't like, but I have a feeling of gratitude. I've become able to be grateful.

DANELY: Like a miracle?

AKEMI: Absolutely! That—that's it. I always say that no matter how many books you read, or things you listen to, your personality doesn't change. You have to return to the origin [*moto*], the soul, and from that place you ask [god] to create the person.

Openness (to the other, to god, or to the world), gratitude, and transformation were all recurrent themes in carers' narratives of counter-worlds. "Opening" was an imaginative window in the "prison" of isolation and fatigue that Akemi described earlier. But this counter-world was not merely a means of escape from the exhausting work of care, but a means toward what Akemi considered spiritual and psychic enhancement:

I am polishing and polishing my future self. I have a lot of underdeveloped parts of myself. But whatever happens, it doesn't hurt me so much. It might just feel like that, depending on the state of my emotions. Same with care. I feel the limits of my strength, emotional anxiety. If I had my family around me, they might be able to help, but [there's nobody]. There's no care for the soul [*kokoro*]. No care for carers. Nothing. Suffering is a kind of training [*shugyō*]. In my case, it's my mother's care. [I realized] life isn't all about good things. When bad things happen, those are the things that open your soul [*tamashi hikareru*]. When there are hard times, I'm grateful. It's not like a test, but there is some kind of meaning. It's important to look at that.

This perspective, the forging of a durable counter-world, was possible not only through many years of dedicated practice in Mahikari, but also through her own experience of bodily brokenness and mental exhaustion. A counter-world of care is not a plaster over the wound, but sometimes an intensification of that wound, a radical openness of dangerous compassion (Danely 2021). Counter-worlds of compassion are not immune to danger (dystopia is never far away from utopia), and while they might generate creative means of adapting to hardship, they might also amplify tensions or produce logics that distort or delimit possibilities for maintaining life in this world. Like others, Akemi in her exhaustion reached the point where she had even thought about a homicide-suicide. "I was with my mother every day, and sometimes I thought about killing her and myself [*shinjū*]. I didn't understand people who did that before, but now I understand. I really empathize with them. I thought it would be easier if we were both dead. There's no medicine for that kind of negative way of thinking." Hitting this low point, however, propelled her further into her faith. Putting aside her ego and continuing to transmit the divine light gradually seemed to yield some relief: "I not only receive the light, but also give it to my mother, [as I have] every day for three years. There was someone else I know who was in the same state three years ago, just bedridden [*netakiri*]. That person is still like that now, but my mother is able to sit up, and it is because I have been doing that."

Akemi transferred the light not only directly to heal her mother, but also to the air and the food, believing that by sending waves of positive light into them, she was changing the chemical structure and purifying them. She reduced most of her mother's medicines, despite the doctor's protests. At this point Akemi's religious devotion may seem reckless, overstepping some boundary of reason into something close to abuse. Without having seen her mother or having the chance to confirm her accounts, it is impossible for me to make a judgment about this. What I do feel is worthy of noting, however, is the way Akemi's spiritual counter-world intensified her relationship with her mother while alleviating it of other sources of care (like medicines). Yet it also appears as a kind of hybrid of compassion and charity. While associations with *shugyō* training and purifying the *kokoro* appear to embody a compassionate orientation, the purpose of this training was to allow the adherent to become a conduit for a more indiscriminate, unconditional grace of the divine light. This mediumship of a greater power more closely resembles charitable care. In the same way that Mahikari devotees hold their hands a short distance away from the body while transferring light, Akemi's hybrid model of care maintained proximity and the space between that allowed her to endure, to become transformed, and to feel a part of a world beaming down love and support:

> Life is just a moment, so when I think that these three years have been so long, it doesn't seem like only a moment; but if I think about that, I really feel like I am given the sense of vastness. I believe there are things like guardian angels, not just ones that we have in our life, but ones that we can't see, so many spirits watching over us! That gives me courage. I am so grateful to all of those people that I cannot see. If you turn your heart over to god, everything changes completely.

Sūkyō Mahikari is by no means a mainstream religious group in Japan, but the ways that it configures suffering, power, and the body, and most of all spiritual resonance with others through the cultivation of the heart, are all narrative themes that surface in other areas of Japanese life. The transcendence of the counter-world was not a means of removing herself from the scene of care or turning away from the face of the other, but an intensification of that relationship that inaugurates *en*-counter-worlds of resonant possibility.

Connecting with the Transcendent

Followers of new religious groups like Akemi, as well as Christians, tended to see their religious faith as exclusive to others. In wider Japanese culture, however, this is more of an exception than a rule. Surveys of religion in Japan are notoriously difficult to interpret, not least because the two dominant religious traditions (Shinto and Buddhism) are neither exclusive nor principally based on matters of faith, but practice and custom (Josephson 2012; Reader and Tanabe 1998). Even then, there appears to be little concern with configuring practices into a coherent system, even if most share the same basic flavor. While anthropologists might see Japanese ways of relating to the unseen as a form of "spirituality," "magic," or "religion," these terms fail to resonate with the heart of the matter, which Jensen, Ishii, and Swift (2016) refer to as "attuning to webs of *en*," or the cosmic connections between beings. For Akemi and others, counter-worlds are also *en*-counter-worlds that produce new ways of meeting and integrating the world into relational experience. Because of the inclusivity of Japanese religion as lived-practice, it is awkward for Japanese individuals to answer questions about their religion as if it were a part of their personal identity, perhaps in the same way individuals might hesitate to identify as a "carer" if they are also the cared-for's daughter or husband. Caring, like religion in Japan, is primarily something one *does* without the need for reflection on the metaphysical and existential implications, even if these do arise in the process (cf. Aulino 2019; Kleinman 2009).

While there is considerable variation across traditions, participating in Buddhist or Shinto practices, for example, need not entail a study of doctrines or sermons, undertaking ascetic practices such as seated meditation, or completing initiatory rites such as baptism or profession of faith. Rather, religious practices may be used to attend to and find connection with others and to the divine, whether that is in the household (though memorial of the ancestors) or community (in festivals of tutelary deities, for example).

Regardless of the religious identity of any individual Japanese person, Buddhism is still very much present in Japanese life. I already mentioned the ways in which Buddhist ontology naturalizes certain cultural understandings of the relational self, the central place of suffering in life, and the virtue of compassion (chapter 1, 25–26). These themes form a pattern across carer narratives and help carers derive meaning from experiences of empathy, fatigue, and care. Buddhist rituals also inform the ways carers and the cared-for understand death and the afterlife, the importance of maintaining attachments with the ancestors (Danely 2014). Yet most carers would find it unusual to consult with Buddhist clergy around issues of caring. Despite the important role of Buddhist institutions in mortuary practices, most Buddhist priests do not engage in counseling carers; counseling with priests or holding ceremonies for the sake of the carer happens only after the care has ended.

A rare exception to this can be found at Hōrin-ji, a small Zen temple located just west of the Kyoto city center and better known as the Daruma Temple. A few years before I had started my research, the abbot of the temple, Sano-sensei, and a small group of monks decided to do more to attend to the community's concerns about aging and caregiving, even going as far as completing a course in practical training in elderly care. After visiting the temple with a group of male carers and meeting Sano-sensei, I arranged another meeting that I hoped would shed light on some of the things carers had been telling me about their religious or spiritual practices. When I arrived at the large wooden temple gate on the day of our meeting, my eye was immediately caught by a brightly colored poster tacked to one side. On the poster was an image of a young mother and father with their hands resting on each shoulder of a silently praying child. Together, they smiled as their arms form a large circle that completed in the joined palms of the child. The caption read, "Gratitude. The debt of gratitude to mother and father, my life here and now."[4] In contrast to the solemn and austere traditional architecture of the Buddhist temples, posters like this, with its whimsical drawing, provided an outward-facing message to the community, promoting the importance of traditional familial bonds and giving no hint of the main ceremonial function of temples of caring for the dead.

Beyond the gate, the low, graceful wooden temple buildings, partially hidden behind neatly pruned pines and flowering bushes, seem to have nothing unusual about them until you inspect them closer. Only then do you begin to notice that the shapes of the windows, the roof tiles, and even the small garden all echo images of Daruma, a semimythical saintly figure in popular Buddhism whose long meditation in the caves of China is said to be the origin of Zen (Ch'an) Buddhism. Daruma is said to have come from India, and is usually depicted in a simple red robe, with his beard and eyebrows long, dark, and unkempt, huge eyes bulging out of his head, and a mouth fixed in an intense scowl of unwavering determination and discipline. And yet images of this ugly monk became a popular meme (a *hayarigami*, or trendy god) during the age of printmaking, when he was depicted as everything from a badger to a prostitute (Faure 2011).[5] One traditional children's toy involves trying to avoid toppling Daruma while using a wooden mallet to skillfully remove the wooden discs he rests on.

His look of fierce determination has made Daruma a kind of patron guardian of those who persevered, and even today, when individuals or groups set a goal, they might purchase a votive image of Daruma, drawing in a single eye and leaving the second to mark the goal's completion. This seemed an appropriate (if slightly intimidating) representation of the spiritual endurance needed to care for older family members. Inside the Daruma temple buildings were thousands of variations of Daruma, from a huge black-ink painting across the ceiling, to lamps and furniture, to tiny miniature statues no bigger than a child's thumb. Many were gifts or votive donations from parishioners (temples are often places that can ritually dispose of dolls, which are thought to possess a soul and might seek revenge if discarded haphazardly) (Gygi 2018). The effect of this uncanny repetition and excess of eyes was like entering a cabinet of curiosities, only to sense that you are the one being watched.

Sano-sensei's appearance couldn't be more different from Daruma: he was tall and cheerful, and his cleanly shaven head and face made him look boyish. He led me to a room where someone had already set out two cups of tea and Daruma-shaped biscuits. A Beethoven sonata softly flowed through an open doorway of a flower-arranging classroom across the hall. I sat on the floor across the low table from him and began by asking what Buddhism could bring to our understanding of care for older people, and what role, if any, he thinks temples can play in the community. He responded immediately and confidently that the role of Buddhism was to attend to suffering:

> I think it was the same in India and the same in China and the same in Japan, but Buddhism and temples were around because people had suffering, everyone in each place had anxiety, worry, suffering. One of the biggest kinds of concern was growing older, falling ill, dying, separating from others [bereavement]. Everyone was different, but these four were what they say are the biggest sources of suffering. In other words, Buddhism *turns toward suffering*. For example, take Japan, this temple, we might have people like that, maybe physically weak, and we might make some rice porridge and give it to them. Or if someone needs medicine, we will give them some medicine. If they are in pain, hurting, we would heal them. So that's why Buddhist priests have been the ones who have played the role of a kind of doctor. Doctor, monk, caregiver, social worker—a monk combines all those faces [*men*]. A temple is a hospital, a care home for the elderly, and then a counseling room for your worries. It was that kind of all-purpose space, I think, a long time ago. Anyway, if there were times when people would feel they were in some trouble, they would first of all go to ask the monk about it. [They would think] I'm in trouble, I better go consult with the monk. Oh, what should I do in this situation? I better go ask the monks, because they were such a familiar presence [*mijikana sonzai*] in everything, they were all-knowing and all-powerful, whatever you needed, they could do it all—like Superman! So, since they were like that, monks might

listen to someone and say, "I see, well in that case, why don't I introduce you to someone I know [who can help]." Well in today's care system, it would be like a care manager. That kind of person is a doctor, a helper; they are right in the middle of this big network, and they can offer this support to the patient. The elder care system, well, you might say, in the old days in Japan, it was the monks who did that sort of thing, perhaps. Today there is a division of labor. Whether you are on the welfare side or the health care side, it is all split up, but truthfully, I think the number one thing that has been lost is turning toward the person's heart [*hito no kokoro ni mukiau*]. . . . The other day at the [male carer support gathering], all that distress, people carrying so much suffering, everyone was facing so much hardship, so we could, a little—of course I could have said, "okay, give to me all of your suffering, I will change places with you," but that would be impossible! If I were to say to you today "I'm in pain!" you couldn't switch [yourself] with my pain [*watashi no itami to kawaru*], in reality. However, you could come close to me [*yorisou*] and say, "Oh, what's happened?"

As Sano-sensei explains, if temples and priests were such an integral part of community life in the past, that role has largely been displaced by modern institutions, and this change has disrupted the resonance between temple and community. For Sano-sensei, modern institutions were faceless entities that could not fully "turn toward the suffering" of the carer; they alienated the person caring from the community rather than integrating them. Sano-sensei's emphasis on "turning toward" or "facing" people echoes the relational ethics that, as I argued in the previous chapter, underpinned carers' motivations for compassion, even reiterating the point that empathetic resonance with the suffering of another person does not mean substitution. Compassionate proximity acknowledges that otherness composes ethical human interrelations.

Sano-sensei realized the need for Buddhist institutions to draw on their history to address those aspects of care that had been lost in the transition to modern social care. This resulted in the establishment of a small group called Sa-ra, which brought together Zen Buddhist clergy, laypersons, and the clinical community to discuss ways they can become better integrated. As part of this, Sano-sensei and some other monks received official certification as licensed care assistants after completing an elderly care training course. These monks offered counseling in the care of a local hospital and performed outreach to carers in their community. While the activities Sa-ra does are still somewhat unusual in Japan, Sano-sensei saw it as part of his responsibility as a monk to "spread the seeds" of compassion, without thinking too much about the results: "It is the practice of compassion, or what we Mahayana Buddhists call 'Bodhisattva practice,' if you want to make it sound fancy. If you lose this [compassion], you're no longer a monk, as far as I'm concerned. The reason you become a monk is [to help] the world, other people, to discard the self and yet live in the world with others. We have to go out into the world and try to make connections [*en wo tsunagu*]" between people.

Like Akemi, Sano-sensei saw compassion arising out of a transcendent connection (*en*-counter-world) with others. He hoped this activity would spread, but he was also aware that many people were wary of religion, and even Buddhists may be closed to the views of sects that differed from their own. As Michael Berman (2018) observed among Buddhist chaplains attending to the survivors of the 2011 Great East Japan triple disaster, performing compassion necessitated a kind of self-censorship that reproduced notions of secularity and undermined their ability to provide spiritual care. In the case of these chaplains, religious particularity was replaced by an ethic of "bonds of suffering" (230). While Sa-ra was not under the same kinds of constraints as the interfaith chaplaincy Berman described, Sano-sensei still felt compelled to follow the same sort of logic, saying "I never ever talk about 'Buddhism' or say 'Shakamuni [Buddha] said this or that' when I talk [with carers]. Instead I say 'Did you eat anything today?' Something really ordinary like that!"

For Sano-sensei, however, this was a practice of accompaniment (*yorisoi*), closing the distance between himself and the person in need of help, and it was part of a Buddhist ethical ontology of non-duality. Carer and cared-for are entangled and intertwined, and the carer's empathetic imagination overcomes the distance of pity and allowed action.

> SANO: So, well, to look after another person, to care for them, is also caring for oneself. Non-duality of self and other as they call it, that is what I have genuinely felt. In Buddhism there is a teaching of non-duality [*jita funi*]. Not two, but one. You and I are in essence one, as a consciousness [*kokoro*], the buddha-consciousness, just one. That sort of thought. [It sounds] heavy! But when I talk to carers, I think, wow, it really is like that.
>
> DANELY: So you feel that caring for another is caring for yourself?
>
> SANO: That's right! It's looking at yourself [as if in a mirror]. When you are caring for another, and you are next to them, you can't say, "I will bear your pain and suffering for you," but if you get close enough, you may be able to feel it as "*our* pain." You start to feel the other's pain and suffering as your *own* pain and suffering. If you just think "Oh, that poor person," you'll always be separated by this space of pity. You see, there you will have a distance like this [*backs up*], not

like this [*moves close and grabs hold of my arm*]. Of course, social welfare, carers, Buddhists, religious people, and even the people of the whole world if they were to [have that perspective], it would be ideal [utopia], I think.

Sano's last comment leads directly to the question of the relationship between personal counter-worlds, care, and larger social, even political visions.

Escape to Solitude

If Japanese carers imagined counter-worlds as *en*-counter-worlds where the connection to the cared-for refracted through unseen networks of the living as well as through spirits and other transcendent beings, English counter-worlds, religious or secular, offered a means of escape from the confinement of caring intimacy, a way back to the self and its singular relationship to god, nature, or the social body.[6]

Allen was the only English carer I interviewed (out of fifteen) who was a regular churchgoer, though some of the other carers had religious upbringings and still occasionally attended church on holidays. For Allen, faith had been the anchor that harbored the boat amid the waves of life, simultaneously a way to distance himself from a turbulent world and a place of refuge where he felt a strong sense of self-identity. Although he and his parents had been regular churchgoers for his whole life, Allen didn't feel like it was something that had bound them to each other, nor did he feel that the church community was there to support him when he began to feel the stress and fatigue of caring for his mother.[7] If anything, caring made his faith more personal, singular, his very own.

Allen's mother had helped care for his father before he died, and just like Allen, she felt that the church turned away from her just as she needed emotional support. Allen had been encouraging his mother to find a new church where she could feel happy, but because they lived in separate villages some distance away, it was difficult even to find people who could help drive her to church. I turned to ask him about his own faith:

> DANELY: In your case, have you found that the community or your faith has been a support for you?
> ALLEN: Faith, yes, church itself, no. It's been very much due to the other things that I've mentioned that have happened with me. Churches very often take a viewpoint on that which isn't necessarily a positive one, and you can be excluded due to that. But for me my faith

is very important for me, and that has helped me through a lot of the tough situations that I've been through, including, you know, looking after Mum and everything else as well. I don't think I would have got through everything I've been through if I didn't have my faith. It's, um, [*breaks off, collects his thoughts*]. An example for you, in that case: When I first got married, I got married in May; in June Dad told he had cancer and was given three years to live. In July he had a breakdown, and in the September my wife had a miscarriage, so to have all those things happen in that short space of time, for me it's my faith that got me through, because it was then a case of you're going to visit your mum and dad, Dad's got cancer, he's got three years to live, you go home and you've got the miscarriage, so there isn't really anywhere you could get away that was happy and light, and that's where your faith becomes important because that is somewhere you've got that is away from everything else and that is just central to you. And obviously that is important going forward with looking after Mum and whatever issues may come up in the future. My faith is solid, and that isn't going to change, whereas everything in the world is in a state of flux, so to speak—anything in the world can change, but my faith isn't going to change because that's just central to who I am.

In this narrative, then, Allen describes the importance of faith as a kind of counter-world to the troubles in his relationships; faith was "somewhere you've got that is away from everything else and that is just central to you." This "solid," steadfast, and unchanging nature of his faith (or his relationship with God) transcended not only his world as a carer, but even the church community.

Allen also contrasted the effortless security of his faith to the constant effort and endurance of caring for his mother. "You've got to get on with life," he told me, "but it's nice to have this solid anchor that you've got, to get through it all, because otherwise it's like a constant battering. This goes on and then that goes on and it's constant. So, yeah, hold steady and knuckle down and get on with it!" In another instance, he explained the constant obsessive pull of responsibility: "You never switch off, you're always thinking it's down to me to sort out."

If Allen's faith could be described as a counter-world, it is one that transports him away from his mother and his everyday life so that he can feel a stronger sense of "who he is." This process has led to a sense of self-discovery and confidence in his faith. Allen, for instance, told me, "I've learnt a huge amount the last few years, just a huge amount of what sort of character I am or what sort of person I am, how I deal with things, how I react to things, which for me has been great because it's like, okay, despite all this tough stuff I've learnt that this is how I am with this or with this, and it's been really good." In this short excerpt from one of our talks, Allen mentioned "I" or "me" a total of eight times, as if the first-person needed to be constantly conjured lest it disappeared into the other. In the context of English society, Allen's journey of self-discovery struck me as both reasonable and completely opposite from what I had been hearing from Japanese carers. Japanese carers' counter-worlds were not places to escape to alone, but ways of being-with, resonating both with the cared-for and with the world in ways that uncovered new feelings and sensitivities. Even when English carers did construct counter-worlds that involved a new sense of embodied time, they described it as solitude rather than relationship, resonating with narrative of the power of a personal spirit rather than the family, or the cared-for.

Charli, a woman in her late sixties who cared for her husband, described how she regularly used her carer's allowance to pay for respite care so that she could get away for a couple of days.

> Last time I went walking in Yorkshire. The time before, I went up to one of the most isolated places in Britain for the week. It is pretty isolated—but Knoydart you can only reach if you walk in for a day, and then you're stuck by the sea—I mean the whole thing was just wonderful. I stayed a night in Glasgow, and then I got the train up to Mallaig. It's a five-hour single-track journey up to Rannoch Moor, um, up to the port of Mallaig that takes people out to Skye and places like that. There is one boat that goes across to the village, but there are no roads up in Knoydart. Just a track, and it's quite a trek—you cannot move to Knoydart and buy a property, you can only go if you contribute to the community. And I just sat. For the first two days I just sat. *I did nothing.* And, and the two days just went—I just wasn't able—and I think that's the stage people get to—there's so much that you're dealing with so that when you haven't got to deal with it you have no energy for anything. So that's what I did in Knoydart. But I didn't need that so much in Yorkshire. I walked and climbed. Only with my legs though, no ropes—only climbing up steep banks with sticks and things. But, yeah. Oh yes, yes, I'm lucky I do have that now, but not everyone has that.

Charli didn't just seek solitude—she sought "nothing," a view from nowhere, a real *utopia.* The isolated village of Knoydart was a counter-world to the unrelenting everyday world of care, a world that she, like Allen, described in the typical English idiom, "just getting on with it," or merely "surviving." Once Charli's life became dominated by care, she, like other carers, grew gradually aware that she had been living with a chronic and uneasy sense of disconnection to this spiritual world. Not only had the time drained away, the slowness replaced by crisis, but the mediums and senses through which Charli felt connected had also been pushed to the side. Charli's counter-world, then, was mediated not only by the visual, but also by the return of something tactile and atmospheric, sounds whose caress was a means of escape, transcendence, the utopic feeling of another possible world:

> I listen to music too. . . . It's strange, it's relaxing, and yet stimulating intellectually, or aurally. That's something that—I've never thought about it before—that's something else that was missing. I didn't have the time to sit and listen to music, and music is very important to me. So when I just sit—actually, I'm not just sitting, I'm listening to sounds, so if it's the sea, if it's the trees, if it's wildlife . . . yeah. That's what I do—it's a sort of escapism, I guess. No, it isn't really, is it? It's reality, because it's there as well. As a small child we had a stream at the end of our garden, and on one side there was a mound with a very old hawthorn tree, and I would go and sit under the tree. I wouldn't mind if it were pouring with rain, I would go and sit under the tree and sit and listen to the rain and watch it on the water, and just sit and, yeah. Listen to, watch the swans come up from the main river. It's all been piped now. Watched the fish. Yes, catch frogs and never quite understand how they would escape from where I put them, yeah. So, I suppose it's something that I've always done, just sit.

The nostalgic innocence of being a child under the hawthorn tree was a feeling Charli described as an "affinity of all things that are alive," through which she herself felt a sense of the spiritual that resonated in her soul. But to find this spiritual resonance with the transcendent, this counter-world, Charli had to find herself stripped of the social baggage of roles and duties, and this meant leaving her husband in the care of others.

Counter-world, Utopia, and Heterotopia

As the examples of Akemi, Allen, and Charli all illustrate, counter-worlds are ways of connecting with the transcendent and may encompass the worlds of dreams, fantasies, visions, hopes, and fears; they are sites of imagination and potential, of natality, where a new story begins to emerge. Alfred Schutz (1970, 245) referred to "the transcendent" as "the open infinite horizons of my world in potential reach."[8] The transcendent is defined, in part, by the ways it exceeds our ability to experience it directly, yet still presents to us a vision of potential, and, as Levinas might argue, an ethical responsibility to that virtual world. The religious worlds of Akemi and Sano-sensei have the familiar ring of highly elaborate moral narrative, the meeting of a collectively composed worldview and the lived experience of the carer in the midst of practice, but these are not the only kinds of transcendent counter-worlds that carers engaged with to maintain and endure while they cared.

Here I want to return briefly to the notion of counter-world, expanding its scope to include realms of the transcendent beyond what would typically be thought of as religious. First, counter-worlds, as the name suggests, emerge as potential alternative or inverted worlds. In this sense, they are indistinguishable from the notion of utopia, though this is a term rarely employed in anthropology and in elderly care.[9] Karl Mannheim ([1929] 1936) argued that "a state of mind is utopian when it is incongruous with the state of reality within which it occurs" (173). Mannheim added a further characteristic in order to distinguish the utopian from the ideological: "Only those orientations transcending reality will be referred to us as utopian which, when they pass over into conduct, tend to shatter, either *partially or wholly*, the order of things prevailing at the time" (173, emphasis mine). This depiction of utopia as something that moves toward the future by partially or wholly "bursting the limits of the existing order" (179) echoes the kind of narrative rupture that carers describe as the gap between norms or policy and practice in lived experience.[10]

Similarly, Japanese philosopher Washida Kiyokazu (2015) described the "counter-world" (*hansekai*) as "dislocating the stiffened and inflexible joints of 'this world,' restoring the world to something plastic and fluid, and as a result, providing an opportunity to braid the world together again" (89). For Washida, the counter-world offers a critical perspective from a "dangerous" place where "things that are inconceivable can be kept as they are without being understood" (91) in terms of reductionistic narratives. Those "stiff joints" of "the world," such as the walls dividing the young from the old concretized as schools and care homes, are for Washida the sedimentation of cultural and historical views on progress and success that has led to the devaluation of the old as anything but the object of care. It is the sensibility (Nortvedt 2003), delicate as the "downy baby hairs of the soul" (*kokoro no ubuge*) (Washida 2015, 118) that carers know so well, that prompts the reconsideration of counter-worldly narratives with a life-or-death urgency. Like the narratives of the Japanese carers I spoke with, Washida's critique of the ideological foundations of modern welfare institutions was premised on an ontological and ethical commitment to interdependence, vulnerability (*yowasa*), and sensitivity (*kanjusei*). The sensitivity emerging from care yields a "gaze of the counter-world" (Washida 2015, 89); not a "view from nowhere" (Nagel 1986), but a view from "manywheres" (Shweder 1996).

Though Washida's ideas of utopia/counter-world come from a phenomeno-logical perspective, Michel Foucault (1986) used a similar analogy of the gaze in his own theory of counter-worlds (what he termed "counter-sites," or "heteroto-pias"). For Foucault, counter-worlds are mediated by a "mirror" that "enables me to see myself there where I am absent" (24).

> From the standpoint of the mirror I discover my absence from the place where I am since I see myself over there. Starting from this gaze that is, as it were, directed toward me, from the ground of this virtual space that is on the other side of the glass, I come back toward myself; I begin again to direct my eyes toward myself and to reconstitute myself there where I am. The mirror functions as a heterotopia in this respect: it makes this place that I occupy at the moment when I look at myself in the glass at once absolutely real, connected with all the space that surrounds it, and absolutely unreal, since in order to be perceived it has to pass through this virtual point which is over there.

Heterotopia is the "over there," a counter-world that constitutes the self from the point of view of the "virtual space that is on the other side of the glass," simultaneously holding the self and the mirror image in a state of connection and separation. Counter-worlds of carers may be heterotopic not only because they present something different, but also because they provide a site of self-reflec-tion, imagination, and even contestation. Leibing (2014) argues that heterotopias might help us understand suffering as something that can "reveal interconnect-edness of place, (aging) body, identity, and power" (232). If Akemi had been at the edge of dangerous compassion and peered into the abyss of exhaustion, she saw something looking back at her. And like Foucault's mirror, the gaze from the counter-world was captivating.

For those carers who did not resonate with religious utopian feelings, a coun-ter-world might still be found in the sense of possibility or broadening horizons found in peer support groups and gatherings that I will turn to in the next section. Not only are these groups conduits for the circulation of novel ways of express-ing and imagining care, but they are the kind of real sites of "effectively enacted utopia" that Foucault was interested in. Carers may come to peer support groups for a specific need or crisis, but for those who stay, the group may be a source of what Ernst Bloch (1986) called "dreams of a better life." In an uncertain world, carers most wished for certainty and order; in a world where the carer's role was ambiguous, they wished for the sense of identity; in a world where there seemed to be no end point, they want a purpose. Utopia is that future realm of possibility located in the real. In the most successful groups, carers can always find someone who has been through worse, or whom they might be able to help through their own experience. Groups console, warn, or give hope, and allow contact with the "not yet become" (Allison 2013, 79–81; Bloch 1986, 144; Levitas 1990).

Tōjisha Support Groups as Collective Counter-worlds

What I am putting under the blanket term "carer support groups" ranges from informal neighborhood gatherings over tea to formal structured sessions with social workers.[11] Carers, new and experienced alike, came to these groups to learn and to provide help, advice, or encouragement, but the main function is to carve out a space where carers could meet, talk, and gain a sense of belonging and connection that they may feel is missing from relationships with other friends and family. Support groups were heterotopic sites of storytelling, which Michael Jackson, after Hannah Arendt, argues constitute "a vital capacity of people to work together to create, share, affirm, and celebrate something that is held in common" (Jackson 2002, 40). For carers, the intensely personal and affect-laden experiences of care made it difficult to feel they belonged in the same world as non-carers, describing this sensation as becoming "invisible," or being unable to voice their experiences without inviting pity, or even disdain, for "complaining" too much.

Even good friends, sympathetic at first, become less responsive or interested as the months and years go on, especially if the carer does not display obvious signs of distress. One English carer explained that after some time it felt like she had "disappeared" again, and this made it even harder to feel she could ask for support. At the same time, trying to keep one's experience hidden from others generated its own kind of stress, denying, in a way, the meaningfulness of care and of the new compassionate self trying to emerge (or survive). The lack of resonance with the world was described by another English carer as life becoming "very compressed and narrow." Carer support groups provided spaces where these carers could feel recognized, valued, and "seen," not just as carers, but as individuals with more complex personal circumstances and histories. In Japan, recognition as part of a support group was sometimes the first instance where a carer identified as a *tōjisha*, a term used in other contexts to identify not only those who fit the immediate target group (i.e., current carers), but also those who have in some way been affected by similar circumstances (e.g., care recipients, friends and relatives of the carer, community volunteers, professional care workers). As Junko Kitanaka (2019) noted in the case of dementia *tōjisha*, this label is commonly used to highlight a group's "agency" and "activism" (120), performing a function of both safety and unified voice, even as it is exclusive, operating on a logic of incommensurability (124). I came to think of *tōjisha* as people who have "been there," or whose experience has given them a personal perspective that resonates with the group's collective narrative.

As mentioned in chapter 1, support groups for carers were more prevalent in England compared to Japan (at least as official registered bodies), with many specifically designated for carers of people living with particular maladies (e.g., Alzheimer's-type dementia, Parkinson's, cancer, stroke, psychological disability). A broad network of local and national charity organizations, council-commissioned NGOs, and employers supported these groups and helped direct carers to them in line with the national 2014 Care Act. They took place in care homes, community centers, and churches, as well as pubs, arts centers, and cafés, and most of the carers I spoke with had attended at least one.

In Japan, formally organized groups, some supported by NGOs like Alzheimer's International, were far fewer in number and were difficult to maintain because of carers' busy schedules. I attended many of these groups, but having never been a carer for an elderly relative myself, I felt very much on the periphery of being a *tōjisha*, even as a volunteer and researcher focused on care. The responsibilities and concerns that I had were somewhat different from those that motivated the others in the group. My role in support groups was as a witness, a listener, and sometimes an ally, whose presence in some small way revealed the value of the group beyond its internal concerns (Sayuri's notion of the "big lighthouse"). As I continued attending, sharing space, stories, and food with *tōjisha*, their hospitality toward me gradually brought me closer to a feeling of being an "insider," or of at least being treated as someone who is "in the same boat" or has "been there"—perhaps not the original "there," but some new "there" constituted out of our relational connections. In this way, the hospitality of the support group constituted a kind of utopian space, or counterworld, where new possibilities for care, comfort, and hope could be perpetually reimagined.

For six months of my fieldwork, I regularly participated in a cross-section of six different carer support groups in the Kyoto area, most of which met only once or twice each month. In all these cases, the mere gathering of a roomful of carers provided a tacit feeling of safety, belonging, and relief. Problems, however embarrassing if shared with others, could be aired and would find sympathetic hearts. Others would share similar stories, nesting words of encouragement, advice, or knowledge in the telling of their own resonant narrative. And everyone ate heartily. "Good food binds people together!" (Oishii wa hito wo tsunagu!), the woman sitting next to me said as she shoveled more food onto my plate. Here I will focus on two groups: the "Hyacinth Group" for women and the "Wednesday Group" for men.

Hyacinth Group

One of the informal support group meetings I attended every month, the Hyacinth Group, was composed mostly of women who were caring for husbands. For these women, becoming a carer was a continuation of gendered household tasks, most of which the women were able to manage, more or less, even as they grew frailer themselves (the "baby" of the group was seventy-six, and most were in their mid-eighties and nineties). However, they also found that even as their responsibilities increased and their bodies became weaker with age, their husbands made no gestures of recognition nor offers to help them.

At ninety-two years old, Takako, the oldest member of the group, was also the most uninhibited and feisty. On the third meeting I attended, she strode in, cane in hand, wearing a huge soft velvety hat with a giant pink flower exploding from the side and a long purple tunic to match her bright purple skirt. She loved poking fun at her husband, a retired professor now living with mild dementia. Her response to my questions quickly sparked a lively conversation among the nine women gathered around the table.

> DANELY: What sort of care do you give to your husband?
>
> TAKAKO: Care? I kick him around! [*Laughs fill the room*]
>
> FUMI: We're not nice, we boss our husbands. Leave 'em alone, they can't do anything by themselves, we had to do everything!
>
> ETSUKO: We were raised to take care of kids, house, neighborhood relations, and our husbands stayed at work. When my husband stopped that he couldn't do anything, just say "Hey!" Or, "Over there!" [when he wanted something]. It was hard.
>
> TAKAKO: That's why they say, "when the husband dies, a woman gets younger" [*more laughs from others*]. It's true! It was hard at first. I would have to make all the food and everything, and the least he could do was take out his own chopsticks, but he just sits there and waits for me!

Others shared similar stories and dramatic whoops of feigned outrage at their husbands' demands, but as it quieted down, a small woman I had hardly noticed seated not far from me began speaking in a low voice to no one in particular. She was new to the group and still a bit shy. Her stare didn't leave the table in front her, and her thick, tinted glasses obscured her eyes. "I was in the hospital and had surgery in the back," she started. "It was so bad, I thought I would die, but when I came back to the house from the hospital, that very day, I had to make food for my husband. I was getting so tired and really thought I would die."

The other women listened, and the atmosphere became tense. Some tried comforting her, telling her she ought to get some help from her care manager and find ways to bring in more paid care while she was recovering, but this too was a source of stress. Like others I spoke with, this woman also found it difficult to get help when there were sudden changes in the health of the carer or cared-for. Short-stay respite often had to be booked weeks in advance, and care recipients like this woman's husband sometimes refused to go out of "pride."

> Aкiko: I went to the welfare officer [*fukushishi*] and asked if there was anything they could do, and she said, well, someone can come and help with the laundry, cooking, cleaning, and so on, but she said that really unless he's got some problem with dementia or something it'll be pretty hard even to get that.
>
> Takako: But even if you get a helper, they have to do everything, clean the house and the cooking and the shopping in one hour! There used to be people in the neighborhood that would just come over and help, but we don't have that anymore. You can do everything you can, but you still have to pay someone, and it isn't cheap! So if you get old without any money, you're in trouble! [*Laughs*]

All the women at the meeting had experienced some trouble with getting access to additional care support when they needed it, revealing another way in which their labor as women and as a spousal carers was both essential and unacknowledged. While the LTCI system in Japan assumes responsibility for the insured person (the care recipient), it does not have a reliable mechanism for recognizing or taking responsibility of care for the unpaid family carer. From the perspective of the women, becoming a carer in later life had as much discontinuity as continuity. It entailed not only a new set of responsibilities that were made more physically laborious because of age, but it was emotionally exhausting, as they felt unable to slip away from the assumed role of women's domestic care. Women like Takako took advantage of their husband's frailty to resist being bossed around, but not all women had her moxie. For the Hyacinth Group, the space they had carved out for lunch together each month was the only chance they had to release these frustrations. "It really is nice to laugh," Takako told me as we said our goodbyes. "You don't laugh very much when you are all by yourself!"

Wednesday Group

Another group I made sure to attend every month was dedicated to men who were carers. While the Hyacinth Group grew organically and focused on a group of neighbors and friends, the Wednesday Group drew participants from across the city. There was a director who was responsible for making sure the meeting happened and for compiling the group newsletter, which was posted on a simple website. On occasion, the director might arrange for a guest speaker to address the gathering. During one meeting, an acupuncturist spoke to us about the need for a program supporting the health of carers, using massage and acupuncture, emphasizing the potential to ease not only the physical aches and pains from lifting, changing, bathing, and so on, but the emotional and spiritual stress as well. Sometimes members of the group would organize outings or tour a care home facility together.

Typically, there were around ten of us seated around tables at the regular café, but if more arrived, they simply pulled up another table. As with the Hyacinth Group, the atmosphere was friendly and upbeat, and direct talk about caring was not the focus. The men talked about the news, about sports or leisure, about their computers. Perhaps the most striking difference between the two groups was that while most of the women tended to use the site to joke about their difficult husbands or other relatives, I have no record of a single instance during the Wednesday Group meetings where men expressed such attitudes toward the person they cared for. In fact, most of the time, they felt quite the opposite, and would occasionally break into tears as they spoke about their wives or mothers. Although every support group had moments like these, it was especially poignant to watch a group of men express such heartfelt vulnerability. Just as the boldness of the women in the Hyacinth Group countered Japanese social norms of delicate, passive femininity, the Men's Wednesday Group was challenging Japanese social norms around emotionally detached and tough-skinned masculinity.

One example of this happened on an unusually hot day in early June after I had already been coming to the group for several months. There were eight of us in the café, sipping iced coffees or sodas when Nori came in and sat in an empty chair next to me, his face flushed and perspiration glistening around his hairline and soaking his collar. He had just come from work and rushed to make the meeting. He looked out of place in his dark suit and white shirt, but he quickly loosened his tie and mopped his forehead with a handkerchief before taking a big drink from a glass of water Hajime had brought him. The last time I saw Nori was about two months earlier. His mother had been waking up several times during the night, and he looked dangerously fatigued, almost unable to speak. I asked how he was getting along lately, and if he had finally been able to get a little sleep.

"Oh, that's over now! I found a group home. She went there yesterday." The words came out quickly, as if he was a little nervous, still breathing heavily from his walk over. His expression reminded me a little of the way I looked after taking my children to school for the first time, equally relieved and apprehensive.

"Nice that you found a good place for her to live," I said.

"She's care level . . ." He mimed drawing the number four on his hand with a finger.

"Four? That's quite advanced, then. A group home ought to be good for her." The others around the table were also listening.

> NORI: Yeah, I got a call the other day, and they said they had a place open. Then I had to ask about the money. Of course, there were some financial issues. . . . Then the care home called and said they could take her for that amount. I didn't call back right away; I thought that might seem a little too casual. So I waited a day, but then I called back, and yesterday my older brother came and picked her up.
>
> HAJIME: She didn't resist or anything?
>
> NORI: Oh, I don't know, since my brother took care of that. But of course, I'm a little lonely. I miss her. It's strange having her gone. I think about her all the time. At night, the thoughts would just go around and around in my head.
>
> HAJIME: But if she's in a group home, that's for the best. You really seemed like you were about to keel over at any moment before!
>
> NORI: But of course, when I think about it, I wonder, is she going to forget who I am? I get really scared. Lonely.

He looked a little tearful as he said these words, and the other men came closer, some offering encouragement, some advice, others humor. Nori knew what he had done was best, but he still felt guilty. The support group members watched and listened. This was a place for a man like Nori to be fragile. After a pause, Hajime smiled and broke the silence.

> HAJIME: You ought to get a girlfriend! [*Everyone laughs*]
>
> NORI: I did my best for ten years! At first I thought I'll care for her just for now, and then it went on. I couldn't see a life after that. I was really scared. Scared of changing. I didn't want anything to change. I was really scared. I'm weak like that. Not wanting anything to change. I have that weakness, so I couldn't bring myself to take her to the home. But how should I live from now on?
>
> KOJI: She can still walk and get around on her own?
>
> NORI: She can do that.
>
> HAJIME: Well, then, she can be there at the home. If she's in a wheelchair, they might not take her.
>
> NORI: It was only ¥140,000 to get her in.

SHIGERU: That's a deposit. But then it's about ¥180,000 each month. Plus extra for diapers.

NORI: I haven't really thought about all that [*laughs*]. But I think we'll be okay.

HAJIME: Well, you've taken off work for so long.

NORI: Actually, I just came from a meeting. I am trying to talk to some people about doing something like a radio drama about male carers. What do you think?

With this suggestion, the conversation turns, and the men start to think about what kind of radio program they might make, who would play the roles, and what sorts of scenarios they might create. From vulnerability, the flow moved to connection and belonging. Even though the care recipient had entered a care home, Nori was welcome as a *tōjisha*, since he shared the same concerns and resonated with the others, born out of a common experience of subjective transformation. Indeed, several men in the group cared for family members who were living in care homes, sometimes because the care recipient's care needs increased after the carer had already joined the group, and other times because the carer only had time to attend the group after he no longer was providing full-time care. For Nori, moving his mother to a care home gave him a chance to recover from the demanding daily care, but it did not change the fact that his subjectivity, the ways he came to exist in and respond to the world through speech and action, still resonated with the other men in the group. Not only that, but through the idea of a radio drama, Nori amplified this resonance by initiating a creative collective action, a space of hope that appeared beyond the individual, a narrative horizon produced by the group. In the space created by their shared company, each *tōjisha* could be a small lighthouse to the others, each face quietly announcing, "I'm here."

Being in the Boat

When life is at its darkest, a "small lighthouse," a "tiny, tiny light of hope" shines even more brilliantly, catching here and there on the edges of the world, creating a relief of shadow beneath the murky darkness. Perhaps Sayuri had a sense of this aesthetic quality, something more intimate, more tactile than bright floodlights of hospitals and care homes. No. The experience of a fellow carer was a faint, fragile light that Japanese novelist Jun'ichirō Tanizaki might describe as "a pregnancy of tiny particles like fine ashes, each particle luminous as a rainbow" (1977, 34). It is a light that embraces mystery rather than seeking to banish it.

For carers tossed by the emotional highs and lows of looking after an elderly relative, the small lighthouse offers a gentle guide back to the shores of ordinary life. What one finds on that other shore, however, is not life as one knew it before, but the counter-world, where new perspectives, visions, and ways of being-with-others can find space of resonance. I describe this transformation as a change in the "world," or in the attunements and responses that constitute one's embodied subjectivity. Not only that, but these are worlds that can hold profound meaning, purpose, and moral value. They are not without their dangers, but they are navigable and, with that, offer the potential to connect with something transcendent. Not surprisingly, these fragile utopias tend to resonate with cultural narratives of transcendence, opening up a deeper, more mysterious sense of connection to one's environment and history.

"Care," Kleinman (2019, 3) writes, is about "vital *presence*—the liveliness and fullness of being—of both the caregiver and the care recipient. Acts of caring call that presence out from within us." While Kleinman points to something rarely acknowledged and even more rarely researched within studies of "carer burden" or "resilience," his sense of "vital presence" calls out for a more precise, culturally situated elaboration. As action that happens in specific moments within particular cultural ecologies, care also reflects the "manywheres" of vital presence.

For Japanese carers (Sayuri, Akemi, Sano-sensei), counter-worlds tended to reflect a sense of invisible connection that was both revealed and sustained by care. The connections of the world encompassed both pleasures and pains of the aging body and its care, but they also meant that one could be connected to a well of power. Cultural narratives offered points of reflection on particular aspects of carers' lived experience in ways that deepened their appreciation for their own hardships and their capacity to love. Through these acts of reflection, carers constructed narratives of future possible selves and the worlds that could maintain those selves; their own invisibility became an entry point to unseen worlds, utopic visions, spaces of relationality. The piecing together of a narrative counter-world not only helped carers manage the fatigue and sorrow of caring in the moment, but provided a bridge toward a more expansive orientation toward the world. The ways in which carers became attuned and responsive to others no longer collapsed the parameters of the world into a dark and lonely place of isolation, but broadened the horizon of imagination and action in the world.

English carers (Allen, Charli) also relied on counter-worlds and a connection with the transcendent for a sense of well-being during care, but rather than proximity and connection that blurred the line between self and other, English carers sought escape and solitude that gave them a steady sense of self. Spirituality, whether religious or more personal, was largely seen as something separate from the practice of care or the specific person being cared for. Perhaps Allen and Charli didn't think of it this way. After all, how could it be that caring both brought them close to the transcendent and farther from the care recipient? Yet these are precisely the "paradoxes of charity" that Trundle (2014) and others have shown create a desire to "escape from reflective action in order to feel in place" (174; see also Elisha 2008). At the very least, they allowed carers to maintain distance without feeling they were acting unethically (quite the opposite).

Finally, I looked at carer support groups in Japan, and the collective work of narrative resonance. Though brief, the vignettes of the Hyacinth Group and the Wednesday Group illustrate different ways carers constructed commonality and overcame incommensurability (Kitanaka 2019) by sharing individual narratives of "being there." As would-be occupants of utopian/heterotopic spaces (in the sense of Bloch or Foucault), carers in these groups were "in the same boat," where their narrative visions of the "not yet" became a means of navigating their own caregiving story, reorganizing the jumble of dark or disordered thoughts, feelings, and sensations by sharing experience, or sometimes by simply listening, being present, finding a course to their own counter-worldly harbor.[12]

LIVING ON

It was Koji who first showed me Fujikawa's book of poems, *Don't Laugh When I Wander* (2013). I had been watching him excitedly showing the book to another regular member of the men's Wednesday support group, explaining how it was all about the writer's twenty-four-year journey of caring for his mother, who was living with dementia. When Koji reached the poem titled "Bird's-Eye View,"[1] he stopped and stabbed his finger onto the page. "This one! This one is really good!" He looked up from the page to me. "Do you know what [bird's-eye view] means? Like stepping back and seeing something you couldn't before? That's what we [carers] need to do more. That's why we come here." I read the page:

> "Bird's-eye view" was a word
> My mother taught me
> Looking down from up high like a bird
> Seeing clearly what couldn't be seen
> Looking down from up on the hill today
> You've gone even higher up than me
> Mother, what can you see?
> What things do you understand?
> (Fujikawa 2013, 101–2, my translation)

This view, with its feeling of height and transcendence, was a common characteristic of the counter-worlds I described in the last chapter, and like Fujikawa's poem, these counter-worlds often continued to broaden the horizon after the death of the person being cared for. Death was not the end of caring, but a return to the initial leap into responsibility when one first became a carer. The bereaved carer must again contend with the question of what makes someone a carer: what does it mean to take responsibility and be responsive when the care recipient has died? For the carer, the world of caring, as it had been constituted in new bodily habits, emotions, and attentions, as well as narrative resonances and counter-worlds, does not come to an immediate end, even when the object of care is no longer living.

Relatively little research has investigated the emotional and physical health effects of what is sometimes called "post-caregiving transitions" of family carers, and the results that are available present a complex and contradictory picture (Ume and Evans 2011).[2] In some studies, bereaved carers experienced greater distress than would be considered typical after the care recipient died (Bass and Bowman 1990), yet other studies have found no evidence that carers experienced higher levels of complicated grief (Schulz et al. 2006; Crespo, Piccini, and Bernaldo-de-Quirós 2013) or depression (Anashensel, Botticello, and Yamamoto-Mitani 2004). Other research has shown that the overwhelming majority of post-carers experience a sense of relief, particularly in cases where the context of the death has been favorable (Mullan 1992; Crespo, Piccini, and Bernaldo-de-Quirós 2013), and in other cases, caregiving was shown to have other positive effects for bereaved carers' well-being (Rubio et al. 2001; Ume 2013).[3]

The simple reason for such varied results is that carers and caring are complicated business. Very few of these post-care transition studies give attention to the influence of historical and cultural contexts of carers and the ways these might afford or inhibit certain narratives to come to the fore in ways that provide meaning to the woundedness of loss. The ongoing narrative work of bereaved caregivers is rarely acknowledged through the formal institutions of social welfare; when the care recipient dies, carer support services suddenly evaporate into the ether. Yet from the perspective of the carer, bereavement and the fragility it exposes continues the process of resonant self-transformation. Not only do counter-worlds that sustained carers prior to the death continue to be meaningful, but the grieving process that may have started when the care recipient's health declined or when the cared-for entered a residential care facility, now emerges fully and in a more public way. The carer is not simply "relieved" of the burdens of care, but experiences the excess of the other's alterity, a haunting presence from which one cannot turn away.

As with care of the living, the "hauntological demand" (Danely 2019, 217) that continues the ethical work of resonance after the death of the care recipient is historically and culturally contingent. As the stories of the carers in this chapter illustrate, elements of compassion and charity continue to weave through the narratives of post-carers in Japan and England respectively. For Japanese post-carers, the cultural practices of memorialization kept the spirit of the deceased close, open to practices of compassion. In England, on the other hand, post-carers perceived their relationship with the deceased to be resolved, even as they kept the memories and experiences close to their hearts. They judged the moral value of their charity on how well they were able to preserve the dignity of the care recipient or manage social services until the end. In both Japan and England, carers' reflections often turned on hopes for the way they would want to be cared for at the end of their life.

For others, bereavement afforded an opportunity for alternate resonances to emerge from further self-reflection. A number of post-carers, both in Japan and England, expressed a desire to continue some kind of caring role, either as a volunteer or as an occupation.[4] Sometimes it is only with some height, or like Fujikawa's poem, the "bird's-eye view," which only the dead can teach us, that the possibilities for making new narratives of living-on can begin to take shape.

Compassion in Loss

Over the course of Tomomi's long stays with her mother, she and her husband had become more and more distant, and they finally settled on a divorce. Tomomi had moved out of their shared flat about a week before her mother passed away. She had been making regular trips back to her mother's house, to help her brother take care of her mother's possessions and to perform the periodic memorial services for the spirit. A lot had happened in the last six months since her mother died, and as a result, we had not spoken for a while. Tomomi quickly accepted my invitation to meet for another interview, explaining that since she moved, she had been trying to get herself to leave the house more, even if it was just to see friends. While her small business, which she mostly put on hold while caring for her mother, was once again picking up a little, I was surprised to hear that she had also recently taken a part-time job, serving food once a week at a small restaurant. "I didn't need a job," she explained. "I just felt like I wanted a way to meet new people, and I like to take care of people."

Tomomi said that rather than sadness, she had been struggling with a kind of restlessness, unsure of what to do with the impulse to care that had dominated so much of her life for the last year.

> [After my mother died] I no longer had someone to devote myself to. I had no one [to think] this person is precious, is there something I could do for this person? Like that. I mean all the time that I was [caring for Mother], it was pretty difficult, but once I got through to the end

of that, it was like, when this other person whom I've poured all my love into was gone, that loneliness and like, burnout [*moetsuki*]. Like that vigilance, as they call it. I was using all my energy to care, but now that I don't have someone to care for, it's like, I want to. Do you understand? It doesn't have to be in the form of elderly care [*kaigo*], just anything, thinking about someone else, trying to think of how to help them. . . . If I can, I think I'd want to do something like continuing elderly care. I'm always wanting to do something to show concern [*hinpai*]. Maybe that's just my personality, I like to be the one taking care of somebody. But when that went away, I missed it. I didn't even have a partner or anything. So, I guess, it's like people are—everyone is alone in the world. We're alone, and we know in our heads that there are times that we just have to get through. Some days are good, some days we feel like we can't do anything at all. It makes me wonder if I can just live a normal life just stacking the days up like that. I had spent so much time paying so much attention to my mother, and now that that is gone, the biggest thing is this feeling of loss.

In previous chapters I described both Tomomi's fatigue (chapter 3) and her dangerous compassion (chapter 4) as processes of inter-subjective and embodied transformation. The empathetic resonance between her and her mother was so strong that it was almost as if they were merged. She described that feeling not as love or affection, but "concern," or "vigilance" to the point of exhaustion.[5] Yet without it, Tomomi was thrown back on herself, and life had become darker, lonelier. Finding a way to do care work seemed like a chance to maintain her compassion in the face of loss.[6]

While adapting to life as a post-carer was difficult at first, Tomomi said that she gradually came to accept the situation.

Now and then I think I'll clean up my room, think about the future, find something that I look forward to. At first it was easy to do that, but the environment changed, my room just has a dim light. It's comforting at night, but when it is dark all day I just feel low, I don't really feel like working, I can't. I have no motivation, I don't have energy. I cried so much, by myself. But, I don't know, after I'd cried as much as I could, I didn't really feel really bogged down in [the feeling] for long. I even felt a little sense of relief. It's fine to have a cry. In all sorts of places, I get lonely, but that's just how it is. Like, I wake up and think, there's nothing I can do about it, my father and mother are dead, and that's just a natural thing that happens. So, if I think like that, I can just be in the present, one day at a time.

Tomomi's narrative tracked back and forth between different turbulent temporal orientations: hope of the future, slow and stuck, then steady and progressive, "one day at a time." As we talked, she continued this cycling of orientations, going back to her memories and then trying, cautiously, to look forward to something new. This process is ritualized in Japanese customs of memorialization, and Tomomi kept a photo of her mother next to a candle in her apartment so that she could remember her daily. Memorialization is not only a way for the living to connect with the spirit of the deceased, but also a way of caring for the spirit in the other world (Danely 2014). It is at once about drawing close and keeping apart, remembering those who were gone as they once were, and imagining their continued progress. In the end, Tomomi felt no regrets about the care she gave her mother and was grateful that she was able to be with her when she died: "There's a feeling of accomplishment [*tasseikan*], you know? That my mother was looked after the best that she could have been. Until [the divorce] I had my husband, and I would make sure he was eating properly and paying attention to him like that, but when my mother was in the hospital with me, and when I was given the privilege to focus on her when I was caring for her at home, that's probably why I have this feeling that I did well, I tried my hardest."

Managing the Good Death

Two years later, back in England, I stood looking out a hospital window with Russell, whose mother had just started twenty-four-hour in-home care. Her dementia and physical frailty had progressed to a point where Russell felt that he and his brothers no longer had the capacity to keep going, emotionally more than physically. He told me he was trying to come to terms with his feelings about this. "The compassion all just sort of leaks out until there's not much left," he sighed wearily, a deeper tone than usual weighing down his words. "And in the background of everything"—he hesitated, looking into the distance—"is that thought that she's going to die soon."

Russell gave the slightest of smiles, softening the somber tone but leaving his words hanging between us. I resisted the impulse to intervene, to offer words of comfort, but stayed with him, trying to maintain a space for these unsettled thoughts and feelings to float there in suspense. I didn't see Russell again for a few months, and when I did, he told me that his mother had died. I instinctively reached out and put my hand on his shoulder, gripping it as if I were holding him up, and told him that I was sorry. He thanked me, returning my gesture with a hand on my shoulder, and I gave him a hug. He was calm, not out of a sense of numbness, it seemed, but of relief. "In the end," he told me, "it was really a matter of managing all the different aspects of her care." It seemed to me in that moment like a rather odd thing to say—what does one say in such circumstances?—but at the same time, it reflected the kind of care work that Russell considered his responsibility. Like Tomomi, Russell was glad that he was able to keep his mother at home, making sure all the care services were in place and things like the wet room and stair lift were all installed. He too had done his best and felt a sense of hard-won accomplishment that buffered the pain of grief.

As I've described throughout this book, English family carers spend considerable time, money, and effort arranging paid care through different public, nonprofit, and private sources, all the while tending to the various aspects of care those sources don't cover, such as companionship, taking care recipients to medical appointments, or managing their finances.[7] Employing paid care workers was not seen as merely a kind of entitlement, much less a social obligation, as it would be seen in more developed welfare states like those in Scandinavia. Rather, for British carers, being involved in managing paid care is a chance to practice a form of charity, beginning at home. The care workers interrupt the carer/cared-for dyad, helping to maintain the autonomy and egalitarian ethical ethos of charity. As care managers, family carers tried to strike a careful balance by providing just the right amount of assistance without appearing to care out of pity or being overly controlling in ways that would make the care recipient feel dependent. This balance often became harder to maintain near the end of life.

In contrast to Russell, Gillian, who lived with and cared for her father during the last three years of his life, recounted her confusion and frustration with the care system in his last months. It began when he was hospitalized for a heart attack about three days after Christmas. He never fully recovered, and was sent home after a week, but Gillian felt "he really just wasn't good." They arranged for hospital staff to care for him at first, but when this came to its limit, they had to arrange care through a care firm. While Gillian was happy with some of the carers, others, she said, "weren't what I would call professional people." As the dissatisfaction and difficulties with her father continued, Gillian felt that, despite help from the carers, it was she who was in the middle, and the stress of managing both sides was overwhelming.

> I had social services around, and they said he wasn't ill enough to go into a care home. And that's really what he wanted. He wanted to go into a care home, where if he pressed a button somebody would come to him. And what I said to them was, if he fell over I couldn't physically pick him up by myself and I'd have to ring a neighbor to come and help—and of course that would distress him. Um, it was all sort of, you know— toward the end I just really did feel very, very sorry for him. I'd always

been definitely against euthanasia, but toward the end I changed my mind completely. I mean, many times he'd asked me to give him a pill [to end his life], and toward the end if I'd had the pill, I'd have given it to him. I just felt so sorry for him. His dignity was gone, and, you know . . . you wouldn't treat an animal like it.

While Gillian spoke often about her father's pride and "old-fashioned" character, her criticism of social services revealed her own sense of wounded dignity that still smarted nearly six months after his death. After her father died, she called up the care firm to tell them they needn't come in, but they still came the next day. As if this wasn't bad enough, two weeks later, grab rails that were ordered from a council grant were finally delivered. The stair lift that was paid for with a £5,000 grant and used for less than a year was removed from the house and scrapped (the council would not take it or recycle it). "Crazy! Absolutely crazy!" she shook her head.

Gillian's resentment was not "merely" complaint. In her own way, it was a way to keep her father and his character alive in her mind, a way to continue enacting the kind of care management that was crucial to achieve a good end of life, even after he died.

Love Letters and Bones

Japanese carers also had to make difficult end-of-life choices in hospitals or care settings, and regrets or uncertainty over whether the best choice was made can make the grieving process agonizing. Emiko, for example, who told me about not being able to fulfill her husband's final wishes to eat eel (chapter 4, 101–2), also had lingering regrets about the hospital where her husband died.

They said, "that hospital's no good anymore." But what's done was done. My husband and I had stayed at that hospital, and they took good care of us in the past, so my husband and I thought that it would be fine to go there again. But of course, the policies had changed, and people were starting to say that it was no good anymore around the time I took him back. I don't know what was really wrong with it, but I didn't really get a chance to talk to anyone, with the nurses going in and out all the time. My husband said "I wonder if they treat rich people the way they treat us." It made me think, if only I had money. I don't care if I have to sell the house to get the money if they look after him well! But instead I told him "I think it would be the same." At the time, that's just what I said. I didn't know if I could change hospitals just like that, or if I did change,

maybe he would end up someplace even worse. I've got so many regrets.
I just hoped he could die thinking "Oh, I'm glad I'm in this hospital."

As Emiko recounted this story, her hands rested on the small kitchen table,
her palms shuddering like leaves, and her voice trembled. Tears began to gather
in the corners of her eyes. She took a tissue from a box at the end of the table and
dabbed her face as she continued.

> I left [the funeral arrangements] all to my daughter. I was just in a daze,
> I couldn't think straight anymore, didn't know what to do. Everyone
> relies on their daughter in a time like that. It was her first time, too, so
> it must have been hard on her. I wish that we could have learned a bit
> more from him when he was alive. We didn't even have a Buddhist altar
> [*butsudan*] in the home! [My husband] was a Buddhist priest and didn't
> have an altar—have you ever heard of such a thing? But we had to learn
> it all from nothing. I had kept in contact with [the funeral company],
> just in case something were to happen, [so they took care of it]. I had
> no idea how to do it. Do it like this or that, the way to arrange all the
> things, [the funeral company staff] taught me. So after I got the *but-
> sudan*, then I visited the grave. "Madam, you've done a proper job of
> making offerings and honoring [the spirit]. Your husband is surely very
> happy!" When he said that, I was just so overwhelmed. I just thought,
> oh, thank goodness! I've done a good job honoring him!

Emiko's tears were now flowing down her cheeks, but she was intent on telling
the whole story. She soon regained her voice.

> Of course, those words after someone had died are so important, you
> know? But some time after the funeral I got depressed again. I lost seven
> kilograms. [*Voice breaking*] My daughter said to me, "He's dead now,
> and you keep thinking about all these things, but there's really no point
> in it. You'd been together more than fifty years, so just leave it at that!"
> But then a priest came by the house to perform the memorial services
> for my husband. When he saw me he said, "Madam, if you don't take
> care of yourself, you won't be able to look after your husband anymore."

Emiko smiled now. For her, this one simple remark lifted her out of what
Larkin (2009) called the post-carer "void" and allowed her to begin again as a
different kind of carer.

When I visited her two years later, she still lived in the same small home at
the end of a hidden alley surrounded by neighbors. She invited me inside, and it
was comforting to see that the kitchen where she and I sat and talked for hours

hadn't changed at all. As it was during the summer holiday of Obon, when families across Japan honor the ancestors and spirits of the recently deceased, a large fresh bouquet of flowers sat next to a framed portrait of Emiko's husband on the *butsudan*. I asked if I could greet him, and she brought me to the *butsudan* and sat with me as I rang the small, cup-shaped bell and bowed my head while introducing myself and thanking him for allowing me to visit. Emiko smiled and thanked me, then gazed dreamily at the portrait.

"He looks so nice in that picture, doesn't he? . . . I don't want to put him in the grave yet. When I die, then we will both go together." She giggled a little self-consciously at her sentimental, romantic gesture. "It is the same with our name," she added, motioning to the small, black-lacquered memorial plaque (*ihai*) set on a higher platform within the altar. The memorial plaque resembled a miniature gravestone, and Emiko showed me that her husband's posthumous Buddhist name was written next to hers. "When I die, my name will be colored in gold, just like his. We'll be together then."

Emiko then started to move, telling me that she wanted to show me something. She bent down slowly, opening a small cabinet underneath the *butsudan* and removing a pale turquoise cylindrical ceramic jar. She set it down between us and took off the lid to show me the bones of her husband inside. I was struck by how beautiful and delicate they were, like fragments of seashell, curved and broken into oddly shaped yet gentle curves. "This is my husband," she said, as she picked up a small piece of paper that was resting on top of the bones.

She unfolded the paper. On it, she had written his posthumous name, the date, and her own name. She looked up at the photograph, still fingering the paper. She unfolded it again and looked at it once more. "Each year I write one of these and place it in here with him, and then on Obon, I burn it, right out here in the garden. It is my way of sending him a message."

On the opposite side of the small room was an empty space. This was where Emiko had cared for her husband, who had occupied a special adjustable bed. In many homes of carers, these large adjustable beds were placed in the same room as the *butsudan*, as this was often the largest and most easily accessible room of the house. This was the case for Emiko, and during our interviews, as she spoke about him, she would often glance over to the spot where he used to lay, as if sensing him still there.

Emiko's case shows the importance of ongoing rituals of care, the symbolic and sensory presencing of the deceased care recipient that anchors the deceased to the world of the living. For those like Emiko, cultural narratives created space for the long transformations of post-care to unfold, like a simple message on a scrap of paper, conveying the message "I am here." For Emiko, there was something particular about the grief felt by a spousal carer, a mutuality developed after decades of living together. As we ended our conversation, she reassured me that the rituals at the *butsudan* had helped her come to a place of acceptance about her husband's last days. The pain of separation still lingered, but she was becoming more accustomed to it. For her, as a spousal post-carer, this was not something she expected to leave her soon.

> When my mother died, they said "it takes one year." It takes a year before your heart can be at peace. Separation [of a child] from a parent, separation [of a parent] from a child, separation of a married couple—you know, they say there are all sorts of bereavement [*shi no wakare*], but they say that there is nothing more difficult than the separation of a husband and wife. There is something like that written in a Buddhist chant, I think. I think a nun wrote it. I read that, and my tears were gushing out! But there is something really true about it.

Togetherness, Undone

Most days, George would sit by himself in the small front room of his two-story, semidetached house. He was ninety-two years old and had lived in the same area for more than half a century. From the window, we could see the rows of identical houses lining the residential cul-de-sac, a somber repetition of brick facades beneath a blanket of dark clouds. Visitors rarely came around, so George was happy to spend the morning with me, even though he had to ask at several moments in our interview what exactly I was asking him about.

George's chair, a wingback tucked into the corner, was pattered with leaves and flowers in dusky shades of red and brown. The only other places to sit down in the room were a dark blue chair set next to his, or a short sofa. I chose the chair, thinking that we would be close enough to hear each other easily, but as soon as I sat down, I felt the unexpected resistance of the hard cushion along with the soft crinkle of something else covering it. I straightened and froze. This was not a young person's chair. I realized that I had just sat in the chair that belonged to George's wife, who had died a few months earlier at the age of ninety-four.

I looked around the room. There was a large clock on the cream-colored wall behind us, and below that a calendar, one month out of date. A telephone with extra-large buttons sat on the table between the chairs, and behind it, a silver-and-blue portable music player sat next to an assortment of medications in their orange bottles. As George began telling me about the two years he spent caring for his wife, the room felt full of her presence. Its familiar, lived-in feeling was their shared world; everything in it seemed to hang on to her. I was suddenly reminded of the front room of my own grandparents' home in Indiana, where my grandmother spent her last years. In my memories of that time, she was always sitting in her recliner, rarely speaking, while my grandfather took care of her and the house. I remember the tenderness and humor in that house, even though their lives were contained by a few rooms, even though I felt the heavy concern of my father when we would visit, even though she didn't believe the man caring for her was her husband.

George was one of the oldest carers I spoke with, and he and his wife had been married for sixty-seven years.[8] He had chosen to care for his wife at home, partly for financial reasons. His pension from the auto assembly plant was just not enough to cover the costs of long-term residential nursing care. But more than that, he was afraid that putting his wife in a home would "finish" her. Instead, he told me that he wanted care to be "real," adding, "I've got no wish to get rid of her—I wanted the opposite!" The opposite, then, is what George called "being together":

> Caring was just being with her, I suppose. And I suppose how I would define it in my opinion is *just being together* and just doing what you can to help and—whether that would be my definition of care I don't know how to put it otherwise. People would say, "Gosh, how did you put up with it?" And I don't know, it didn't seem long to me, and it was every day, every day was a new day. I suppose we just—that's just what life is about. Just made it through *togetherness*.

George's repeated emphasis on "togetherness" caught my attention, as it seemed so different from what I had been hearing from other English carers, whose views about maintaining independence, dignity, and choice reflected the normative orientations of a society centered on the individual. Instead, like Emiko, George lived a life so intimately enfolded into that of his wife that they moved and felt as one. In caring for her, George told me, he felt he was being cared for as well:

> At the start of this, people thought I should have her put into a home, but she was my wife, and I had a great pleasure looking after her. So, toward the end she had dementia in a slight way, but she was ninety-four, and you could gradually see her slipping away. But as I say, the pleasure was mine, because, as I say, I looked after her. I—I don't know how to explain it, but it was just, what she wanted, obviously, I did give to her, and I cared for her. I looked after her, and she, I think she appreciated it because it lifted her. Caring is difficult to explain, I think, because everyone possibly would do it differently. As I say here, well, she wanted to die at home, and that's what we did. She went into hospital for a

short spell, and the hospital provided us with a bed and all the necessary things [to take home], and she slipped away. She didn't suffer at all,
which is good. No, I wouldn't change it for the world. I wouldn't, and
I'm really glad I did [care]. You really got together, you know. But as
I say, we had a nice—our life was full.

The way George concluded this story at first sounded to me almost as if his life
had ended together with hers: "*our* life *was* full." George was able to bring her
back home from the hospital before she "slipped away."

George admitted that he had never done much cooking or housework before
he began caring at age ninety, but having shared so many meals with his wife,
he didn't see this as a difficulty. They lived modestly but comfortably, and for
George, the mutuality of care, the togetherness, grounded them so profoundly
that time passed quickly: "It just flowed." Visiting with George, it was easy to
imagine how his life and his wife's could flow into each other. This deep life resonance was never questioned by George, though he was aware that for others, the
residential care home was the expected path of charity:

> I know when people would say "You're going to put [your wife] in a
> home?" And I was probably thinking myself, if I put her in a home,
> who's going to look after me, you know? [*Laughs*] It's going to take
> all the benefits away! We went to a club, and it was for dementia, and
> I would say, where's so-and-so?—Oh, she's gone in a home. And so-
> and-so? She's gone in a home. And I saw it then that they're so willing
> to plonk their missus in a home, and as I say, mind you, when they
> say "home," I think maybe a lot of people have a lot of money better
> than I have. It depends what sort of home that you put them in. There's
> homes and "homes," isn't there. For us, I think a lot of [caring] was just
> togetherness—because I think that's what it's all about, it's together-
> ness. That's what life is about. We just made it through togetherness.
> And [in the end], she had a quiet death, and I suppose everything went
> smoothly, if you can refer to death like that. No, as I say, it was just part
> of life, looking after her. It was *an extension of the other.*

George's story points out what may be at stake for a society that depends on the
separation of unpaid carers and care recipients by care homes, instead of recognizing and supporting the care that can be provided by willing family members.
The separation, as George sees it, comes down to wealth: "If you've got plenty of
money," he explained, "the word 'care' can mean, 'oh I'll look after her, I'll put
her in a home, and that will care for her!'" George's different opinion about care
homes may have also been influenced by his working-class background and ethic

of thrift. If charity is an ethic that arose historically from the work of wealthy phi-
lanthropists, then the ethic of care may have developed quite differently among
the working class.

Despite his satisfaction with the circumstances of her death, the pleasure of
caring for his wife seemed to have made the pain of bereavement all the more
acute. When I asked him about his life after care, he described it as "empty," adding, "I don't know what to do with myself. Life is gone, you know? There's nothing for me to look after. You know? I had—well, as I say, I just miss her, simple as
that. I can't put it any other way, you know." As I took notes, George gestured to
my chair. "She liked that chair."

While the walls of the house still hung with vacation snapshots and memories,
George brushed off my questions about them. His reaction was similar when
I tried engaging him with some of the objects in the house. It seemed that unlike
Emiko, George's house of memories had become empty, a place he could no
longer inhabit. George died nine months later.

George's and Emiko's cases helped me to appreciate the resonances between
the experiences of spousal carers in England and Japan. For both of them, being
together, as an "extension of the other," exposed the extreme existential disruption posed by hospitals and care homes. As post-carers, George and Emiko both
experienced the emotional and physical weight of the "void," but while Emiko
was buoyed by ritual memorials, George struggled to find a way to find meaning. His case points to the importance of continuing care after death, of creating
social spaces for mourning and memorial that could extend his "togetherness"
past death.

Another World of Care

I first met Yoshie at a coffee shop where I went daily to write during my fieldwork.
She and her middle-aged daughter sat at the table near to mine, and seemed to
be continuing an argument about a medical appointment they had just come
from. Yoshie had short-cropped, light gray hair, and her cap and trousers completed her boyish look. When her daughter got up to use the restroom, Yoshie lit
a cigarette, and then, to my surprise, swiveled on her seat and greeted me, curious
about what I was working on. I explained that I was interested in family carers,
and she nodded.

"Getting old is hard!" she said, her face growing grim. "I went to the doctor
just now for a physical exam, and I hurt my back!" Yoshie was setting the stage,
placing her body and its vulnerability somewhere in the scene. When I asked why

she saw the doctor, she introduced the characters of the story, bringing them into a narrative that I didn't expect:

> I went because I want to climb Mount Fuji in August—and I don't like being told no! So, I won't quit! This will be my third time. I went ten years ago, when I was seventy-one, and before that when I was seventy. Do you know the reason that I want to go this time? Well, I was going to go a third time, but my husband said that he was worried about me, so I didn't end up going. But last year, May, my husband passed away. So, this time, I have decided to take his photo and climb Fuji-san again. You see, when he died, I really felt like there was no reason to go on living. It was better to die, I thought! I was really down. Until the forty-ninth-day anniversary ceremony, it was just really bad. But when I figured it out. I felt my energy come back. Now I am living for this. Climbing Fuji-san with his photo is my goal.

Yoshie's goal was not simply about a project of self-improvement or even of "generativity," one of the psychosocial hallmarks of adult development that identifies age-related desires to create a lasting legacy. Indeed, the climb, which her doctor and daughter both advised against, was an adventure in dangerous compassion. For Yoshie, the climb was a way of incorporating her relationship with her deceased husband into an emotionally powerful symbolic order, encoding the landscape in ways that elevated their connection to a cosmic level.

Although Yoshie first came up with this plan after her husband died, the inspiration was rooted in a promise made on a visit to the Grand Canyon not long after her husband's retirement and before caring for him:

> My husband saw the Grand Canyon and he said that he felt that he should forget about all of his worries, all his feeling bad for himself, just think about living from that day on, taking care of each other. It was just so tremendous. You look out and just see sky. We rode one of those little planes over it, and I couldn't believe how huge it was. So, it was all thanks to the Grand Canyon![9]

Yoshie went on, gradually becoming more and more choked up.

> He's watching over me even now! The weather, when I have to do something and it looks like a little rain or something, it will just clear right up. Thanks to Papa. I know that it's him watching out for me. So I'm not going to give up on climbing Mount Fuji. No way. I don't want to just be alive, right? You can't just do that. And I was all alone, I needed

something to live for. It is really hard going up, but once you see the view, it is so incredible. So that's why I want to just keep going. Keep going.

Eventually Yoshie did make it up Fuji-san with her husband's photo, but not on the first try.

On the first attempt, the weather was poor, and the trip was harder than she was prepared to endure. Try as she might, she only made it to the seventh rest station. After she descended, feeling understandably defeated, a strange cloud formed over the mountain, like a brilliant white halo floating over the crater. Yoshie knew the cloud was more than just a random meteorological event. It is at times like these that one finds the world animated and alive. It was a sign, she told me, that her husband was there and he knew she had tried her hardest. The next year, Yoshie completed her ascent to take a photo of herself, her daughter, and the portrait of her late husband.

Yoshie's story, one yet to come to any closure, is not merely an example of the power of perseverance and endurance in old age—a story of enduring endurance—though it is that, too. Like Emiko's memorial rituals, the climb up Mount Fuji crossed temporal vectors from the past toward futures reimagined. Yoshie was both a post-carer for her living husband and a carer for his spirit. This is not a radical transformation, but part of an ongoing process of self-formation and re-narration of the self—refiguring, reconstituting, and recovering the self by moving possible selves into a field of culturally valued social relations.[10]

Yoshie's gesture might be seen as a kind of resistance to this narrative and its implications that older people are just heavy weights or burdens. Climbing the mountain was a form of memorial, and although it entails effort, discomfort, and risk, it is also a form of caring for the self in old age, making use of those final stores of energy and will and living them into a project of moral becoming. It is the photograph of her husband that animates the landscape, making the mountain and its surmounting more meaningful and memorable. As we see in her first attempt, the mountain is hardly just a mountain, but is itself something that speaks in images, cloud formations, signs from elsewhere and beyond that point to a world and life otherwise. The image brings the mountain life.

Mournful Resonance

The photographs of deceased family that Emiko and Yoshie both held dear were images of mournful life though which relations of care were imagined and sustained. They brought forth memories and desires, but they also gave a face to the world of bones and letters, mountains and meteorology, a face that called from beyond and demanded a response.[11] Living alongside the dead meant recognizing them and taking responsibility for them, not as they were, but as they continue on, gazing down from the bird's-eye view of a magical cloud.

For George, there were no rituals, and the old photographs were not the same as being together with his wife, belonging to and extending each other, even in care. While George's sense of purpose appears to have been strong enough to carry him through the work of care, it lacked an afterlife. His days would be spent not in the care of others, but sitting next to her chair, answering the phone when the companion services called. While I have never seen nationwide estimates of the numbers of post-carers like George, they must number in the millions, and yet so often their experience becomes lost. Family members do not ask about it, and formal care support groups are not meant for the bereaved. The fact that post-carers like George become cut off from places and communities of resonance is not mere coincidence; it follows a logic that assumes the post-carers will be relieved and liberated from the "burden" of care, free to independently direct their life. This is the danger of constructing models of aging personhood without considering the journey of carers and its long influence on their lives.

In Japan as well, new revisions to the LTCI social insurance system continue to reinforce individuating logics of responsibility, prevention, and independence, with no support provision for older carers or post-carers. Rather than building resonance, the system remains one that separates. In the final chapter, I examine the LTCI from the perspective of paid care workers before considering two cases of institutions that challenge the values and logic of LTCI, embracing a broader view of social interdependence, resonance, and mutual care.

7

THE POLITICS OF CARE

Thus far, this book has focused on the experiences of carers and care recipients as they engaged in the ordinary and even routine practices of care, as well as the personally transformative potential of these practices, which train embodied empathetic attentions and motivate creative narrative resonance.[1] This cartography of care has stayed close to the foot-worn paths of carers' experiences, tracing lines that connect and diverge and connect again.[2] The map that emerges is both topographical and political; it reveals the peaks and valleys of care, as well as its borders and bridges. After all, embodying responsibility for care and inhabiting counter-worlds are not only about feeling the world differently, but are political acts, in the Arendtian sense of creating spaces of appearance between actors (Arendt 1998, 198)—the very stuff of shared lives.

While each care encounter yields a slightly different tone to the political spaces it inaugurates, I have argued that bringing carer narratives into juxtaposition with one another allows us to discern the cultural and historical patterns that have shaped those spaces. From the moment carers take responsibility, they look for narrative clues about how they should feel and respond; they seek ways to make sense of this new role. They learned this foremost by being open to the face of the cared-for, a face that can bring new worlds into being; but there were other relationships that mattered as well. In both Japan and England, few carers based their actions on any explicit intergenerational transfers of knowledge about caring, although some had memories of seeing a parent or a sibling provide care at some point. Most, however, relied on a sense of social expectations or consulted with a few trusted friends, neighbors, or other family members as they became more settled into their role. Carers also relied on the advice and expertise of doctors, nurses, and formal social care services to help them understand when they could access additional paid care support or how to navigate the difficult ethical and emotional decisions around residential long-term care or end-of-life options. While the relationship between the carer and cared-for was at the core of Japanese carers' subjectivities, this relationship also transformed and initiated other relationships and political spaces that further expanded or constrained the capacity to endure or flourish as a carer.

In this chapter, I look at how the politics of care are shaped and constrained not only by historical and cultural norms and values, but also by social welfare institutions and policies. One typical assumption is that the boundaries between private, familial, unpaid care and publicly supported, institutionalized, paid care are clearly and explicitly drawn, and that practices and values of care are largely consistent across the two domains. You would not expect to be financially remunerated for feeding your elderly father, for example, nor would you expect paid carers to express emotional attachment for their clients. Yet here I want to trouble this distinction by arguing that in both Japan and in England, unpaid care has become incorporated within the welfare system as a means of perpetuating social inequalities and enacting governmentality through the family. Furthermore, relationships between unpaid carers and the state are not fixed and absolute, but often expose contradictions, complexity, and contestation. Similarly, paid carers may not be explicitly asked to perform familial intimacy, but the nature of the work as feminine and domestic may produce these associations and expectations, while paid carers may see themselves as filling a role vacated by family and expected to fulfill and even value a nurturing and emotionally involved kin-like role (cf. Buch 2015a; Mazus 2013).

Decades of research on the politics of paid care work shed light on the ways care produces contradictions: it can be at once nurturing and dominating, egalitarian and hierarchical, loving and violent.[3] Part of the problem with paid care has to do with the bureaucratic rationalization of profit-driven institutions, which reduces the more holistic functions of caring to specific measurable tasks and distributes them based on specific qualifying criteria such as income or "activities of daily living" (ADL) (Glaser 2019; Lopez 2013). The rationalization of care stems in part from its categorization in most places as "unskilled work" that employs a large number of precarious, part-time or on-call workers. As a result, elderly-care workers often earn only minimum wages (or less) and contend with heavy workloads, poor working conditions, and high staff turnover (Broadbent 2014, 2010; Shirasaki 2009). The large majority of care workers are women, often migrants from less economically developed countries, who are assumed to have a natural skill or disposition for care and nurturance as well as a better tolerance for intimate bodily care (Glenn 2000; Twigg 2000; Kittay 1999). This is not to say that women should not choose to work in care professions or take pride in the skill and value of that work. Rather, the problem is the combination of a severe gender imbalance with low-status, high-risk work that reveals a continuation of historical disadvantage of women in society.[4]

In comparison to this impressive body of forceful critical works on the politics of paid care work, far fewer anthropologists have examined the political context that reproduces and controls unpaid elderly care (Aulino 2019; Brijnath 2014; Cohen 1998). Part of the problem may be that apart from these few ethnographies, the family has been treated as a bounded unit of intervention rather than one that is actively involved in dialogue with health and social care providers, as well as with volunteers and neighbors. Yet just as family carers have shaped the subject position of the paid carer, paid carers are also affecting the ways that family members make judgments about their own care.

I did not conduct interviews with paid carers in England, but they were key to gaining access and introductions to family carers during my fieldwork in Japan, and a few became some of my most insightful interlocutors over the course of my fieldwork. All the Japanese paid care workers I spoke with were aware of the difficulties faced by family carers and were often critical of the formal care system. Some were able to use personal networks and connections to bypass or subvert obstacles to obtaining care for their clients. Many of these paid carers I came to know best were also active volunteers, carers, or post-carers themselves, further blurring the boundaries between paid and unpaid, private and public, family and state.

The politics of unpaid care cannot be fully understood and appreciated without the perspectives of the paid care workers, who every day must straddle the gap between worlds of practice and policy. I will begin this chapter with the stories of Japanese paid carers as well as the ways their work figured into unpaid carers' narratives. Finally, I will turn to examples of how political action is being reimagined in Japan in ways that enhance the voices of ordinary carers and dissolve barriers between all of those involved in care.

Entwined Precarity

Japan's Long-Term Care Insurance (LTCI) system was rolled out in 2000–2001, opening the market for new care services and providers (Campbell and Ikegami 2000; Long 2008). By 2015, the number of elderly care service provider businesses (*kōreisha kaigo jigyōsho*) rose by about 450 percent, from 9,726 to

43,406; between 2015 and 2018, it had nearly doubled again to 76,812 (Tokyo Shoko Research 2018). In 2015, there were approximately 1.83 million paid carers working in Japan, about one-third of whom are home care assistants (most working part-time or on call), while the other two-thirds worked in various elderly care service businesses. This is around 400,000 fewer than what the Ministry of Economy, Trade and Industry (METI) estimated were needed, however, and future estimates look much more alarming (METI 2018).[5] The aging postwar baby boom generation and shrinking population are likely to result in a care worker shortage of nearly 800,000 by midcentury (Kiyokawa 2020). One consequence of this shortage of workers is that over one hundred care-sector businesses have failed each year since 2016, with some analysts estimating that about half of all for-profit care homes would be closing over the next year (*Shūkan Asahi* 2018, 18). The main reasons for this downturn are the inability to hire enough new staff and the high turnover rate. About 60 percent of care workers quit within the first three years—hardly surprising, given the low pay and highly stressful conditions.

Working in elderly care is not always a decision taken out of a sense of calling or a desire to do good. In the words of one former care worker, it was work for the "scrap heap" (*hakidame*) (Danely 2016, 207) of those who lost jobs or couldn't find work elsewhere, those who felt little commitment but needed temporary or part-time work.[6] Like family care, care work also came, in a way, as a surprise. Some new care workers were former laborers or farmers, but others I met had also been in white-collar work or were university graduates. On one afternoon, I met a young, former care worker while sitting at the counter of a café. I had been talking about my research to the woman serving drinks when she motioned to another customer sitting alone at the other end of the room. It was a man in his twenties dressed in a black shirt and jeans. She called him up to the counter, saying, "You used to work in a care home, didn't you?" The young man looked up and nodded as he took his cup of coffee up to the bar. "He's a DJ now," she said, then added on the side, "When I get old I want to be at a care home with a DJ and dance club! And a place where you can play mah-jongg and enjoy yourself! That wouldn't be so bad!" She did a little twirl to the big-band jazz music playing on the café's stereo.

Her playful fantasy was punctured, however, once I started asking the DJ about the kind of work he did when he was a carer. Over the din of kitchen noise and the wailing horns of the music, the DJ told me that he took the job when he was just out of university, despite not having any strong interest in care. Someone he knew had worked for a care home and offered to help him get a job. The DJ wasn't having luck with music at the time, and he saw that it only took a couple of months of training and that he could start right away (training on the job). He ended up working in care homes for four years. I asked why he quit:

> DJ: I just couldn't do it anymore, physically. It was hard work. My shifts were usually seventeen hours.
> DANELY: Seventeen hours? That's hard.
> DJ: It is.
> DANELY: You'll die—
> DJ: They're dropping like flies from exhaustion. It is scary.
> WOMAN AT COUNTER: Like a horror movie!
> DJ: It's a crazy world.
> DANELY: Almost like dying people looking after dying people!
> DJ: It is dangerous. Collapsing like that.
> DANELY: There was that incident recently in Chiba. That was horrible.[7]
> DJ: Yeah, that was scary.
> DANELY: That was someone who used to work at that place, right?
> DJ: Yeah, [care home managers think] there's not enough applicants, so anyone will do. So that's what happens. It's scary.
> DANELY: Sometimes I hear that people who haven't been able to do well getting other jobs—
> DJ:—they get jobs [in care]. There are still a lot of people who don't have any certification to do care work. [Pause] But in the end, most people can't do the job for long. Seeing people who are dying, it's really—[pauses]. There were four or five people [living at the care home] that I got pretty close to, and they've all died. It's not really a good thing to see. Well, it's a good experience, but it isn't really a pleasant thing.
> DANELY: People who are bedridden [netakiri]?
> DJ: Sometimes people who are bedridden. The last place I worked at was a terminal care facility. The hospital wouldn't take care of them anymore, so they ended up with us. They would come and, in a week, they'd be dead.
> DANELY: Four years seems like a long time to do that sort of work.
> DJ: It was hard, but on the other hand, I learned a lot. Young people here don't have many chances to be around older people. Just people in their own family, but not many people outside of that. So, in that respect, it was a really great job.

While several aspects of the DJ's experience working in care homes mirrored the experiences of family carers (fatigue, grief, a sense of self-improvement, for example), there were also important differences. First, although he did form a relationship with some of the clients, worker shortages meant that most of the time he had to hurry from one client to the next with no chance to develop an intimate dyadic bond that would approach the attachment that families described. His responsibilities and attention were spread across several individuals with varying needs, and each individual client came to rely on several different care staff. The second related difference was that although he worked long hours, it still did not amount to the 24/7 care many of the Japanese family carers provided, nor did it last for years (sometimes less than a week). His responsibility and responsiveness for each person were therefore tightly constrained by rationalized institutional structures. The DJ stayed with the job longer than most, however, and consequently, like family carers, he learned the value of being close to older people and the dying. While Japan has the largest proportion of older people of any large country in the world, the spatial politics of urban settings meant that outside of care institutions or private homes, younger people would rarely have a chance to interact with them. It seemed as if the precarity of the DJ's work did not overwhelm his capacity for appreciating the fragility of care.

Sho, another care worker I spoke with, voiced similar concerns about working in a care home, and since he was also the primary carer for his grandfather, I asked him what he thought the main differences were between caring for family and caring at his job:

> I totally hate the care at work. Well, saying I hate it is a little rude, but— say you had a client who took a lot of work, well, even if that sort of person was there, you do your eight hours, putting up with them for eight hours, then you can go home, can't you? You just say [to the next shift], "Take care of the rest of it for me, okay?" But when you're at home, that's not the case, is it? And then the care at work, whether it is diapers or the bath or the size of the room, everything is more or less set up and organized, right? At home, it's not set up at all [for caring], so right now I have to think about how I'm going to [help him] get into the bath in this narrow bathroom. I have to think about things like how I am going to stop my grandpa from getting up and trying to leave the house in the middle of the night while I'm working. No matter how much skills training you have, caring at home, when it comes to the person [you care for], how do I say it—you have to have the ability to come up with clever tricks [*kufū*], if you don't have the power to endure [*nintai shite iku chikara*]. I don't think you could keep it up. All those [paid] care skills, for example, like how to quickly change a diaper and so forth, I can see how that is necessary and all [at work], but when

you are caring at home, it is only for one or two people. So, whether you change them quickly or slowly, well, it doesn't really matter. In the worst case, even if you were to neglect them a little bit, people say it can be forgiven because you're just [caring] as a family, and it's treated like a family problem. So, the home is not about your skills, it's more about how you can keep on providing good care, like it's more about the mental [strength]. I think the skills are what is needed for care outside [the house]. However good you are at the job, I think it's a different thing doing well at home.

Sho's reflections were frank and flowing; I wondered if he had been asked this question before. In some ways, his sense of incommensurability between unpaid home care and his paid care work was even starker than the view of the DJ, yet both recognize the malleability of care (and the carer) that allows them to fill up differently shaped political spaces. For Sho, the workplace was about skill and efficiency: the body of the carer is disciplined to fit the rationalized *techne* (practical application of knowledge through discrete skills) of the occupational role. Caring for a family member, in contrast, produced care as both *mētis*, a situated and practical knowledge of the "clever tricks," or even how much one could "neglect" the cared-for, as well as *poiesis*, as in the art of "good care," which requires a long process of enduring commitment.[8]

Other Japanese carers, men and women, working in day service centers, geriatric hospitals, nursing homes, and community care, all shared similar stories about their working experiences. Some of their experiences were shocking, including cases of abuse (both of and by older clients), neglect of clients, ignoring excretory needs, and frequent sedating of clients with only minor problematic behaviors. Care workers also had to contend with family members who could be uncooperative or neglectful, or client's homes that were dangerous or belonged to hoarders. If I heard these stories mainly from professional carers, it was only because they had seen more cases of those with the most advanced and complex care needs. All these things happened within families as well, and with estimated greater frequency than in paid care settings.[9] There was no evident or easy solution.

When I caught up with Sho two years later, he had moved on from his role as a care worker to a more administrative role as a social worker for those on public assistance, about 40 percent of whom he estimates are elderly. Since he was still in his first year, he saw only about ten clients each week (out of about forty total), but because of staff shortages, many of his more experienced colleagues had to deal with caseloads of around a hundred clients. His grandfather had home care assistants and attended a day service center, but these services were also dealing with staff shortages and would sometimes cancel at a moment's notice.

The shortage of workers was also a concern for care managers, whose work included conducting needs assessments, drawing up care plans, and utilizing networks of different care services to help older people and their families make decisions about the kinds of paid care they might want to use. Similarly, Comprehensive Community Support (*chiiki hōkatsu seikatsu shien*) staff, whose role it was support community-based initiatives for older people, also found their time dominated by the complex needs of individual carers and care recipients. These actors had both expertise and insight, moving between layers of the care ecosystem, and were often able to find ways to navigate around the hurdles and hoops of the bureaucratic apparatus in ways that other care workers could not.

Japan is haunted by stories of the ways elderly care becomes violent, like contemporary echoes of *obasuteyama*, the folktale of abandoning one's elderly parents to die in the mountains (see chapter 1, 32). How unpaid family carers fit into this picture is not entirely clear. For some, a "familialist" welfare system like that of Japan (Kodate and Timonen 2017) perpetuates the precariousness of paid carers (particularly women) and ultimately the suffering of older people (Glenn 2000). In other words, as long as paid carers are doing work that family members do without wages, they will continue to be seen as unskilled and their wages will remain low.

To others, it is the rationalized care system and the marketization of care, not necessarily the prevalence of family carers, that must be dismantled and reformed. Yet, while state-provisioned socialized care may protect recipients from some of the profit-driven abuses of care service providers, it does not mitigate rationalization (and indeed, may exacerbate it) (cf. Christensen 2020).[10] Policies similar to those that give security to new parents, allowing them to provide child care, might be applied to unpaid carers of elderly relatives, but again, any such system must ensure a just division of care and support.

The stories of unpaid and paid carers reveal the tensions and overlaps between two different and imperfect solutions to complex ethical questions of how society should respond to suffering and dependence. Whether paid or unpaid, regulated by policies or by traditions or social norms, care is a site of biopolitical power in the sense that it shapes carers' subjectivities, their sense of responsibility, their horizons of possibility and ethical belonging to their society (Neilson 2006; Stevenson 2014; Hromadžić 2015). To draw too sharp a line between paid and unpaid care work would reinforce this biopolitical misrecognition of family and private domestic life as separate from public institutional care, which legitimates the disinvestment of resources from both.

The Everyday Ethics of Care Management

The Apricot Club, a regular monthly social group for seniors in the neighborhood where I lived, had changed venues yet again, this time filling up the main hall of a small, traditional Japanese building with sliding paper doors and woven tatami mats on the floor. The group, which was organized by neighborhood volunteers, including some women who worked in the paid care sector, had moved venues three times in the last year, unable to secure enough funding from the city to establish its own dedicated meeting room. The new venue belonged to a religious group, who discreetly shielded the shrine from view with a screen while we used the space. Some volunteers prepared tea to fend against the chill February drafts that seemed to whisper in from every corner. Other volunteers greeted participants and helped them remove coats and get to their tables, where a tidy packet of crafting materials and a box containing scissors and tweezers were already laid out for each of them.

I recognized the tall, slender woman wearing a dark blue track suit and keeping watch from the end of the room as a staff member from the day service center where I had been volunteering. She herself had just turned seventy, and also volunteered with the monthly meal delivery service. "Good morning, everyone! Let's start with some open and close for our hands!" she announced, stretching her long limbs forward and clenching and opening her hands to a rhythm. As she ran through the warm-up routine, her thick reading glasses bounced around her neck on a long red beaded cord.

After the warm-up, one of the other group organizers, Ryoko, walked to the front. She wore a puffy black down vest pulled over the top of a bright red sweater, giving her husky stature an outdoorsy roughness. Ryoko addressed everyone with a loud and lively greeting, apologizing for the change in venue but promising to find something more permanent soon to keep the group going. As she finished speaking, more volunteers began to quietly circulate among the tables, distributing tubes of glue and small wooden sticks to the participants, many of whom were already diligently bent over their craft materials, mumbling in concentration. The group regulars didn't wait for the activity leaders to explain the task, and Ryoko stepped away from the tables and poured herself a cup of instant coffee, sitting on the floor next to me at the edge of the room.

Ryoko had a swagger in her walk that announced she was used to being the boss. Since the beginning of LTCI, she has worked as a care manager. Clients are assigned care managers after they are released from hospital stays or if they are assessed as having care needs, and work together with managers to develop a bespoke care plan. Managers might refer clients to certain care providers or services, help clients access assistive technology, and coordinate care arrangements between different agencies. Like Ryoko, almost all care managers are private contractors whose role as a mediator between LTCI administration and the market of providers is critical to the functioning of the formal care system. When I was allowed to sit in on care manager consultation sessions with clients, the atmosphere was friendly but focused, and never took longer than fifteen minutes. Clipboard and files in hand, the care manager (usually a woman) would ask the client if anything had changed in the last month before running through her care plan list, asking if each item was still adequate or needed. Clients were expected to act as self-advocates, but articulating their concerns made the clients I observed visibly uncomfortable; just the fact of inviting the care manager into the house meant that clients also felt the need to play host, and asking a guest for help was no doubt awkward. Even when I knew clients were having difficulty, they seemed to find it was simpler to just say that everything was fine and send the care manager on her way. Experienced care managers might be able to sense subtle cues and open spaces for clients to speak more freely, but this could not be guaranteed, especially in light of the heavy caseloads.[11]

Ryoko was not only experienced, but her approach was direct and never soft. She was not afraid to speak her mind. When we spoke at the Apricot Club meeting, she was managing a caseload of thirty-nine people, fewer than other care managers, but she was sure to add, "All of them are difficult cases!"

When I asked Ryoko if she felt there were parts of LTCI that she was unhappy with or would like to see improved, she looked at me a little dumbfounded. "I'm unsatisfied with everything!" she suddenly burst out, as if I should have known better than to ask such a thing. "There are so many things, I don't know where to begin!"

Just then, the two of us were joined on the floor by a young man who had just arrived late, looking sullen, or perhaps just tired (I wrote "hungover?" in my field notes). His long hair swooped around his face, and he wore a black leather jacket smelling of cigarette smoke. He and Ryoko greeted each other casually, like old friends, and she introduced him as Hiroshi. He was there to play guitar for some songs the group would be singing after the crafts. Hiroshi was a civil servant in the ward office, and Ryoko had persuaded him to come along to the Apricot Club (she is a hard woman to refuse). Ryoko told him about my question and asked him where she ought to start. "There are so many things!" she repeated, without a hint of sarcasm.

Hiroshi nodded. "When you think about the care system, you have to take in the perspectives of the ward office [yakusho], the care service providers, the family, the insured, the hospital, all of that."

Thinking that I might have been misunderstood, I explained, "I'm trying to get the care manager perspective."

"That *is* the care manager perspective," he replied. "They have to work with all of those people and manage all of their different rules and roles and positions." Ryoko made some instant coffee for Hiroshi, and he slouched against a wall, explaining how care managers are in the middle of a "huge gap" between the official policy and what actually goes on in places of practice (*genba*). Ryoko agreed, adding that the most common issue that arises because of this is that clients need support beyond what LTCI will cover.

She shrugged her shoulders. "I can't help, but simply say we can't do it. That's it. We just can't. I'll ask the people at the ward office for help, but they won't come out and do anything." She nudges Hiroshi. "When this guy was at the office he helped a lot, but the section chief changed, and now they never come out to help. So, I just have to say that nothing can be done."

Care managers like Ryoko must not only persuade older people and their families to make use of care services like respite or home care assistants, but she must also be sure that these services will qualify for LTCI coverage (i.e., that they match the needs assessment), which is managed through the ward office. Spanning the gap means negotiating with both sides, translating the family situation into a narrative that will be acceptable to welfare administrators, while trying to gain the trust of family members who may be reluctant or uninformed about services. Even when Ryoko felt that they she was repeatedly failing to change the system, she tried to protect against losing her identity by projecting confidence. "If you go in there shaking and hesitant, [the client and family] are going to pick up on that right away," she explained. "You need to go in and say, 'I will take care of everything.'"

The results rarely satisfied both sides. Having help from allies at the ward office could smooth the negotiation, providing alternate routes to care, but these relationships depended on particular sympathetic individuals, on friendships, or on the willingness of some administrator to go against the system. But the ward office insurance administrators avoided interactions with care recipients at the *genba*, and LTCI had no provision for supporting family carers directly. If the help that the insured care-recipient needed was support for the family carer looking after them, then this would likely be denied. When I sat in on care manager consultations with older clients, none of this backstage work was apparent. Ryoko explained the way the family carer ends up falling through the gap:

> For example, there are some people with families, and if you live with your family you can't get help with daily tasks under the LTCI system, right? Not if you are living with family. But some people are living with really chaotic family situations. There may be problems when the family is gone all day working and don't do anything like prepare meals,

or maybe people in the family have mental or relational problems and can't really take care of the insured [elderly] person. I just have to resolve whatever I can right there. I may suggest a day service for someone, and if their family member can't see them off to the day service, I'll see about getting a helper that can come at those times and see them off and arrange for that. Sometimes all I can do is suggest that they hire someone [and pay out of pocket], and that's really it. But where is that money supposed to come from? One client with dementia was left alone all day and started losing things and forgetting where she put them, and she would think that someone had come in and stolen her things. She'd call the police, and then the police car would come. This happened almost every day for this woman. And the family couldn't do anything. And what would the neighbors think with a police car called to the house every day? They'd start to think that something bad is going on there, because they don't understand. If the ward office can't really help, I have to do what I can. I am always fighting with the ward office! I can tell the ward office to help with something like that, but even when I can see there is abuse or neglect happening, they just stick their heads in the sand [*shiran kao suru*, lit. "make a face like they don't know anything"].

Hiroshi listened to Ryoko, adding his own perspective from the ward office.

You see, the issue is that we are depending on the insured [elderly person], and their family, and the administrators aren't very conscious of the situation [in practice]; they leave everything to the insurance rules and the care manager. If there is something that doesn't fit the rules, they just push it over to the care manager to figure out. For example, Ryoko comes to me and says I have a little complicated situation with this one client, can you come and look in on him? I will decline. Why will I say no? Because from the point of view of the ward office, this is unequal treatment. And so if we make an exception for this one case, we have to go through and check on all of the others as well. But in reality, I know about that, and I will say that there is nothing we can do, but let's talk about it, and then Ryoko and I will talk, and she'll bring up this case, and I may go to look into it more, but in a lot of cases there is nothing I can do. We are good at making up a lot of reasons why we can't help at the office! It is not really manageable for the care manager as well, since each person has to look in on so many clients, and they can't spend all their time with this one person and not go around to see the others.

Care managers like Ryoko, welfare administrators like Hiroshi, and others inhabiting the gaps between policy and practice struggled to uphold both their moral duty of care toward specific families and the principles of social equality and universality of the LTCI. Their struggles reflected the everyday ethical dilemmas that anthropologists have observed among social care workers in different medical, psychiatric, humanitarian, and social work contexts (Brodwin 2013; Knight 2015; Stevenson 2014; Ticktin 2011). The dissatisfaction and frustration with the inability of the system to adequately address the needs of older people were constantly being weighed against the value of the care that was provided and the moral identity of the role of the care manager. The ethical tensions that pervaded the work of care managers in the "gap" produced particular performances of care and suffering. How does one translate and make legible the anxiety of a person with dementia who calls the police every day? Or the shame and worry of a child of that parent? And what happened to the family when these efforts at translation failed to produce care?

At first, I wondered why Ryoko and the other care workers would spend their "days off" in neighborhood volunteer services like the Apricot Group. "I want people in the neighborhood to be healthy, so they don't become one of my clients!" Ryoko half joked. But the ethical work of volunteering also had benefits for these paid care workers. Informal events also served as occasions for care workers with different roles in the care ecology to build bonds of trust and friendship that smoothed over recent conflicts at work, and often spilled over into meals and drinks after the volunteering. Like the family carers in support groups, these paid carers needed friends who understood and could resonate with stories about work, and those friendships became the start of a network of reciprocal relationships that greased the wheels of support for her clients.

Learning more about her background, I also wondered if volunteering was Ryoko's way of preserving the sense of holistic care that existed prior to LTCI and the introduction of the care manager system. Before LTCI, Ryoko had worked as a *tsukisoi-fu*, or "hospital companion," whose role it was to accompany and care for recovering patients after they had been discharged from the hospital and no longer needed extensive medical or nursing care. Caudill (1961) described the *tsukisoi* in Japanese psychiatric hospitals as occupying an ambiguous role below the level of nurses yet giving more support for well-being than one would expect of a domestic housekeeper (205).[12] Older carers I spoke with had especially fond memories of this system, which provided more comprehensive and personalized care for the patient, as well as a sense of security that should problems arise, someone was watching over them, and only them, around the clock. Unlike current home care assistants, whose visits are typically no more than thirty minutes long, the *tsukisoi*, true to their title, provided a constant reassuring presence and accompaniment meant to resemble that of a caring family member.[13]

One day while I was visiting Ryoko in her small office, the two of us were joined by Mayu, who had begun work as a care manager at the same time as Ryoko. She too had worked as a *tsukisoi-fu* for several years, and the three of us naturally began discussing the differences.

> RYOKO: I think people back then who had that sort of job had much more of a caring feeling from the bottom of their heart, don't you think?
>
> MAYU: I think so.
>
> RYOKO: They had a kindness, you could say. They think, "I have to look after this person"—not like now, where it is just like any other kind of business-type relationship. The world has gradually become more and more, what should I say? [That feeling] has just become *diluted* [*kihaku ni natta*].
>
> MAYU: I did that too, but how long ago was that now? About thirty years ago? When they started the new elderly care welfare model, just at the start of Heisei [1990]. At that time I was at the hospital and did *tsukisoi-fu*. I was looking after people who couldn't move and just before they died. Then we'd get paid some amount for a twenty-four-hour period. I can't quite remember everything, but at that time the image was a kind of a housekeeper [*kasei-fu*] or something. It was an on-call position, so I'd be called by the hospital from the dispatch center. But nowadays, you need to have a home care assistant qualification, a welfare officer qualification, but back then we didn't have certification for anything like that. The idea was that you would be there accompanying them.
>
> RYOKO: But at any rate, the *feeling* was different from elder care workers today.
>
> MAYU: Sure was. But why? That's complicated.
>
> RYOKO: So, the reason there was this kind of transformation in the feeling [*kokoro no hensen*] of care, well, maybe because nowadays it is all about certificates, certificates. It was just about the 1980s when they started coming out with those, and then you needed this and that and the other, and it turned into this whole complicated hierarchy.
>
> MAYU: Yeah, but on the other hand, if they didn't have that kind of system, there wouldn't be any hope of taking care of as many elderly people as we have today.

For Ryoko and Mayu, the pragmatic need for a sustainable national elderly care system legitimated, to some extent, not only the frequent problems it generated, but also the shift of the "feeling" (*kokoro*) of care from the intimate presence of the *tsukisoi* system to the rationalized efficiency of LTCI. The ambivalence many care workers as well as unpaid carers felt toward the LTCI system did not appear very different from British attitudes toward the NHS. Both systems are, for all their faults, still considered some of the most successful health and welfare systems in the world, and are staffed by dedicated and caring individuals who believe in the right to equitable lifelong care. Yet both systems have suffered under a rationalized management system that has favored third-sector subcontractors (including charities, NGOs, for-profit services, and corporations) without corresponding protections for care staff and clients.[14] While the "logic of choice" (Mol 2008) centers responsibility on the care "consumer," the weight of the ethical obligation has shifted away from the care recipient toward the larger social obligation to the social care system, leaving much of the risk to be absorbed by the mediating care managers. The close emotional involvement that made care meaningful for both unpaid and paid carers in the *tsukisoi* system has become decoupled from the tasks of care and relegated further into the private sphere of the family and to voluntary initiatives like the Apricot Group. As another care manager bluntly put it, elderly care "is really just a business these days. Lately in the care service world we no longer use terms like [service] 'user' [*riyōsha-san*], but rather an 'honored client' [*o-kyaku-sama*]." When I began to respond that "it has become a consumerist—" the manager's reaction was quick:

> That's right. So some people don't feel comfortable with that, people who came into welfare a long time ago because they liked helping people. But new businesses are growing out of it since care has become socialized, and even ordinary companies have become able to develop business, so they use terms like "customer" ever since LTCI was established. And the services are good, but I can't help but feel something may have been lost along the way, perhaps? Care managers' jobs are the same way; they've become rationalized [*warikitteru*]. I think we all have to consider seriously what has been lost.

Care managers like Ryoko and Mayu increasingly struggle to enact ethical care as the LTCI system has become increasingly bureaucratic since its introduction. Informal events like the Apricot Club buffer the effects of these changes and provide critical spaces-between to reflect on and cultivate the feelings of care, compassion, and resonance; but just like the physical relocation of the club every few months, these spaces tend to be transitory, fragile, and locally bounded. As the care system comes to rely more and more on locally managed informal voluntary preventive care in the community, this unevenness and tension will deepen, further threatening the system's sustainability.

Care in a Time of Brexit

In my last research interview with Russell while he and his brother were both still looking after their mother, our conversation drifted easily from family care to the state of British politics one year after the referendum to withdraw from the European Union was passed in what became popularly known as "Brexit." After some trial and error, Russell had found a home care assistant whom he and his mother liked so much that they happily increased her hours to cover five days a week, thinking they had found a solution to keeping their mother at home. As a Portuguese (EU) migrant, the care worker could legally work in the UK, but Brexit had suddenly put her status into doubt. Already, thousands of NHS-employed health and adult social care workers who had migrated from EU countries for employment had left the UK, only a year after the referendum (Holmes 2021). For Russell, national politics was suddenly a very personal matter: "The rest of the world is looking at [Brexit] and thinking we're stupid, you know? Politically we're in disarray. The world is an interconnected place, but people just want to build a little fence around themselves, and now we can't go back. And it will affect absolutely everybody and everything."

Russell looked grim and exhausted, holding his head in his hands. It's as if the fatigue from pondering the political situation had compounded the fatigue he felt from thinking about his mother's care. "The world is an interconnected place" reverberates from one site to the next, down through the scales of experience. Russell explained that after his mother had another fall, they had to "move on to more active care," all the while telling his mother, "This is going to help you with your independence." He rolled his eyes wearily. "You say all that, but actually, you're taking it away." Was he talking only about his mother? Or was he still talking about Brexit?

Russell was far from alone in his concern over the consequences of the referendum on adult social care in the short- and long-term future. As the process of Brexit negotiations dragged on through the months and years, the entire country seemed to sink into a dense, heavy fatigue of its own. This mood of uncertainty and anxious waiting seemed to hold both paid and unpaid carers captive, refracting and amplifying their own personal feelings of loss of control.

Carers knew well that policies around carer support were often poor indicators of what care actually looked like in practice, and that political promises and platitudes rarely delivered real results. Carers' critical views of the British politics of care could be seen as an extension of their own charitable role managing and advocating for paid care services for their family care recipients. By bringing their firsthand experiences of the day-to-day work of care into the political conversation, they were able to more effectively demand better care. To the extent that British family carers were actively mediating between the care recipient and various state welfare and other agencies, care was a matter of citizenship as much as kinship (Thelen and Coe 2017).

The enthusiasm for Brexit, like other national populist movements elsewhere in the world at the time, was driven by widening economic inequality and hardships following the decline of industrial manufacturing and the post-housing-crisis austerity measures that began in 2010 (Fetzer 2020). As an extremely rare national popular referendum, Brexit not only gave a voice to those frustrated with the status quo, but it became a symbol of patriotic identity. Brexit supporters, for example, identified the source of the nation's troubles in the collusion between European liberalists and the growing number of immigrants and refugee asylum seekers arriving in the UK via Europe, ignoring consequences this would have for the care services sector (Goodfellow 2019). Russell's frustration resonated with my own experience. The referendum vote took place during the year my family and I moved to the UK, and part of the shock I felt when the results were announced came from the way it seemed to suddenly address me personally. Reading the results in the morning newspaper, I felt like the country that had welcomed me had also passed judgment on me, as if my family and I were now a threat to the existential sovereignty of our hosts. And like many others, both Russell and I were shocked by how much this result threw us into this baffled state, despite all the information that should have prepared us for the outcome. It was a loss, and we were in a state of grief.

European immigrants, some of whom had been living in the UK for decades (but who were not allowed a vote in the referendum), were thrown into even greater chaos as their rights to live and work and be with their families had suddenly come under a cruel yet ambiguous threat. In the weeks that followed, news of hate acts against immigrants and their children were daily features of the newspapers. The scope of British charity had become much smaller and more segregated than Prime Minister Cameron's grand utopian vision of the "Big Society."[15] Among those who voted for Brexit, some would have been carers who had struggled to access support from local authorities because of austerity. "Vote leave" campaigners addressed them directly, assuring that Brexit would bring billions of pounds flooding into the NHS and other social welfare services once the UK departed the EU. As of 2021, despite issues of underfunding and failed infrastructure starkly and tragically revealed by the COVID-19 syndemic, the conservative-led British government is still struggling to adopt new policy measures to improve social care or to fully fund the National Health Service (the "Brexit dividend" for public services is yet to materialize).

English carers were most engaged with politics on a local level, doing the work of Japanese care managers to move back and forth between the local authority and the care market. But they are also aware of the connections between national political sentiment and their ability to access social welfare support. Chris, a single man caring for his mother, who lived with dementia, received a small carer's allowance, participated in support groups, and attended a six-week seminar on Alzheimer's disease that was paid for by his local council. He had previously received small, one-off grants of £300 here and there, which he used to pay for transportation to see his sister, but he had not applied in recent years. While he felt that all the support he received had been helpful, he had a less favorable impression of the local authority, who he felt should be making better-informed policies rather than simply "saying here's some money, get on with it." Chris imagined that a better support strategy would be to take a more active or collaborative role (with more secure funding) in the activities currently run by charities.

> CHRIS: People on the councils, . . . they would never understand, they've absolutely got no idea. That's why you see such policies sometimes, don't ya? Yeah. And they need the advice of people who understand to pass on to them to make the right decision, don't they, because if you don't know yourself, right, then you got to rely on somebody else who does know to tell you how to do it, haven't you? Yeah. . . . Because it is amazing from twelve or fifteen people sat around in a room exchanging ideas and exchanging experiences how fulfilling that can be for you. And for some of the people like myself I felt really great in this sense, because when I see the many problems these other people had, it made mine seem like nothing, you know? And I've just stubbed me toe compared to them, you know? And that is why I say that, why I *wish* that there was more funding around for just bringing people together. Not having to rely on charities and voluntary organizations and that to do it, but you know to have it as an organized part of the health care of the nation. It'll never happen unfortunately, certainly won't with Mr. Cameron's [Conservative] government because they're determined to save every penny that they can anyway.
>
> DANELY: And do you have any help with the caring?
>
> CHRIS: Nope. I get no help whatsoever. Getting help is like trying to start your own gold mine in [my town]. It's great, they all say yeah, you can do this, you can have that, you can have something else,

right, and then when it comes to actually getting it, no one wants to fund you, and no one wants to pay for it. When was that, that was two years ago, wasn't it. . . . Two years ago my mother had a blood clot in her leg that caused a lot of problems, and for a little while we got help to help get her back on her feet and that, but six weeks they gave us of help coming in, and helping to bathe and clean her a little bit, but after that they said "no, she's fit enough now, bye-bye, we're off!"

While local authorities might have considered their obligations fulfilled if they could get their funding out the door to carers, for Chris and others, without consideration of the needs of carers, the money (if and when it arrives) can feel almost like an insult. Whether it was carer support meetings, or using the grant money to visit his sister, the connection and resonance of "just bringing people together" were what made him feel supported.

Because of the extraordinary costs of residential care homes, and because the value of one's home is not included in the means test for social care benefits (as long as that is where one receives care), many individuals try to remain at home as long as they can.[16] While "aging in place" has replaced institutional care as the preferred paradigm of long-term care in both England and Japan, in many ways the logistics of making a house a place of care muddies the line between private and public, the responsibilities of the family and those of the state. If an unpaid carer co-resides with the care recipient, local authorities might deem house remodeling, for example, to be unnecessary, leaving it up to the carer.

Charli, who requested a grant from her local authority to make her home more accessible for her husband's wheelchair, was denied support on the basis of their household income. Even telling me this story, Charli began tensing her fists with frustration. The letter she received from the council indicated that she would have to spend £88,000 before she and her husband could receive any support for the house. "I still feel very angry about that," she seethed, "that lack of concern." The council had made its decision based on a means test of the entire household, rather than just the care recipient. After that, the council began requiring back-payment for care assistants.

We have these two carers in the morning and two carers in the evening, and suddenly we had a letter to say that because he has to pay toward that, it's not free, it was going to be augmented 600 percent, what we had to pay. Which would take all of his pension. But they're not meant to consider my income, by law they're only meant to consider his income.

But they were going to—county council was going to take all of his pension for his care. And we were so outraged. First, we thought there was a mistake. We went back and said how is this?! And county council justified it, and that's why we were so outraged.

Not only did Charli take her case to the national press, but she also had a position on a local panel for carers and began advocating against proposed budget cuts for care. The political challenges were considerable. As she lived in an area with many wealthier conservative households, increasing funding for social care was not necessarily going to win popular support. Local and national politics could not be separated from what it meant to be a carer. Carers like Charli may be rare, but they embody a wider sentiment among English carers that direct political engagement was what was necessary to ensure support. For unpaid carers, this responsibility was just as important as the warm, intimate care of holding a hand or a spoon. As Charli put it, sometimes being a good carer wasn't consistent with being a passive, obedient citizen:

> They have all been very good little boys with the exception of this one [*pointing at herself*]. "Good little boys" and girls following the government's line and proving that they can do what the government wants, and as a result they have nothing—no finances to fall back on—they have nothing to fall back on—and whereas other county councils, particularly up north, they've got around the government demands. They've said we're not doing this to people—whereas [here] that hasn't happened. And so there's no room for maneuver. On the other hand, they've been put there by the government, and really it comes back to what this government wants to do with any kind of strategy that enables people to fare well. They conflate welfare with scrounging, but actually if you take it apart, it's about *faring well*, about living well, having a social conscience—a society that has a social conscience and social support.

By invoking ideas about welfare as means of enabling people to "fare well," Charli challenged the neoliberal logic of self-reliance and independence that stigmatizes those receiving support as "scroungers." Her plea for a society with a "social conscience" and her work to actively bring about justice, not only for her husband, but for other carers, gave her a sense of solidarity and resonance with carers across the country. I have argued that for unpaid carers in England, charity begins at home, but charities have also been important political actors for human rights and the "social conscience" throughout British history.

Tsudoi no ba Sakura-chan and the Mischievous Magic of Care

The lack of official recognition of unpaid carers in Japan made me curious about the small pockets of political activism that have arisen to challenge government policy and to raise what Charli called a "social conscience" around carers. This led me to "Sakura-chan," an ordinary-looking house on the corner of a quiet street in Nishinomiya, near the city of Kobe. The only hint that the house was special was a small placard next to the door identifying it as a "gathering place" (*tsudoi no ba*). Maru-chan, the owner and energy behind Sakura-chan, met me at the door with a broad smile, welcoming and a little mischievous. "Come on in!" she said, and pointed to the fuzzy leopard-print slippers she'd already laid in front of me. I liked her immediately.

The narrow entryway was decorated with posters bearing inspirational slogans written in bouncing calligraphic script, stuffed animals, and a large Shinto good-luck charm. The atmosphere of the space was not so much political as playful, or maybe it was politics-as-play. It was homelike and enclosing, rather than an open storefront in a commercial district.[17] This disruption of boundaries that allowed the public into the domestic reinscribed the spatial ecology of care, with a feeling of intimacy and hospitality typically reserved to private spaces. The "gathering space" of Sakura-chan is one of many informal spaces of resonance and belonging, or *ibasho*, that have emerged to address the displacement and "dis-belonging" faced by carers and those they cared for (Allison 2013; Kavedžija 2019).[18] Unlike carer support groups, Sakura-chan keeps its space open every day and welcomes not only the carers and those they care for, but people of all ages and backgrounds who are interested in building community.[19] If Sakura-chan is trying to address a social problem, it is not carer fatigue, but the systemic ageism of rationalized and marketized care that forecloses counter-worldly narratives of collective emergence (Puig de la Bellacasa 2017, 139–40; Haraway 2016; brown 2017; Tsing 2015) and instead concentrates our attention only on the administrative particulars of fees and forms. The space of the Sakura-chan house not only disrupted the status quo, but reimagined itself as a pastiche of human resonance.

Maru-chan and I were joined by two other visitors, and we were all seated at the long wooden dining table in the main gathering room of the house. On one end, the table was covered with a jumble of books, magazines, papers, copies of articles, and other items Maru-chan had gathered in her work on Japanese elderly care. Resources overflowed the tables onto chairs and shelves as if to announce the disorderliness of information about care (not the way you might see it neatly presented at a social welfare office or care home). The room folded these texts into the cozy interior space of the heart of the house, deliciously mingling with the smells of Maru-chan's home cooking. The walls around us were papered with dozens of photos of smiling carers and care recipients, including several posed group photos at various outings and activities.

Maru-chan was very much at home, standing at the stove on the other side of the room, where small pots simmered and steamed. Before Maru-chan started Sakura-chan and began writing books and articles advocating for changes in the elderly care system, she spent fifteen years in Tokyo working in the food industry. When her mother was diagnosed with cancer, she moved back to Osaka to care for her and to realize her dream of starting her own restaurant. Just as the restaurant was set to open, the Great Hanshin Earthquake of 1995 destroyed the restaurant along with thousands of other buildings in the area. Not long after the disaster, Maru-chan's mother's cancer returned, and for the first time, Maru-chan became a full-time carer. Nine months after the earthquake, her mother died, and within a year, her father suffered a second heavy stroke. For the next nine years she cared for her father as well as a brother who lived with mental illness.

Like so many of the other carers introduced in this book, Maru-chan also struggled emotionally during this time, experiencing depression and isolation. After her father died, however, she felt not only a greater confidence in her ability to care, but a sense of motivation to try to improve the system of care. At first, she decided to study to become a paid carer, but during one of her first sessions of practical training, she was shown how workers would forcibly restrain a client during washing. She was horrified, she said, as she was made to watch a naked and confused woman with dementia screaming and struggling for help while the workers went about their business, holding her tightly. This experience convinced Maru-chan that not only were unpaid carers being ignored, but paid carers were learning the wrong ways to care. Maru-chan echoed the other carers I spoke with, explaining that care was something to be learned from the cared-for, not violently forced on them:

> I was really worried about how these care work students are being edu-
> cated. There is too big of a gap between what they are told and the
> reality, so they get all this education and training and spend money and
> time, but in the end they don't have enough learning from experience,
> and when they realize this they quit! They can't take it because the gap
> is too big. But there is so much that you can learn from the person
> [receiving care] themselves. That's how I felt after I had been caring for
> my mother for a while. There is nothing you can learn so much from as
> care [for older person].

Maru-chan never finished her course, but instead started Sakura-chan, which she called a place where informal carers and the person they care for can spend time meeting others, sharing information, talking, crying, laughing, and most of all, eating. It was a "space for carers to heal" (*iyashi no ba*).[20]

She set out some beer as well as pungent chunks of chewy squid and other savory dishes, each beautifully set on its own small brown or blue ceramic dish. She kept talking as she walked back to the stove. "When I was a caregiver, I would feed Mother something soft so she could eat it, and something without much taste. Then at night I would want to eat something crunchy, like peanuts, or something with a little toughness, like squid! That feeling [of soft food] just builds up in your mouth, and it's hard to bear—so first and foremost is eating!"

Maru-chan's food was not only for sustenance, but for stories, memories, and sharing. As she tended the cooking, she conjured images about her life and work with the honesty, boldness, and humor that had become a trademark of her writing. Her books take aim at the ways LTCI, care institutions, care managers, and end-of-life care have been made to fit business models rather than an ethics of care. Sakura-chan was a grassroots attempt to develop an alternative model of independent local political space (*ma/ba*) where people were not consumers but companions, a counter-world that pointed beyond party politics. The food was not only a way to nourish, but a way in which this counter-world was embodied and shared. She explained with several short accounts of the transformative effects of this space:

> I'll tell you the kind of place this is. A carer came in with her father the other day, and he was sort of giving her a hard time. He had dementia, and we were talking about it. She was trying to give him a glass of tea, and he kept on saying he didn't want it. So, we decided to give him a cold beer. He took a long drink of beer and looked completely content, then fell asleep. If young people would see that sort of thing, they might think, "oh, it is possible for old people to live a contented life [in the community] like this," and they wouldn't be so averse to old age.

Simple, small stories. But stories, nonetheless, that can instantly reveal the problematic assumptions about aging, disability, and care. The politics of Sakura-chan were about creating and sharing these stories not only to critique the dominant models of care, but also to nurture intergenerationally integrated communities and consciousness. In order to maintain her autonomous vision of community, Sakura-chan is not registered as a care service and, unlike many other groups, does not accept money from LTCI or the municipality. It is registered as a nonprofit organization and charges a nominal membership fee of ¥500, and ¥500 for those who would like lunch. Maru-chan also refuses to get involved in political campaigns, and when she came back to the table with more food, she told us, "All the politicians use older people in their campaigns because they know that they are the ones who are going to vote. They talk really well, like Kyoto University graduates, about how we have to protect pensions and improve care, but in reality, they hate children, the elderly, disabled people. As soon as they get elected they forget all about those promises!"

As she walked back to the stove she added, "There is a new person running for mayor around here doing just that, and everyone thinks just because they are young, things will change, but we'll see!"

The telephone in the kitchen rang, and as soon as she heard the voice on the other end, we all watched her smile, saying, "Oh, we were just talking about you!" She held the receiver away, and she turned to us. "It is a campaign worker calling about the election!" She rolled her eyes before telling the person that she could not talk and hung up. We were all left speechless for a moment by the magical way she seemed to conjure the coincidence.

When I asked Maru-chan what she thought about the role of care managers and other services, she was sure not to criticize individuals, but rather pointed out the accumulation of systemic deficiencies. She brought up the case of a woman she knew who worked as a care manager but quit because she was sick of writing *sakubun* (long creative essays), making up notes saying that the case was going well and ticking all the boxes. With caseloads of as many as one hundred clients, it was impossible for her to get to know individuals and keep up with the paperwork. At their worst, she says, care managers are "cheap salesmen" brokering deals for particular care services and taking their own cut on the side.

While supporters of LTCI point to its success in increasing service use (Campbell, Ikegami, and Gibson 2010; Tamiya et al. 2011), critics like Maru-chan point out that a reliance on services has resulted in removing chances for older people to be integrated into their communities and have opportunities for intergenerational engagement.

> Family who put their relatives in a home just dump them there and never come back to visit. People in that situation end up becoming *boke* [out of it], and then they can't communicate and get stuck in a room alone with a television they don't know how to operate—and that's what they call welfare? In the old days, grandpas and grandmas used to have things to do, they had a role in society, but these days care homes are just keeping people alive [with nothing to do]. Would you really give your life over to these people? They have no idea what they are doing and no sense of the meaning of a person's life. The biggest mistake the welfare system makes is that it makes caring separate, when it is *part of life*.

She set down a bowl of rice and a dish of pickles as if to punctuate her statement with a final course. "There is a different tempo of life when you do care, and *they* don't get that."

Sakura-chan is not only a gathering place, but also runs volunteer services to do small errands to support people caring for family at home, and even arranges visits by "listening volunteers" for people in hospitals or care homes who do not normally have family visiting. "To get the tempo of life right," she told me, "you have to really listen to people. Listen with acceptance and openness. It's not easy to do. People can't do that when they are putting [the cared-for] in a home; it's even hard if they are alone, but they can do that here." Maru-chan called this art of connecting different people and building relationships *majikuru*, a portmanteau of the Japanese words for "mix" (*majiru*) and "swirl" (*kuru*), as well as a phonetic approximation of the English word "magical."

While Maru-chan's critiques of the Japanese welfare system point out serious problems with the paid care system, some may find her "magical" vision overly sentimental, nostalgic, or simply unrealistic in a time when fewer family members are free to provide care. In Japan, LGBTQI+ individuals and others who do not have children may be especially disadvantaged if they rely on unpaid community support.[21] At a time when inequality between women and men remains a major problem, reducing paid services, for all its potential advantages of disrupting the gendered division of paid care labor, will also make it harder for women to become independent by increasing their responsibility for unpaid care. Additionally, if care becomes more distributed among local grassroots meeting places, families, and paid services, this might exacerbate regional inequalities, with resource-poor communities unable to achieve the same level of care as others. These are serious considerations and underline the interconnectedness of welfare with other political and economic factors.

The biggest contribution of Sakura-chan and other grassroots community actions like it is the way in which it reimagines life where happiness is not about the pursuit of wealth and autonomy but caring relationships, relationships that can be vulnerable and that have space for sadness as well as joy. Spaces that resonate with life. If we extend this ethic of breaking down barriers and making greater connections by sharing our space, our food, our stories, we can imagine a counter-world where other barriers can begin to dissolve, including those that reproduce other social inequalities.

Dōwaen and the Vision of Shared Life

Dōwaen, a large Buddhist care home nestled in the forested mountains of eastern Kyoto, celebrated its hundredth anniversary in 2021. While elderly care for those who were poor and without family had been a function of Buddhist temples over much of Japan's early history, it is rare for an elderly care home to be run by Buddhists today. The director of Dōwaen during my visit there in 2016 was Hashimoto-sensei, himself trained as a Buddhist priest, who continued to carry on Dōwaen's philosophy of holistic support, including support for unpaid family carers. Like Sakura-chan, Dōwaen dismantles the boundaries and roles that structure rationalized, profit-driven care services, integrating family and clients into the community of the home in ways that enhance its capacity for generating resonance, or what Hashimoto-sensei called "imagining" (*omoi wo haseru*) others' lives. Dōwaen has also become especially well known for its philosophy of terminal care, which emphasizes a natural death without the use of life-extending procedures. Regular Buddhist funeral ceremonies for residents were held at the care home with other residents in attendance; the transcendence of boundaries applied not only to the living, but between the living and the dead.

When I arrived at Dōwaen to speak with Hashimoto-sensei, I was a little surprised by the building's unadorned, even drab appearance. The low ceilings and exposed pipes reminded me of some of the Japanese schools I'd taught in many years ago, but as I was led through the corridor, my eyes fell on a tall stack of bright yellow plastic crates with beer logos printed on the side. When I asked Hashimoto-sensei, he smiled. "We have a bar for residents or their families if they want to use it. If people like to drink, they're free to drink!"

The bar, and indeed the freedom given to the residents to move about and even have romantic relationships with other residents, were not matters of fulfilling hedonistic pleasures in one's final days, but rather extensions of the ethical principle of providing humanistic and holistic care for dying persons, recognizing and respecting their capability and desire for love and pleasure even when living with frailty, disability, or cognitive impairment. This principle was not viewed as an abstract principle of human rights, but rather as an ontological feature of Buddhist non-duality and interdependence that produces compassion. I was interested in how Dōwaen managed to maintain such a unique approach despite the pressures of LTCI and the new landscape of elderly care it had ushered in. Hashimoto-sensei sat me down in his office and explained:

> LTCI started in 2000, and so [welfare] became an insurance system. As a result, we became a "service." Now, a service is something you pay money for. On top of that, it's a contractual agreement. When you have a contract, it's between you and the individual person signing the agreement—well, in our case most of the insured people don't have the capacity to sign an agreement, so it's the family that has to do it. So, from the family's point of view, they've hired the experts and paid the money, and so they turn everything over to those experts. So, these days, if a person goes into care, the family steps back a little. I felt that happening.

But here at Dōwaen, our conviction is [care is about] family support. Not just support of elderly individuals—those people have family, and we have to wrap the care around the whole family.

Lately what I've been thinking about is that human children care for their parents. Out of all the living things on earth, humans are the only ones who care for elderly parents. Ordinary animals would just get old and leave the group and die. So, the essence of being human is that we raise children and then grow up and have children, and then they take care of their parents and so on. And so this cycle is what it really means to be human. So maybe this whole LTCI is wrong?

In the past, care homes were only for people who didn't have any relatives. But now in Japan, our aging population has grown so quickly and children are busy working, so they can't care. So now care is socialized. It might have been better if they chose a kind of community social care system or something, but now we have this LTCI system that follows market principles, so the experts become care service providers, and the family are one step removed from the care process, they just buy the goods. But if children choose to take care of their parents and it's difficult for them, we want to support them. That point is really important. So, for example, we have a lot of terminal care cases. The family comes and stays overnight. They can eat with them, help them in the bath, and so on. It's as if we have just moved the place where the older person lives to Dōwaen, but the role of the child is no different than if they were living on their own. If the family carer is getting stressed and anxious, we'll do the care tasks. If they come in, we'll do it *together*.

He tells me a number of stories of families coming to Dōwaen initially to accompany a dying family member, but finding a sense of ease and community as they participated in care, even taking on general tasks around the care home, like sweeping floors.

"We don't force anyone to do these things," Hashimoto-sensei explained, "we just say, 'you're free to use the cleaning equipment, help yourself if you like.' Then if one person starts doing it, sometimes another will, and soon family members who don't clean feel left out, and it just goes like that!"

The walls between family and service provider were lowered, and as a result, the weight of caring became lighter. In one case, Hashimoto told the story of a woman whose father died at Dōwaen but who continued to come because she felt it was her *ibasho*, or the place she belonged. The staff allowed her to continue coming, offering her little jobs to do and inviting her on outings or to special occasions like the late summer holiday dance (*bon-odori*). "She didn't know what to do with her life after her father died, and for her, the staff and I and the counselors were family." This woman eventually spent her own final days as a resident of Dōwaen, helped by the care of her daughter.

There were a few other cases of multiple generations of a family who ended up staying at Dōwaen, and it was also common for the staff to take care of their own elderly parents there as well. Not only did care create family ties with care recipients in a more vertical relationship, but family members created ties with other residents, horizontally. This family ethos emerged organically over time as a result of the principle of family support. Family carers often remarked that after coming to Dōwaen, they felt closer as a family, that their relationships with each other became easier. "That's the meaning of welfare," declared Hashimoto-sensei proudly, joking, "We're like Gaudi's Sagrada Familia! We don't know the ultimate goal, but we've got to keep building something! This is the meaning of karma. We can't focus on the results we want; all we can do is trust in the process."

While places like Sakura-chan are also able to cultivate a consciousness of mutuality and belonging, as a Buddhist care home specializing in end-of-life care Dōwaen was able to extend this feeling to the death of the care recipient and beyond. This continuity of spiritual care was again something I had only come across in discussions with Buddhist clergy, like Sano-sensei (chapter 5), perhaps because hospice care was still relatively new in Japan at the time (T. Benedict 2018). By 2014, the number of deaths due to "old age" (*rōsui*) was three times what it was in 1999. This rise corresponds with data showing a significant increase in the proportion of people dying at home or in care institutions and a decrease in time spent in hospitals. This change has been largely initiated by changes in medical care aimed at cutting costs on expensive end-of-life procedures, but it also reflects the majority preference for dying at home. The culture of care homes, however, has been slow to respond to this change, and many still do not understand the importance of providing grief care and spiritual counseling to family members.

"Human life is finite," Hashimoto said, so from the Buddhist point of view, "end-of-life care should be about taking things one day at a time, continuing to provide care in the moment [*ichigo ichie*]" Hashimoto-sensei went to his shelf and brought back a large black binder, spreading it on the table between us and opening it to a photograph of a funeral ceremony. "That's me, there!" he said, pointing to himself, dressed in long saffron robes and brocaded sash, at the head of the ceremony. In the center of the altar was a framed photograph of the deceased, flanked on both sides with offerings, flowers, lanterns, and candles, all arranged in an intricately carved wooden setting. More bouquets on stands beside the altar bore inscriptions from mourners. "We are the only care home in the country that holds these funerals in the care home, Hashimoto said, "and we've been doing it ever since we've started. For the families, the grief care begins before the death. We engage with them and stay involved so that when we get to the funeral, they can attend with a smile. Staying involved before the person dies is the most important part, not after."

He turned the page again and showed me another funeral photograph. In this one, a family is gathered around the simple rectangular wooden casket; the body has been draped in white and is surrounded by white and pale-pink flowers. Staff can be seen aiding residents in attendance, some of whom are approaching the casket. On one side, a woman with thin white hair falling over her ears looks into the casket with her hands raised to her mouth, palms together in a respectful gesture of *gassho*. The woman is seated in a wheelchair, and the staff member assisting her is also bowing his head in *gassho*. On the other side, an elderly man grips the side of the casket as an assistant, dressed in dark clothing and a black apron, helps him out of his wheelchair to lean over and look inside.

"That was his wife [who died]," Hashimoto-sensei tells me, pointing at the man. "She was also staying with us." Both of them had Alzheimer's disease, and ordinarily, those living with Alzheimer's or other forms of dementia would not attend a funeral for fear that they would become agitated and disrupt the ceremony. There was no such concern at Dōwaen, however, and the family had agreed to have the ceremony there, allowing the husband to attend and say a proper goodbye. "After we took him back to his room," Hashimoto said, "he would still ask where his wife had gone, and the staff could remind him that they went to the funeral together. They would show him the photograph, and he'd say, 'Oh yes, that's right, that's right,' and he would be relieved for a while. If he hadn't gone to the funeral, the staff would have to make up lies and say that he was at the funeral, but there was no need for that."

We turned another page, and I read it out loud:

「共生」
　共に楽しみ、共に喜び、共に生きることを願う人々の営みを
とおして自他の尊厳に目覚め、生命を全うする
　仏教社会福祉辞典より
"Mutual Coexistence [*kyōsei*]"
Awakening to the dignity of oneself and others and fulfilling one's life through the actions of those who wish to live together, sharing their pleasures and joys.

—Dictionary of Buddhist Social Welfare

I looked up from the page to meet Hashimoto-sensei's face, both of us still as he watched the words sink in. Over the last decade, since the Great Tōhoku triple disaster, the term *kyōsei* had been creeping into mainstream political rhetoric as a counter-discourse to the crisis of the "relationless society," or "disbelong-ing" (*muen shakai*) (Allison 2013, 8, 17). In the same year I visited Dōwaen, community mutual coexistence (*chiiki kyōsei*) had become a key pillar of Prime Minister Shinzo Abe's cabinet's "Plan for a Successful 100 Million," a manifesto of economic and social schemes based on demographic projections of Japan's shrinking population, including increased support for paid and unpaid carers. For Hashimoto-sensei and Dōwaen, this approach was doomed to fail because it not only reduced the notion of mutuality to particular measurable outcomes such as increased numbers of volunteers and decreases in those leaving work prematurely to care for elderly relatives, but it also placed the desired results in front of the process, leaving the heart and art of the plan empty.

"For Buddhists," Hashimoto-sensi explained, mutual coexistence means "whatever happens is the results of karma, and our will has nothing to do with it. We don't presume if we act the right way we will achieve the results we want, so we let go of [controlling] the results, and [concentrate on] the process. If we do that, then we are able to take responsibility for and accept whatever happens without judging it as right or wrong." This openness and vulnerability in the encounter with the other, the one I take responsibility for and care for, pres-ent a radical onto-ethics that imaginatively deconstructs categories like "family," "staff," "carer," and "cared-for," mingling them together in ways that allow them to all resonate with each other.

Hashimoto-sensei's vision of mutuality—the karmic "Sagrada Familia" build-ing, connecting and nurturing lives without attachments to goals, outcomes, or end points—imagines a politics of vulnerability grounded in ordinary lived experiences of care. Drinking together, working together, mourning together. Life and death at the care home were less about expert knowledge than every-day intimate practices that synchronized bodies and spirits to a shared tempo. As fundamentally relational and responsive, care at Dōwaen resonates with the stories of carers in both Japan and England and challenges the political liberal-ism of care systems based on values of individuation, self-reliance, and market capitalism. The stories of unpaid family carers, whose lives are so often underval-ued and invisible, reveal the same transformative potentials, each one a different voice worth listening to if we are to envision another possible world, one worth living in and caring for.

CONCLUSION

New worlds then, open to our listening, difficult or enchained, neither normal nor disabled, a flowering of surprise, worlds becoming polyphonies, resonances, different yet compatible, worlds finally returned to their plurality. Don't tell me I'm dreaming or that this is poetry.

Julia Kristeva, "Liberty, Equality, Fraternity, and . . . Vulnerability"

I returned from fieldwork in Japan with hundreds of pages of notes, sketches, clippings, photographs, and dozens of hours of recorded interviews. These came with me to England, packed preciously into a blue, hard-shell carry-on suitcase, where they stayed until they settled into my new office. Before I began the second stage of my research, I needed some time to organize this mountain of data, but most importantly, to transcribe the recordings. My first transcription assistant had arrived in Oxford around the same time I had, accompanying her husband, who was a postdoctoral researcher at Oxford University. She was timid but very friendly and well educated, and while raising her two young children in a new country kept her very busy, she was eager to take on a little work that she could complete at her own pace. Raising two young children myself, I was happy to be flexible, and when she agreed, we worked out a schedule that we thought would be manageable.

Things went smoothly with the first transcript, but the second one was delayed several times, and I was starting to find it difficult to get clear responses when I wrote or called to follow up. Finally, after two weeks without a response, I received an email from the assistant, explaining what had happened. "Listening with so much concentration to the interview," she wrote, "I started sympathizing with the suffering they were talking about, and I felt miserable." The letter went on to describe symptoms of a full-blown panic attack: heart palpitations, dizziness, labored breathing, and difficulty seeing the screen. I felt terrible, and made sure immediately that she knew her health was more important than my transcripts. Had I grown so numb to these stories that they no longer moved me? How could I have so badly misjudged the effect these stories could have on someone, how deeply and dangerously they might resonate? After we agreed to end the contract, we met again informally on a few occasions, and I was relieved to hear that she had not experienced any further distress. I thanked her for helping me to be more conscious about my research and for reminding me about the power of these stories.

My second transcription assistant, Eriko, had a more gregarious, sociable personality, and had been living in England for several years. Her work was professional and punctual, and helped move my analysis forward tremendously. While she had spent most of her life in Japan, Eriko's reaction to the carers' stories was completely different. This became evident a few months into her contract, when we met over coffee to look at the transcript together and discuss any issues or questions. When Eriko arrived at the café, she slapped a hard copy of the most recent transcript on the table between us and sat down.

"These people don't even have a self!" she told me and frowned as she leaned back in her chair.

"You think that they are sacrificing too much in order to care?" I asked, a bit unsure if her comment was meant to be critical or not. At the very least, it sounded unsympathetic.

"They don't *feel* they are a sacrificing because there was no self to start with! Japanese people are only what those around them want them to be. They just waver in the wind [*kūki*]."

I asked what Japanese people do with their "selves," or their own desires and wishes in these cases. She didn't hesitate in her answer: "We forget them. Forget we even have our own wishes!"

Eriko's response to the interviews affirmed some of my own impressions about compassion and self-displacement as modes of ethical endurance, but it also forced me to reckon with the fact that not all Japanese people (and women in particular) will see this as a positive outcome if it means stifling one's own self-expression, desires, and aspirations. Different as Eriko's reaction was from that of my first assistant, both would probably agree that even "good" care wounds.[1]

I wanted to begin my concluding reflections on care with these two anecdotes because they remind me that this book emerged out of a collaborative journey where experiences of fragility and connection refuse to stay on the page and instead hit us in the gut. This was not always a pleasant experience for me and the research assistants I employed, and it did not always teach us things we thought we wanted to learn. There were many times when I left an interview or a support group meeting and wanted nothing more than to collapse and sleep through to the next day. The more time I spent volunteering in care settings and spending time with carers, the more I began to resonate with them, not because my experience was the same, but because my way of feeling and acting in the world, the resonant properties of my being-with-others, had slowly become reconfigured.

The research assistants' reactions also reminded me that just as each carer's story is different, different readers will also respond to these stories in different ways. Some readers may feel that I've overstated either my representation of carers' hardships or their capacities to adapt. Others may remain unsatisfied with my "comparative" account, or feel that it relied too much on notions of culture that do not give enough room for singularity and heterogeneity. These have all been concerns of mine as well, and exactly the kinds of debates and discussions that I think more anthropologists ought to be having.

When I asked Japanese and English participants in the study what kind of a book they would want to read, each one agreed that it was the stories of carers themselves that should be the most prominent. They weren't as interested in my telling them what to think about those stories or giving advice on how to care better or differently. They just wanted to connect, to resonate.

I have done what I could within the limits of this book not only to place carers' voices in the foreground, but also to link their stories to each other and to a larger body of research, through themes like responsibility, endurance, ethics, and imagination. Any comparative account of unpaid care of frail older adults must contend with at least some if not all of these domains of experience, and perhaps others that arise in response to other local conditions and concerns. Yet, despite this, the stories and lives of carers and those whom they care for overflow even these domains. In my experience, some of the most important stories are not only the ones that "break your heart" (Behar 1997), but also those that leave space for questions.

Looking Back on the Path

I began this book by considering what it would look like to write an account of unpaid care "from the path," rather than from the "summit." I imagined that such an approach could make space for "the shadows of uncertain lives" (Mattingly 2014b, 216), particular lives of particular people whose stories reveal the ordinary ethical work of care. I would not measure each carer on a scale of "burden" or "well-being," or set family care in opposition to paid care. The perspective from the path, instead, would begin with the "fleshiness and fragility of life" (Mol 2008, 11), the ways carers learned to sense and respond to suffering and pleasure, to frailty and vitality.

Resonance, I argued, occurs not only as an empathetic or sympathetic current running between the carer and the cared-for, but also as an openness to cultural and historical patterns (narrative resonance) and to what Kleinman (2009) called a sense of becoming "more human" (cosmic resonance). Resonance depends on a harmonic likeness of structures; intimacy, proximity, and the embodied rituals of care transform carers toward a more resonant being-with-the-other (Rosa 2019). While this resonance repeated itself again and again in carers' stories, it was not always without a sense of danger and concern; resonance did not provide a solution against pain, fatigue, moral dilemmas, tragedy.

While the final chapter highlighted some of the instances where paid care workers and family interacted, and how broader political events (like welfare restructuring or Brexit) influenced the nature of those interactions, much more could be said about the ecosystem of care that composed carers' worlds. Much of what I learned about community care, volunteering, and care within religious communities in Japan was left out. My visits and observations of standard residential care homes and the more flexible "small-scale multifunction" care homes had to be left for another time. Several carers cooperated with other family members, such as siblings, while providing care, and other carers complained about family members who were critical or demanding (especially when they were not providing the care themselves). This too is an important part of carers' experience, but unfortunately was one that I found too challenging to capture ethnographically, given the way families were dispersed.

Perhaps the most glaring omission, however, has been the voices of those receiving care, the frail or disabled men and women who were often hidden in the background of the interviews.[2] For a book focused on resonance, this imbalance between the perspective of the carer and cared-for is conspicuous and no doubt leaves many questions unanswered. Bringing in the perspective of the care recipient would have been especially illuminating in the early transition to dependence, when the carer and cared-for were still negotiating their roles, adjusting to new rhythms of responsibility, and starting to imagine a shared vision of what may lie ahead in the future. Some of this was evident at the day service where I volunteered, where many participants were still being cared for by family but were no longer sufficiently independent to be left alone for long periods. Some of them questioned why they had to attend, or felt a sense of abandonment by their family, while others were grateful to have company and enjoyed the bath, meals, and activities provided. Family carers also felt some ambivalence about these services, unsure if they were doing the right thing. Who was to say what that right thing is? No response to these questions could be final and definitive. But they are questions that remind us of the fragility of family relationships, their intimacy and their wounds. In the final section, I discuss the implications of this research for improving the lives of carers and those they care for.

Justice and Love

Anthropology speaks most clearly and forcefully when it follows what Cheryl Mattingly has called the "histories of the nearly invisible" as they emerge in the "illuminating drama of everyday life" (2014b, 206). An anthropology of care descends into long folds of the ordinary, repetitive, ethical work of endurance, but also ascends through the transcendent in ritual and heterotopic counter-worlds. The stories of unpaid carers in Japan and other aging societies are compelling because they reverberate with both the ordinary and the extraordinary, revealing how care comes to matter profoundly, and how it is so often hidden from researchers, policy makers, and the public.

The key insight that can be gained from taking these stories seriously is that family care can be both devastating and transformative. For Japanese carers, to be compassionate meant becoming open to the other's suffering as one's own suffering, and the care of the other as one's own care. But while many of the carers I spoke with saw the fatigue and hardships of care as a foundation for their transformation and maturity, others struggled in situations that became exhausting, isolating, and dangerous. Fiona Ross (2010) reminds us that compassion, like hope, calls on us to accompany one another, and that it is this "act of accompaniment, rather than co-residence or kinship or even shared histories per se, that accomplishes 'the community'" (2010, 200). Supporting carers with compassion, then, would mean to wrap them in a community that works with them, rather than taking control away from them, a community that can make space for their grief and uncertainty and help them to see this as a part of their claim to belonging. Support of this sort is fragile yet durable—it stays with carers, following along with them on the path, resting with them when the light grows dim.

In the parts of this book on counter-worlds and on politics I briefly introduced places where this is already happening, in support groups and neighborhood volunteer organizations, among post-carers and faith communities, but even today there are still too few of these groups, and they lack organization that might help them share resources and knowledge. In Japan, the Comprehensive Community Support system, introduced in 2006, which was supposed to do this work of organizing local community initiatives and connecting them with market-based services, found itself making up for understaffed services elsewhere in its locality, especially helping solo-dwelling older adults (some post-carers) who were most at risk of isolation, frailty, and a "lonely death" (*kodokushi*) (Nozawa 2015; Danely 2019). Hiro, a social workers from one of these centers, lamented to me,

> People are going to need help, and if the services are not there, they'll go to hospital, then to a geriatric hospital, then to a home or to older persons' housing where you can heap on all sorts of services. Then you're in your own place but you're imprisoned in solitary confinement [*zashi-kirou*]. . . . We're becoming a dying society. The population will peak at 2025, and the low fertility rate will continue, so people after eighty will start dying. There won't be the family there to watch over them, or the family will be old themselves. We're worried about what lies ahead. [*Saki yuki fuan*] . . . the country hopes people who have dementia or are bedridden will die in the community, receiving care from local groups, so they don't have to use hospitals and care facilities. So they tell the local people to do something about these people. People living alone are increasing, lonely deaths and things like that.

This is a bleak forecast, but one that is increasingly common as the population ages, shifting away from institutionalized care in favor of community-based care. This means that reliance on family and other unpaid or informal carers will continue to increase. As Hiro recounted the various steps a person descends, from having a small need to dying alone in "solitary confinement," his voice was weary from a story he had heard far too many times. Neither the existing LTCI system nor the compassion of unpaid family carers was sufficient for addressing the issues. Compassion required justice, a social conscience that responds to the other and realizes that "we ourselves are always already an other" (Levin 1999, 334) and are therefore not alone in the world.

If the compassion of carers finds its social complement in justice, the charity of English carers finds its complement in love. Charity, as I have used the term in this book, aligns with English carers' values of autonomy, egalitarianism, rights, and dignity. Unlike compassion, which is generated through a process of self-displacement, charity requires agency and intention, though the help it provides ought ideally to be disinterested and not based on criteria of deservingness. While I have argued that this moral, cultural foundation, partially and imperfectly translated into the ethics of being-toward-others existing today, can explain some of English carers' reliance on paid care (as well as their reservations about "socialized care") and the prevalence of charities and support groups, it was also clear that, again, charity was not enough to meet the needs of an aging English society. Although the 2014 Care Act assured carers that carers would be cared for, it still appears that many are either not taking full advantage of this entitlement or are unable for other reasons to secure sufficient state support.

Nonprofit groups contracted by local authorities to support carers (similar to the Comprehensive Community Support centers in Japan) are struggling with staffing and retention. If trends over the last decade hold, continued cuts to funding will mean that local authorities will again resort to raising eligibility thresholds for support or dropping or reducing services. Family carers will find themselves taking on more responsibilities for longer stretches of time.

English carers, however, found it challenging to maintain a sense of intimacy and kinship while giving care. In stark contrast to the Japanese carers I spent time with, English carers not only voiced greater discomfort about providing personal (bodily) care, but they also remarked very little on feelings of aesthetic resonance with the care recipient. Even so, love was not absent from these caring relationships, at least in the sense of attachment, commitment, and tenderness. Penny, for example, who cared for her husband in their home, complained about how uncomfortable it was to get into the adjustable hospital bed for "cuddles," but she still felt that their relationship was able to deepen as a result of the care. She told me, "In those four years we were together more than we ever had been in our active life! And it was really very companionable, and I miss that in a way."

Paul, whose experience of caring for his father was one of the most harrowing cases of the English carers I spoke with (chapters 2–3), told me early in our first meeting that he was not caring out of sense of "love," and yet he trembled as he told me much later that between the panic and aggression there would be moments of peace, and his father would say things like, "I really love you [Paul], I really love you." When this happened, it was so uncharacteristic that Paul was dumbfounded: "You know, Jesus Christ, he'd never said stuff like that to me before! And I'm sure that was a result of his illness, we'll call it." While Paul doubted that his father really understood what he was saying, the fatigue of care had made Paul so sensitive that he couldn't help but be emotionally moved anyway.

Bianca Brijnath writes that love in care "is neither as contained nor as simple as it used to be" but is "linked to power and framed by age, illness and loss" (2014, 189). Writing about the role of love in political work, Keahnan Washington (2019) writes that love is about "affective potential, interaction, and interdependence," and it welcomes "those whose capacities are different or otherwise" (22). When I say that English care needs love, then, I mean that it needs to free itself from the notion that the care is bounded by social institutions and resources and that other qualities of affection are at best supplementary and at worst disruptive to accessing quality care. Love needs to exceed the boundaries of charity and create meaningful spaces for mutual vulnerability, intimacy, openness, and emotional resonance. Starting from these qualities we might imagine a welfare system that looks very different from the rationalized, bureaucratic, and anonymous one that has proven so inadequate. We might instead ask what it would be like to design care support that starts with relationships rather than autonomy, an abundance of unpaid care rather than its scarcity. Healer and activist adrienne maree brown (2017) argues that love is essential to justice and liberation, a "core function" of what it means to be human, leading us "to observe in a much deeper way than any other emotion." Similarly, Jarrett Zigon (2013, 203) has written about love as a "demand for ethically remaking [our] moral subjectivities." In this kind of formulation, we see that love is more than just desire or sentiment, but a mode of being-with and resonating that is morally transformative.

My purpose in reflecting on these ideas of justice and love here in the conclusion is not to simply introduce new (and age-old) buzzwords for the virtues of care, as if this was enough to heal its wounds. Rather, I bring them up to help us consider how existing ethical commitments like compassion and charity might be expanded and enhanced in order to address the political and institutional obstacles faced by carers like those I came to know in my research. Their stories revealed that abstract concepts like compassion, charity, justice, or love need to be understood within the contexts of everyday lifeworlds and the cultures and histories enfolded around and through them. These worlds must also be allowed to exceed our precise definitions at times in order to suit local circumstances and become catalysts for creative counter-worlds that can produce real and sustainable change.

These key words—compassion, charity, justice, love—also help us to locate and identify those projects that have already realized ways to care that challenge state- and market-driven divisions, such as Sakura-chan and Dōwaen in Japan, and to learn from them. Hilary Cottam's (2019) vision of "radical help" and the Care Collective's *Care Manifesto* (2020) present two similar alternatives aimed at British carers and their communities. Cottam make the case that the current British welfare system, devised in the aftermath of the Second World War and an inspiration to the Japanese postwar "Beveridge System" (Makita 2010), is no longer "fit for purpose" (Cottam 2019, 14). For Cottam, the problem is that the "current welfare state does not try to connect us to one another, despite the abundant potential of our relationships" (2019, 18). By creating initiatives that enhanced existing capacities rather than focusing on deficits, Cottam's social experiments have revealed the potential for small actions to nurture interconnections rather than divisions, an ethos of shared responsibility for others rather than autonomous self-reliance. When it comes to responsibility, endurance, and compassion, carers have experience in abundance, but for this to change society, their work and its complexity need to be recognized and valued. As one British carer told me, "There are history books about doctors and nurses, but I've never seen one about family carers!" And yet care, as Kleinman puts it, is the "invisible glue that holds society together" (2019, 236). We must ask ourselves, then, is this fact evident in our lives, our families, our workplaces, our communities?

What I have found is, echoing Cottam, the current long-term social welfare systems in both Japan and in England, for all their virtuous aspirations, rely on rationalized bureaucratic and market mechanisms to deliver care. The biopolitical subject produced by these regimes of care, as many other critics of the neoliberal state have observed, is the independent, self-reliant individual as rational consumer (e.g., Mol's [2008] "logic of choice"). Yet, as the stories in this book have illustrated, family carers' subjectivities are not determined by state-driven biopolitics, but have another "life beside itself" (Stevenson 2014), one of sense and attention, fatigue and love, of mourning and of presence.

Key words can bring us focus, but resonance brings us hope. As long as we age, frailty and death will remain with us, our dependence and vulnerability will leave us hurt and wounded. Yet, in our fragility, we are able to see and touch others; in seeking resonance, we affect and are affected by others, and our world is transformed. Whether in the empathetic resonance of carer and cared-for, the narrative resonance of support groups and cultural counter-worlds, or the cosmic resonance that brings hope for social justice for carers around the world, resonance had a way of preserving and at once transcending difference. And if such fragile resonance is possible, we are not only closer to a comparative anthropology-ecology of care, but we are engaging in a new politics of relational possibility, one that opens new worlds to our listening.[3]

Notes

INTRODUCTION

1. While my formulation of resonance and its relationship to the cross-cultural comparison of caring emerged independently, from my own process of working through my notes, as always such epiphanies are tempered when one finds that others have already advanced similar ideas. Unni Wikan (2013), for instance, wrote that she is "convinced that resonance is a way for the future: Only when we recognize the distinct humanity of the other, however inhumane or incomprehensible her actions may seem, can we hope to bridge worlds that are seemingly incommensurable" (26). Wikan develops her notion of resonance as both a new paradigm for comparative anthropology and as a methodology that goes beyond the limits of a Geertzian narrative approach to pay attention to silences and sensations occurring between actors as they inhabit everyday life. In the field of sociology, resonance has found renewed interest through the work of Hartmut Rosa (2019), whose approach is rooted in the Frankfurt school but draws on phenomenologists like Marcel Merleau-Ponty and Emmanuel Levinas as well. In many ways Rosa's formulation of resonance as a "mode of *being-in-the-world*" (2019, 34) that is at once familiar and fascinating (beyond our ability to "philosophically *nail it down*" [458]), and that is at once rooted in our potential for interrelatedness and mutuality and limited by conditions of domination and power, is perfectly aligned with the kind of resonance I outline in this book. However, rather than simply using ethnography to provide an empirical grounding for Rosa's notion of resonance, I have chosen, in this book, to keep resonance more closely situated in the specific context of the care of older people, and return to it only briefly in the final chapters.

2. I use "fragility" here primarily in the way it has been taken up in ethical philosophy (e.g., Anderson 2003; Matsuoka 1995; Nussbaum 1986; Ricoeur 2007), which is similar if not interchangeable in most cases with "frailty" (Arendt 1998, 188; Grenier, Lloyd, and Phillipson 2017) and constitutive of "vulnerability" (Browne, Danely, and Rose now 2021; Butler, Gambetti, and Sabsay 2016; Butler 2021; Ferrarese 2016; Gilson 2014; Harrison 2008; Han 2018; Kristeva 2010; Laceulle 2017, 2018; Laugier 2016). But fragility also points to the importance of the fragility of the frail or disabled older person (Kaufman 1994; Pickard 2014, 2018; Pickard et al. 2019), as well as intersections with other forms of social fragility, perpetuating the reliance on family carers while also withholding support for them (Danely 2017, 2019, 2021).

3. This approach follows calls from anthropologists inspired by phenomenological and existential approaches to ethics, relationality, narrative, and well-being (Desjarlais 1992; Jackson 2002, 2013; Mattingly 2014b, 2016, 2019; Throop 2017). While phenomenological and lived-experience accounts are not alien to research on elderly care, they tend to be overshadowed by a dominant biomedical "evaluative approach" (Seaman, Robbins, and Buch 2019) that aims to make improvements in care interventions, often by optimizing carers' performance on validated measures that will translate into clinical practice. Initially, many anthropologists researching later life had, as a matter of both entering into dialogue with mainstream gerontology and making a case for the new subfield of "geroanthropology," taken a similar problem-based approach (Cohen 1994, 140–43), but the anthropology of aging is now a much richer field both in terms of theory and breadth

of empirical cases (e.g., Lynch and Danely 2013; Sokolovsky 2020). In particular, the field has been shaped by problematizing the relationship between culture, person, and the body (e.g., Cohen 1998; Gubrium 1993; Leibing and Cohen 2006; Lock 1993) and consequently has brought up important questions regarding care (Buch 2015a, 2015b). In this context, phenomenological and existential approaches aim to preserve the complexity of experiences and to suspend assumptions about the nature of "good care" by considering the lived experiences in cultural context (Aulino 2016, 2019; Gill 2020; Grøn and Mattingly 2018; Grøn 2016; Kavedžija 2019; Meinert and Whyte 2017; Wijngaarden et al. 2018).

4. I am indebted to Günter Thomas, William Schweiker, and the John Templeton Foundation–sponsored Enhancing Life Project for introducing me to the term "counter-world," which I explore later in the book in greater detail.

5. Uncertainty was a prevailing feature of elder care in its fragility (Wijngaarden et al. 2018) and of the potentiality for moral transformation afforded by counter-worlds (Mattingly 2014b). Biehl and Locke (2017) describe this quality as lines that entangle as they "make up concrete social fields, mutually constitutive and dependent[;] each type of line comes with its own openings, dangers, and dead ends." The uncertainty and unfinishedness of these entangled lines leave room for moral reflection, or what Zigon (2007, 2010) describes this as "moral breakdown," an "ethical dilemma" that "occurs in moments when one is forced to reflect on the kind of person one wants to be in one's social world" (Zigon 2010, 70). Mattingly's (2014b) virtue ethics approach echoes this idea of reflection, noting that carers "undertake circumstances that are fraught and uncertain, when it often seems impossible to find any best good that is worth acting upon, but where, nonetheless, people continue to care about and struggle to obtain some version of a good life" (5). Cultivation of the good life, she explains, is "communal" and inter-subjective, and that as a consequence is also "full of frailty and uncertainty" (10).

6. The same question and approach is raised by Cottam (2019), brown (2017), and others who argue that social transformation emerges from the potential in our mutual interdependence and interconnections.

7. Philosopher of communication Amit Pinchevski (2017) describes resonance (in contrast to other forms of resounding, like echo, reverberation, or reflection) as a relationship between the internal vibration of a system and another vibration emerging from outside: "resonance is always selective: to resonate is to resound with the outside *in terms of the inside*" (2017, emphasis mine). Pinchevski draws on Niklas Luhmann's (1993) theory of "ecological communication" describing resonance as "conservative, and hence any transformation it brings about is always bounded by anterior consistencies of the resonating system."

8. In these kinds of cases, the practices and feelings of care could take on an uncanny tone, more like an echo, or a "relation that is disjointed: the resounding of echo is always out of place and out of synch—yet still firmly in relation with—that which it echoes" (Pinchevski 2017, n.p.).

9. As Puett and Gross-Loh (2016) argue, "the path" has a long history in East Asian thought, and this has highly influenced Japanese aesthetics and worldview. *Michi/Dō*, "the path" or "way," is a highly developed concept that describes not only the ongoing process of disciplined moral improvement, but also the embeddedness within a shared lifeworld (*kyōsei*) of people and objects that extends one's path infinitely and imbues it with transcendental value. The path is formed through use, bears the traces of past use, and disappears if it is not used.

10. See Ingold and Vergunst (2008) and Ingold (2011, 2016) for one possible answer to this rhetorical question.

11. Puig de la Bellacasa (2017), responding to Latour's uses of "matters of fact" and "matters of concern," uses the phrase "matters of care" to bridge the material and

NOTES TO PAGES 9–18

affective space of care, particularly in the case of human interaction with "more than human worlds" (18). Her "speculations" on mattering are pertinent here as well: "Ways of knowing/caring reaffect objectified worlds, restage things in ways that generate possibility for other ways of relating and living, connect things that were not supposed to be connecting across the bifurcation of consciousness, and ultimately transform the ethico-political and affective perception of things by involvement in the mattering of worlds" (18).

12. Tsukui Lilly Garden was a care home for disabled persons, many of whom were not elderly. See Reynolds (2018) for a Levinasian perspective on these events and the double response to the face (violence and care).

13. *Obāsan* can be glossed as "grandma," or even just "old woman," but in Fumi's case, she is referring to her mother-in-law.

14. For more on Kyoto as an ethnographic site of social imaginaries of tradition and modernity see, e.g., Brumann 2013, Danely 2014, De Antoni 2011, Hareven 2002.

15. The elicitation and analysis of narratives is a well-established approach for qualitative research, especially for those who work in the field of health and illness, where narrative structures, metaphors, and associations can provide important hints about the relational links between culture and subjective experiences (e.g., Becker 1997; Charon 2009; Frank 1995; Kirmayer 2000; Kleinman 1988; Mattingly 2008, 2010, 2014a; Ochs and Capps 1996, 2002; Phoenix, Smith, and Sparkes 2010).

16. D'Andrade (2008) calls this the Fujita-Sano effect, after a study by Fujita and Sano (1988) about child socialization for individualism in US and Japanese nurseries. The researchers used video footage in each setting, then showed the footage to nursery staff in the respective comparison countries to elicit discussion. They found that respondents interpreted the scenes in ways that highlighted their own values rather than an understanding of the other culture. For example, while the Japanese material could have been seen as evidence of socialization for individualism, the US respondents interpreted it as interdependence.

1. CULTURAL ECOLOGIES OF CARE

1. Chief editor of the *Lancet* Richard Horton (2020, 874) has argued that to limit our view of COVID-19 to a pandemic excludes the critical interactions between the biological and the social (including racial inequality, education, employment, housing, food, and environment) and argues for the adoption of what medical anthropologist Merrill Singer and colleagues have called a "syndemic." Given that the purpose of this chapter is to establish a broad ecological frame to questions of care, I have adopted Horton's logic in addressing COVID-19. To call this an "ecology of care" means recognizing that individuals and their environment are part of a dynamic system that poses both affordances and constraints (Bateson 2000; Dewachi 2021; Duclos and Criado 2020; Hacking 1998; Hankins 2013; Ingold 2000; Puig de la Bellacasa 2017; Raikhel 2015). An ecology of care also recognizes the root of *oikos*, or the domestic sphere of relationships and spaces that forms the basis of broader social economics and for hospitality (M. C. Bateson 1989, 135–36; Danely 2019; Derrida 1992). This emphasis on the broader systemic nature of care focuses attention on the interaction among its elements as contributions toward the enhancement of the environment, including the natural and built environment.

2. The "successful aging" paradigm (a precursor to what is now referred to as "active aging") has been the dominant paradigm in gerontology since the 1980s. Lamb, Robbins-Ruszkowski, and Corwin (2017, 2) summarize its core premise as the notion that "you can be the crafter of your own successful aging—through diet, exercise, productive activities, attitude, self-control, and choice. Aging well becomes a vital personal and moral project, benefiting not only the individual but also one's broader family, society, and nation."

This paradigm looks at aging not as a kind of natural decline of bodily functioning, but as a time when activity and lifestyle can maintain good health and independence until just before death (compression of morbidity) (Neilson 2003). The successful-aging paradigm has been criticized both by social scientists who argue it downplays social inequalities and blames "failed" agers as irresponsible (Katz and Calasanti 2014; Rubinstein and Medeiros 2015), and by geneticists who argue that it overemphasizes the degree of plasticity in later life (Masoro 2001). Several anthropologists have offered alternative visions of what "success" might mean that depart from some of the problematic assumptions of the successful-aging paradigm, such as "growing old with God" (Corwin 2017), "Foolish Vitality" (Danely 2017a), or "Nurturing Life" (Farquhar and Zhang 2017).

3. Despite the growing need for unpaid family care, there is still very little research on the topic, especially within anthropology (notable exceptions are Aulino 2019; Brijnath 2014; Kleinman 2019). Rather, anthropologists have focused almost exclusively on critical examinations of paid carers in long-term care settings like nursing homes (McLean 2007; Rodriquez 2014; Shield 1988; Stafford 2003; Thang 2001; Wu 2004), or on migrant domestic workers (Mazus 2013; Parreñas 2015) or home visiting aides (Buch 2013, 2018). There are about 410,000 residents in 11,300 care homes in the UK (Competition and Markets Authority 2017). Japan, which has roughly double the population of the UK, also has about double the number of care homes (21,560) and residents (close to one million) (MHLW 2016). Both countries are expected to experience a sharp rise in demand for nursing homes as the post–World War II baby-boom generation in those countries enters more advanced age (over seventy-five). In the UK, the number of people who need twenty-four-hour care is expected to double by 2035, yet current austerity measures mean that hundreds of care homes are closing their doors or raising the eligibility criteria. Some estimate that half of Japan's for-profit care homes will go bankrupt by 2030, in large part because they lack sufficient staff (*Shūkan Asahi* 2018, 18). Many of the social care workers in the UK are immigrants from Europe, Asia, or Africa and have faced considerable uncertainty due to tightening controls on immigration and increased deportations. Japan's strict labor immigration laws make it very difficult for care workers to come from abroad, and policy changes in 2018 specifically to encourage care worker migration have been controversial and inadequate. By 2025 (the key year in Japan) there will be an expected shortage of at least 370,000 workers.

4. Mattingly (2010) describes the interaction between felt and lived experience and storytelling as "narrative phenomenology." The strength of this approach is the way it "connects small-scale dramas—particular historical events as experienced by particular historical actors in particular contexts—to larger social histories" (217). Narrative phenomenology is therefore consistent with the ecological approach's emphasis on mutually constitutive relationships, but it adds a dramaturgical element that grounds those relationships in practices, performances, and improvisations.

5. Tronto's definition and its implication that care leads us to live "as well as possible" may strike some as obscuring the "moral ambiguity" (Cook and Trundle 2020, 178) or inevitable "conundrums" of care (Arnold and Aulino 2021). Similarly, Duclos and Criado (2020) make an important critique of Tronto's notion of "repair," which they argue can be co-opted by nationalist political actors (e.g., "Make America Great Again") as a tool of violence. Similar critiques have been made about the political use of "compassion" (Berlant 2004) and "vulnerability" (Han 2018, 338). I tend toward a more generous reading of the ethics of care that emphasizes relational processes over the strict policing of narrow definitional boundaries. As shown by scholars like Puig de la Bellacasa (2012), who also adopts Tronto's definition, a care ethics approach can be productively combined with other ecological models of care.

6. Saba Mahmood (2015, 23–24) writes, "In my view 'understanding' in anthropology implies not simply objectively recording how people in a given society think or behave, but juxtaposing the constitutive concepts and practices of one form of life against another in order to ask a different set of questions, to decenter and rethink the normative frameworks by which we have come to apprehend life—whether of one's own, another's, or those yet to be realized." While Mahmood refers to juxtaposition of different forms of religious and secular life in Egypt, and I am using the concept to examine other kinds of historical and cultural difference, the principle that comparison needs to not be formal, but part of a creative process of interference and question-asking, still holds.

7. See Kavedžija (2019, 77, 173n3) for more on the social history of self-cultivation in Japanese community life.

8. It could be argued that both compassion and charity are terms typically reserved for acts of care toward relationally distant "others," or strangers. Informants rarely used the terms "compassion" and "charity" to describe their care. Care retained an ambiguity and floated between these modes, making it both flexible but also difficult to compare within or across cultural and historical contexts. Compassion and charity have received scholarly examination primarily in institutional contexts such as in religious organizations (Benthall 2012; Elisha 2008; Mittermaier 2014, 2019; Trundle 2014) or in humanitarian and development organizations (Bornstein and Redfield 2010; Bornstein 2012; Fassin 2005; Livingston 2005; Ticktin 2011). The approach that I take is relatively unconventional in that it is examining how these modes of caring play out in intimate domestic kin-provisioned care contexts.

9. The Buddhist practice of meditation, for instance, has been found to enhance "altruism," measured as a sense of connectedness to others, in ways that can even bring about changes in neurological structures responsible for perception and attention (Keltner, Marsh, and Smith 2010; Mascaro et al. 2015; Mascaro et al. 2018; Trautwein, Naranjo, and Schmidt 2016; Weng et al. 2015). In other words, compassion is less a set of abstract ethical principles than it is an embodied and evolutionary product that can be enhanced through contemplative practices.

10. In this respect, Buddhist compassion more closely resembles the ethical ontology of phenomenologists Emmanuel Levinas and Watsuji Tetsuro (both of whom were critical of Heidegger), wherein personhood (*ningen sonzai*) emerges from the response of care to the ethical demand of the "other" (Danely 2016, 2017b, 2021).

11. It is interesting that the term for "suffering" used in the word "compassion" is not the same as the one used to convey the Buddhist noble truth of *dukkha* (Japanese: *ku*). Instead, it is a more ambiguous term that covers a wide range of emotional suffering. H. Nakamura (1954), Takeuchi (2009), and others, for example, have looked closely at the historical usage of the Japanese word for "suffering" (*kanashimi*), the second character in the composite word compassion (*jihi*), pointing out that its meaning indicates not only sadness, but specifically pain of losing the object of one's affection, attachment, and love. The characters *aware* (translated variously as pity, pathos, grief, fascination) and *ai* or "love" can also be substituted for this standard character for suffering with the same phonetic pronunciation (*kanashimi*).

12. Also noteworthy is that in English, "the word 'care' is a noun derived from the Old English (*caru*) and the Gothic (*kara*) and means 'lament, sorrow, suffering of mind, grief'" (Connell 2003, 13). This aligns to the meaning when we use phrases like "He didn't have a care in the world!" So, much like the Japanese word *jihi*, as van Manan (1990, 58, cited in Connell 2003, 13) notes, "the term 'care' . . . possesses the dual meaning of worry, trouble, anxiety, and lament on the one side, and charitableness, love, attentiveness, benefice on the other side."

13. In the Vimalakirti Sutra, each of the most revered of the Buddha's students visits an ailing layperson named Vimalakirti. But rather than offering him their great wisdom, they find that they must humbly accept what he teaches about the nature of compassion. In one passage, the wisest of the Buddha's students, Manjusri, inquiries about the nature of Vimalakirti's illness. Vimalakirti responds, "The bodhisattva loves all living beings as if each were his only child. He becomes sick when they are sick and is cured when they are cured. You ask me, Manjusri, whence comes my sickness; the sicknesses of the bodhisattvas arise from great compassion" (Vimalakirti 1976, part 5). In this explanation, Vimalakirti not only expresses compassion as the embodiment of the world's suffering, but he calls attention to the fact that this state has provided a chance to teach others, or translate compassion into practice. See Cheng and Tse (2014) for an example of a modern counseling framework based on this sutra.

14. While Berlant (2004) offers several examples, including the "compassionate conservativism" in the US, it is worthy to note more-recent example outside of this context. In 2015, for example, the UK prime minister David Cameron delivered a statement to Parliament celebrating the "extraordinary compassion" of the British people "always standing up for our values and helping those in need" (Oral Statement to Parliament, September 7, 2015). (Cameron's compassion, however, extended only to accepting a maximum of twenty thousand of the millions of refugees and asylum seekers who had been displaced from Asia and Africa to Europe.) It is also worth noting that discourses of compassion as a kind of emotional labor become woven into narratives of resilience, exhaustion, depletion, and replenishing. Research on compassion in the context of health and social care has escalated over the last decade alongside the growing focus on person-centered care and explicit policies that employ the term "compassion" as a guiding practical aim. Lown (2014), for example, reports that England's chief nursing officer established "Compassion in Practice" as a primary vision for the National Healthcare Service, requiring employees at all levels to "foster organizational cultures of compassion and create incentives that advance compassionate care" (7). Lown herself outlines "seven guiding commitments" for making health care compassionate, including the "commitment to support caregivers" (IV), and "Deepen our Understanding of Compassion" (VII) (2014, 8–12). Empirical studies that take up this last commitment have tended to focus on "compassion fatigue" (Figley 1995; Coetzee, Knobloch, and Klopper 2010) and, to a lesser extent, "compassion satisfaction" (Stamm 2002), sometimes substituted with qualities like resilience. Medical research, policy, and education construct compassion as both a highly valuable and desired skill—a subtle gentleness that is also potentially dangerous if practiced in excess. Such studies are interesting because of the way they shift the "problem" of elder care away from the patient as a cause of "burden" to the carer who must learn how to better sustain the emotional stress of care. Accordingly, the locus of intervention also shifts from the cared-for to the carer.

15. One might argue that the Samaritan was also compassionate, as the text states he was "moved by pity" or sympathy. That is, he was affected by the suffering person in such a way that it disturbed his travels and motivated care (Zimmermann 2015, 301–2). It also ought to be noted that the parable is Jesus's response to the question "Who is my neighbor?"—itself prompted by the command to "Love thy neighbor as thyself" (echoing the Torah). Thus, although the text does not contain the word "love," the parable should be seen as a demonstration of love or charity, rather than focusing on the moment of pity or compassion.

16. For a more detailed discussion of this work and Weber's notion of "world-denying" religion and "acosmical love" see Bellah (1999).

17. C. S. Lewis explains this absolute primacy of God's charity by referencing Luke 14:26: "If anyone comes to me and does not hate his own father and mother and wife and children and brothers and sisters, yes, and even his own life, he cannot be my disciple."

18. Here, narrative resonance resembles Robert I. Levy's (1975) notion of hypocognized and hypercognized emotions. One might argue that in Japan, compassion is hypercognized and charity hypocognized, while the reverse would be the case in England. This allows us to bridge the public discourses that elaborate these terms and private emotional and embodied states that they are supposed to inspire.

19. During this time, the imperial government sought to incorporate Gyōgi and his followers by providing limited numbers with official status while at the same time discouraging taxpaying farmers from leaving their land to become ordained (Sakuma 1994, 8–9). Those who sought to emulate Gyōgi, such as Eison, restricted the scope of welfare activities to those benefiting "*hinin*, such as beggars, orphans or the elderly left on their own, and lepers or others with grave illnesses or physical impairments who had no regular means of support" (Quinter 2008, 49). In a "non-discriminatory" ceremony held at a temple next to a *hinin* community, Eison is reported to have quoted a sutra that read in part, "The Dharma-Prince Manjusri turns into an impoverished solitary, or afflicted sentient being and appears before practitioners. When people call to mind Manjusri, they should practice compassion. Those who practice compassion will thereby be able to see Manjusri." According to Quinter (49), Eison explains, "You should know that compassion and Manjusri are two different words for the same thing. To promote compassion, Manjusri appears in the form of a suffering being. This is the basis for the origins of such charitable acts (*segyō*)." *Segyō* might be translated more precisely as "almsgiving" or specifically giving to the poor. We might notice in this exegesis on the Bodhisattva a resonance to the words of Jesus in Matthew 25:40: "Truly I tell you, whatever you did for one of the least of these brothers and sisters of mine, you did for me" (NIV). While the contrast between Gyōgi's development-oriented compassion and Eison's focus on the suffering of socially marginalized groups indicates a tension between interpretations of compassion, in many cases clear distinctions are impossible. For example, throughout Japanese history, Buddhist figures and laypeople have been involved in projects to aid people affected by natural disasters, offering both pastoral care for grieving survivors as well as rebuilding shelter and infrastructure. This tradition appears to have revived following the 1995 Hanshin earthquake and the 2011 Tōhoku earthquake and tsunami (McLaughlin 2011; M. Berman 2018).

20. Both these names contain the syllable *den*, represented by the Chinese character for "rice field." This identified these institutions as places for the cultivation of one's heart, just as one cultivates a field, through care and compassion. Self-cultivation was inherent in this early idea of social welfare, although at some point the term changed from *fukuden* to *fukushi*, implying a less agrarian, corporate institution.

21. The principles of Buddhist care are rooted in the "Four Bases of Sympathy" (Japanese: *shishōji*, Pāli: *catur samgraha vastu*): generosity (*fuse*), loving speech (*aigo*), acts that benefit the cared-for (*rikō*), and empathetic cooperation (*dōji*). Each of these weaves compassion into the separate components of care, from the provision of basic needs (e.g., giving alms), to speech, act, and mind. Generosity is sometimes glossed as "charity," but while acts of generosity might include giving (directly or indirectly) to the poor or needy, the ethical logic of this "charity" must be understood within the specific context of Buddhist economies of merit-making (Aulino 2019; Bowie 1998).

22. While Shinto and other traditions maintained their importance in everyday community life, Buddhism flourished as a religion of healing, compassion, and care through its influence in social welfare. Buddhist temples continued to play an important role in supporting poor, sick, and disabled older people for another eleven centuries, until the severing of state ties to Buddhism and the establishment of modern secular state institutions in the late nineteenth century (Hardacre 1989).

23. Large employers began to provide their own pension benefits as early as 1904, but the current two-tiered universal pension system started in 1961 (Makita 2010, 83–84).

This system ensures that anyone who has lived in Japan between ages twenty and sixty and who has been employed for a total of at least twenty-five years within that period has the right to receive payments after the age of sixty-five. Those who do not meet these criteria are eligible to receive a national pension. Despite this pension provision, Japan has the largest proportion of people over seventy still in employment. About 27 percent of older persons' households have income below the poverty level—an incidence of poverty about 40 percent higher than that of younger adults (*Nippon Keizai Shinbun* 2018). Social security (*seikatsu hogo*) payments can be three to five times as much as the basic national pension and do not require the enrollee to pay LTCI premiums or copays. Currently, about 45 percent of those who receive this public assistance are over sixty-five.

24. There are very few modern Buddhist care homes (Dōwaen in Kyoto, discussed in chapter 7, is an exception). Buddhism remains associated with funerals and memorial rituals and has kept its role in health and social care marginal, even in regard to grief care or hospice care (T. Benedict 2018).

25. For those who wish to know more, I highly recommend the rigorous and enlightening research on the modern development of institutions for the care of older people in Japan and England by Mayumi Hayashi (2015).

26. As of the latest revisions, the large majority of those enrolled still pay the lowest copay (10 percent). Those with annual incomes in excess of ¥2.2 million (about £16,000) would pay double. For those whose income is from pensions and from other household members sixty-five or older, such as a spouse, the threshold is ¥4.63 million (£34,400).

27. Ministry of Health, Labour and Welfare 2003 guidelines for admission to *toku-yō* specify that those living with family or who have family carers will be given lower priority (Yuki 2012, 34–35). In addition to *toku-yō*, LTCI covers stays at smaller group homes specifically aimed at care of people living with dementia, and "small-scale multifunctional homes" (*shōkibo takinō*), which combine residential care with short-term care and supplemental community-based care. There are also a number of geriatric hospitals (*rōjin hoken shisetsu*, or *rōken*) for those who require more advanced nursing care. Unlike hospitals, which discourage stays that exceed three months, *rōken* allow indefinite stays. There is also a range of private residential care homes and apartments for older persons that provide a menu of care services (at a cost) to people who can live mostly independently.

28. The important exception, of course, was charitable actions to raise money to aid those affected by the March 11, 2011, Tōhoku earthquake, tsunami, and nuclear meltdown that killed sixteen thousand people and displaced hundreds of thousands more. Similar grassroots relief work was started during the 1995 Hanshin earthquake as well.

29. This is partly because panhandling puts one at risk of violating stringent Japanese laws regarding fraud, but also, according to some ethnographic accounts, because unhoused people are trying to preserve a sense of dignity.

30. Hayashi (2016) would probably categorize this as a quasi-NGO or a *quango*, a type of arrangement that is prevalent in Japan.

31. The representation of older people in premodern England, as in Japan, is ambivalent. They are both honored for their wisdom and experience and demeaned as useless and repulsive. For some family members, care was considered a good Christian duty, but abuse, neglect, and abandonment were also common. A number of instrumental factors no doubt also played a strong role in shaping the care of the elderly. First was the unavailability of children. In the sixteenth and seventeenth centuries, one in three older persons would have no surviving children at all (Ben-Amos 2008, 29; Thane 2000, 136). Individuals in preindustrial and premodern England were very mobile, so few children lived close by (only half, according to Thane 2000, 136). So, a second instrumental reason families did not care for elderly relatives was the low rate of co-residence (Ben-Amos 2008, 64). Older widows, however, might have taken in lodgers or

sojourners, so the role of non-kin in supporting older persons' independence remained important.

32. Hayashi (2016, 16) notes that "of the 2,100,000 persons aged sixty-five or more in the United Kingdom by 1900, 1,750,000 were living in poverty, with 613,000 in receipt of poor relief."

33. Some premodern charitable houses for the poor were specifically for older people. Ben-Amos (2008, 120) notes that in "London, new institutions for the aged rose from 41 in 1599 to at least 100 in 1700"; these were built by charitable actions of guilds (haberdashers, brewers, fishmongers).

34. The Institute for Fiscal Studies estimates a 17 percent cut between 2010 and 2020 (Harris, Hodge and Phillips 2019).

2. BECOMING A CARER

1. About two-thirds of carers whom I conducted interviews with were women, both in Japan and in England. This approximates the proportions of the latest available census data estimates of unpaid carers of elderly relatives: the 2019 *Kokumin Seikatsu Kiban Chōsa* (Comprehensive survey of living conditions) conducted by the Ministry of Health, Labour and Welfare, which found 65 percent of carers were women, 35 percent men; the 2011 UK census found 58 percent of carers were women and 42 percent were men (2021 census data was not available at the time of publication). The UK census data, however, did not distinguish between those caring for older family members specifically (although they estimate that around 84 percent of carer respondents fit that category). While this is still far from equal, it is interesting to note that for Japanese carers, 2016 was the first year that the average amount of time spent daily on caring for a frail or disabled older family member was higher for men than it was for women (two hours and thirty-two minutes, and two hours and twenty-eight minutes respectively) (Sōmucho Tōkeikyoku 2017, 3), although men still do far less general housework or child care. Despite the longer average healthy life expectancy (HALE) of women and the tendency of husbands to be older than their wives, spousal care is roughly equal between men and women. According to the UK census, women constitute the majority of carers in every age category *except* for those age eighty-five and older. Similarly, in Japan, 22.8 percent of male carers are age eighty or older, while only 12.6 percent of female carers were eighty or older (MHLW 2019, IV 25). Caregiving in Japan, especially since the postwar period, has tended to be closely associated with both the practical tasks of domestic reproductive labor (cooking, cleaning, managing household finances) and cultural gender norms of feminine nurturance (Ochiai 1997). Most accounts of women's unpaid elderly care in Japan stress the same kind of social pressures linked to traditional household ideology, as well as the ways women have found to adjust, cope, or make care meaningful (Elliot and Campbell 1993; Hashimoto 1996; Jenike 1997; Lebra 1979; Long and Harris 2000; Makita 2010; Yamamoto-Mitani and Wallhagen 2002). While this might strike some as a kind of codependency, where the woman's identity becomes dangerously dependent on care of everyone in the house, the cultural value placed on the role of carer and on selfless endurance also means that this is not necessarily considered pathological (Borovoy 2005). The only instance where a Japanese woman I spoke with mentioned problems of codependency was in the context of paid care work. According to this woman, codependency was a serious problem in care work, perpetuating the tolerance for sexist verbal and physical abuse from patients/clients, which leads to burnout among female care workers who try too hard to make their (often male) client/patients happy and comfortable.

2. Emmanuel Levinas (1905–1995) is a philosopher whose work accompanies me throughout this book, and although it is not my intention to use the anthropology of

compassion to extend or critique his concepts, I find it helpful for his voice to interject here and there like a provocative echo. Responsibility was a recurrent theme in Levinas's ethics. Critchley (2004) writes, "Levinas's one big thing is expressed in his thesis that ethics is first philosophy, where ethics is understood as a relation of infinite responsibility to the other person" (6). Responsibility can be called "infinite" in the sense that the face of the other to whom I am responsible always exceeds my capacity to know or control it; I can be in "proximity" to the "alterity" but never penetrate it fully. Levinas makes clear that being a responsible subject in the sense he uses it is not simply "a matter of an obligation or a duty about which a decision could be made," but rather "the I is, by its very position, responsibility through and through" (1996, 17). For Levinasian ethics then, responsibility is not a matter of being responsible *for* or *to* someone or something but a matter of being woven into the encounter. Further, Levinas argues that this responsibility in the encounter is a means to transcendence: "The structure of responsibility will show how the other in the face, challenges us from the greatest depth and the highest height—by opening the very dimension of elevation" (1996, 17).

3. This echoes the question that prompted the parable of the Good Samaritan: "Who is my neighbor?" Like the Good Samaritan, then, we care for the one who suffers before us, who calls out for our response, or who is difficult to deny. Some philosophers, like Emmanuel Levinas and Martin Buber, have argued that it is only as we encounter the other that we become aware of this responsibility, first to the singular other (i.e., the cared-for), then to all of society.

4. To the extent that *kokoro* also approximates the English words "mind," "heart," "consciousness," "conscience," "subjectivity," and "intentionality," it gathers together all the qualities of psychological interiority. The defining property of the *kokoro* is that it is invisible: although one cannot see the *kokoro*, or truly know it fully, one can "read" it because one also possesses a *kokoro* (Doi [1971] 2001, 107). This capacity to empathize, identify, and intuit the other through the *kokoro* makes care and a mature relationship with the other possible.

5. See Goldfarb (2016) and Nozawa (2015) for examples of two Japanese modes of relatedness (*kizuna* and *en*).

6. Some have argued that in Japan, the sense of responsibility for care comes not from moral obligations of filial piety, but from social inter-subjectivity (*sekentei*) (Asai and Kameoka 2005). *Seken* has been described as a "force that pressures the individual to conform to following the group" (Sato 2015, 10). Sato argues that prior to the introduction of modern formulations of "society" and "individual" in the late nineteenth century, this concept of *seken* was so all-encompassing that the majority of Japanese people could not think outside of its confines.

7. While unusual, it may be more often the case of men who marry into their wife's family, or *mukoyōshi*. These men and their children will take on the family name of their wives and carry on the duties of the patrilineage of the ie (*honke*). While Hideki did not fall into this category, he was also not an eldest son, so his identification with his wife's family was also not necessarily a violation of household norms.

8. Historical evidence suggests that men actively cared for older relatives at least since the early modern period (seventeenth to nineteenth centuries) in both countries. Records from the Japanese Edo period (eighteenth century) show that many male members of the samurai class requested leave from their duties or retired entirely in order to assume care duties for elderly parents or grandparents (Yanagiya 2011). Guidance manuals for the care of the sick and old from that time, as well as the diaries of samurai, show that this was not merely an expected duty of a male head of household, but that affection and compassion were traits that earned men respect and honor. In England, Ben-Amos (2008, 33–37) found numerous references to sons and grandsons who cared for older family in

the Newgate narratives (documents related to Victorian crime and punishment). In these cases, the men co-resided with their poor and ailing older relatives, supporting them at least materially. Men's place in work, family, and nation would shift again in the twentieth century, as military conscription, mass industrialization, urbanization, and other forms of nation building reinforced strictly partitioned gender roles. The "lost years" of following the collapse of the 1980s bubble economy left a new generation feeling more adrift in the "liquid" landscape of flexible and precarious labor (Allison 2013). This generation of carers straddle the pre-/post-bubble worlds; they want to preserve a sense of rootedness in the values of family and perseverance, while at the same time they are less likely to adhere to sharp divisions between gendered labor. The manga *Pecoross's Mother and Her Days* (Okano 2012), written and originally self-published by Nagasaki native Okano Yuichi (b. 1950), tells his story of caring for his mother, who was living with dementia. The local popularity of the manga caught the attention of a larger publishing company, and it quickly became a best-seller and, in 2013, a feature-length film (Morisaki 2013). Both the manga and film depict the humor, frustration, and intimate sorrow of the son as he muddles through the day-to-day tasks of caring, now and then seeing small glimpses of his mother's past singing through the fog of memory. As he reflects on her life and their relationship over the years (including the complex ambivalence toward his hardworking alcoholic father and his mother's silent endurance), his commitment and affection deepen with his grief, and the family drama of injury and care crescendos in the deafening silence of wordless pauses. Pecoross (a nickname meaning "onion," referring to his bald head), depicts himself as a man who has failed at manhood: a poster boy for the lost generation.

9. Hideki worried that his mother-in-law might be uncomfortable having a man touch her, but such a sentiment was not a frequent among other male carers in Japan (in contrast to English carers). This discomfort was, however, mentioned by daughters-in-law taking care of their husband's fathers, so it may be the case that sensitivity has more to do with consanguineous versus affinal relationships.

10. Among the current Japanese carers I conducted interviews with, seven had either moved into the home of the person they cared for, or moved the care recipient into their home for at least six months in order to provide care. This included one woman who traveled from her home in the US to stay with her mother for two years. In almost every other case, like that of Yoko, the carer and older care recipient lived together already prior to care (only two lived separately from the person they cared for). Among my smaller English sample, one in five associated moving with the start of their caring, but only one (Paul) moved the care recipient into their home. In two cases, children lived with the older care recipient before they began providing care, and all spouse carers lived together prior to care.

11. ¥110,000 covered rent, while other services such as the nighttime monitoring staff were an additional ¥70,000. For those unable to pay even that, there would be few options outside of residential care homes, which usually provided only shared rooms (curtain-separated), or geriatric hospitals, which would be covered separately through the national health care insurance.

12. The original phrase came from the English sociologist Joseph Harold Sheldon's study of the living conditions of older people in the city of Wolverhampton (Kawai 2015, 32). While Sheldon referred to a distance close enough that a "hot meal" would stay warm, the Japanese have adapted this to "soup" (*sūpu*), but most are unaware of the origin. While residence is a norm during the care of bedridden elderly (*netakiri*) (Long and Harris 1997), living close by is considered ideal for less intensive care.

13. Aneshensel et al. (1995) is one of the most extensive qualitative studies of unpaid carers (*n*=555) based on their narratives over a three-year period. While acknowledging the limits of this study for delving into individual cases over the full "career" of care, they

stress the diversity and complexity of care. That said, the framework they use to analyze and present their findings is problem-centered, focusing on stress and its "containment" through utilization of paid care, culminating in institutionalization. Their goal is explicitly policy driven (i.e., cost-saving) and reproduces biomedical views of aging and the accumulation of deficits and frailty (Rockwood and Mitnitski 2007). While this may be a normative model in the United States, it does not necessarily match the "career" of carers in England, Japan, or elsewhere.

3. FATIGUE AND ENDURANCE

1. Many women are choosing to marry and have children later in life as well, increasing the likelihood of "double responsibility" (see Yamashita and Soma 2016), or what Plath (1975) called the "Confucian Sandwich."

2. Compassion fatigue is sometimes referred to as "secondary traumatic stress" (although some consider the two to be separate conditions). Halifax and Byock (2008) and Marr (2009), who examine caregiving in the context of palliative medicine, have argued that from a Buddhist perspective, "compassion fatigue" does not make sense, and that an alternate phrase such as "empathic distress" is more appropriate.

3. Although care fatigue does not carry the same pathological implications that compassion fatigue does, it has been successfully used to reduce sentences in some cases of care homicide (*kaigo satsujin*).

4. *Gaman* is composed of the characters for "ego" (*ga*) and "slow" (*man*), as if the desires of the ego are slowed down, controlled, or suppressed.

5. This is a frequent motif in Japanese mythology as well as popular medieval ghost stories and contemporary horror movies. The attachment and love of the mother endures even past death! (see Creed 1996; Dumas 2018; Iwasaka and Toelken 1994).

6. If care is an event, it is dispersed across so many subtle moments, muddled feelings, and memories that it eludes attempts to pin it down. As Povinelli observes, quasi-events trap or suspend subjects in sometimes dramatic efforts toward futile or tragic ends (she offers the metaphor of riding a leaking boat that needs constant bailing); ultimately these efforts bring about "modes of exhaustion and endurance that are ordinary, chronic, and cruddy rather than catastrophic, crisis-laden, and sublime" (2011, 132). Yet as Povinelli goes on to argue, and what I want to emphasize here, is that enduring or persevering in such tragic situations is a form of hope. This hope, however fragile, allows carers a space for reimagining the possibilities for being-with the cared-for, stepping into new narrative forests. See also Nixon (2011) on "slow violence."

7. Levinas ([1947] 2001) writes that fatigue is "a numbness, a way of curling up into oneself" but also "an impossibility of following through, a constant increasing lag between being and what it remains attached to, like a hand little by little letting slip what it is trying to hold on to, letting go even while it tightens its grip."

8. Csordas (2008, 117) uses the term "inter-corporeality" to describe (inter)subjectivity in terms of bodies, a "mode of collective presence in the world."

9. Funahashi (2013) has also linked fatigue, and more specifically the recent emergence of "burnout" syndrome, to an inability to identify as oneself, arguing that not only is this alienation rooted in neoliberal capitalism, but that liberal therapeutic regimes of self-reflection might further reinforce this alienation. Similarly, Povinelli (2011, 32) identifies fatigue (or "exhaustion," to use her terminology) and endurance as forms of life that emerge from the "spaces and zones of late liberal exposure and abandonment" that foreclose on the possibilities for self-recognition and self-fashioning. In Paul's case, his confrontation with this father's alterity—a confrontation that is very much about bodies and their energies on the threshold of sacrifice—throws his own self (not just his capacity

to fill a role of carer) into doubt. His fatigue (or burnout or exhaustion) is an expression of this sense of dislocation, vulnerability, and exposure.

10. English carers often went to great lengths to live separately from the person they cared for. According to the 2019 Japanese census, almost 54.5 percent of those receiving LTCI benefits co-resided with an unpaid carer, either a spouse (23.8 percent) or an adult child (sometimes with that adult's spouse or family) (28.3 percent); only 12.1 percent relied primarily on paid care services (MHLW 2019, IV 25). Actual numbers might be even higher, since about 19 percent of those surveyed did not answer. About one in five (18 percent) older people receiving care lived in a three-generational household, down by over a third since 2000. In England, "multifamily households," such as three-generational households, represented only 1.1 percent of total households, and most sources agree that while there has been a rise in unpaid care and a decline in residential paid care, there are still few family carers who co-reside with the person they care for, and the trend is toward a decrease (M. Hirst 2002).

11. Kondo (1990, 109–15) describes the way these same ethical scripts of endurance and physical exhaustion are channeled into narratives of transformation and growth. In her case, these scripts were woven into the ideology of her company as a means of extracting labor, loyalty, and cooperation in the workplace. She reminds us that "selves are produced through specific disciplines and transgressions elicit particular punishments, just as the ethics doctrines offer particular, compelling, and satisfying pathways to self-fulfillment" (115).

12. In *Existence and Existents* ([1947] 2001), Levinas writes, "But the notion of the struggle for existence is . . . a struggle for a future, as the care that a being takes for its endurance and conservation." The connection between futurity and endurance is discussed further in chapter 6.

4. DANGEROUS COMPASSION

1. While risk has become understood as a defining theme of speculative market capitalism, I am thinking of it here in the sense of a moral economy of care and reciprocity (Danely 2014; Douglas 1994; Ryan 2018). Yet in both cases, risky relationships generate value and reproduce trust, anticipation, fear, and desire.

2. In his memoir, *Bring Poison to Yourself* ([1993] 2002), the eighty-two-year-old Japanese artist Okamoto Taro captures something of this spirit of dangerous compassion. He writes, "It is in times of facing and confronting dangers, hardships, and death that a person thrives [lit. "burns up"]. That is what makes life worth living [*ikigai*], and what surges forth in those times is not happiness, but 'bliss'" (63–64). He celebrates taking the "dangerous path" (*kiken na michi*, 18) that comes from responding to the present moment, free from the attachments to our pasts or futures, or even to the drive for self-preservation that might cause us to close off from the world in a perpetual state of "one of these days" (*izure*). To Okamoto, persons who live in this mildly hopeful state of "one of these days" have not only forfeited their passion and creativity, but more importantly, lost a sense of *responsibility* and *responsiveness* to the world (51–52). The danger is there because, as Okamoto asserts, it is what makes life worth living.

3. Tahhan (2014) critiques discourses around these and similar idioms of bodily oneness as feeding into essentialist and orientalist notions of Japanese uniqueness (and non-Japanese/Western difference). She does not deny that these discourses might influence the lived experience of Japanese people insofar as they are part of the structure of social habituation, but she calls instead for a more ethnographically and phenomenologically grounded notion of these concepts that might account for more nuanced variations in their experience.

4. Phenomenological philosopher Bernhard Waldenfels defined "responsivity" as a basic feature of speech and action. Anthropologists and philosophers have applied this notion of responsivity to contexts of care (Grøn 2016; Rosa 2019, 35; Wentzer 2014).

5. The form of dance Naomi had studied and performed for fourteen years was a kind of avant-garde, often improvisational dance genre originating in Japan called Butoh. While there are many styles of Butoh, they share a daring sense of freedom of expressive movement that is the polar opposite of classical Japanese dance based on the mastery of set forms. In Butoh, dancers are encouraged to feel and respond intuitively to forces or energies arising out words or images and to observe the body rather than controlling its actions (T. Nakamura 2012). Furthermore, the dance troupe typically live a communal lifestyle premised on a relational model of the social body.

6. Tahhan (2014, 80) describes the openness between bodies as a relational space that preserves both difference and empathetic connection through the potential for "oneness" (*ittaikan*).

7. This changing perspective also evokes the kind of play of third-person typifications and categories becoming worked into first-person experiences (Grøn 2016; Mattingly 2019).

8. Throop (2012a, 163), commenting on the moral phenomenological work of Alfred Schutz, explains that "according to Schutz, in dynamic moments of face-to-face attunement that characterize the co-presence of a 'we-relationship,' there are moments of possibility in which another may perceive aspects of my own self-experience that I am not yet aware of myself." The hypersensitivity of the cared-for and the attention needed to adjust behaviors that Naomi mentioned seem consistent with this kind of analysis, suggesting the primacy of perceiving and responding to the other in face-to-face encounters of care.

9. For children (but also for adults) this is captured in the prepared lunch box (*obentō*) that conveys the sense of the mother's care through the body; see Allison (1991); Tahhan (2014, 116).

10. See, for instance, the film *Kyō mo iyagarase bentō* (*Bento harassment*) (Tsukamoto 2019), where a mother uses elaborate lunchboxes to send messages to her belligerent teenage daughter (making their relationship the unwanted object of scrutiny of her classmates). Tokyo Gas also produced a series of award-winning advertisements about cooking that binds the family together (*Kazoku wo tsunagu*), including one in which a mother communicates with her son over the years through her encrypted lunchboxes assembled before dawn. The son's only "response" is the empty box after each day, until the final day, when he leaves a note to say, "I'm sorry I never said 'Thank you.'" Seeing this, the mother is moved to tears. Emiko Ohnuki-Tierney (1990) has expanded the relational quality of food in her discussion of the Japanese "ambivalent self," which is literally and symbolically embodied through practices of food preparation and ingestion. Food is a medium through which one might imitate (imperfectly) the foreign other, or aspire for authenticity (though this is often only a reflection of foreign expectations). It thus always separates and connects the self and other in ways that are often multilayered and ambiguous.

11. Much has been written in anthropology about the various ways of eating food. This most mundane aspect of our survival condenses complex meanings about kinship, class, and history (Bourdieu 1984; Douglas 1972; Mintz 1985; Mintz and Du Bois 2002; Sutton 2001, 2010), especially in Japan (Bestor 2012; Cwiertka 2006; Gasparri 2020; Gould et al. 2019). Feeding is seen as critical for the physical and psychological development of children, as well as their socialization into cultural norms and values (E. Berman 2019; Chapin 2014; Lancy 2015), but feeding is less frequently mentioned in ethnographies of old age. Lamb (2000, 165) describes the ways older Bengali women include more "cooling" foods

in their diet, embodying the associations this brings with purity, asceticism, and death. Brijnath (2014), also working in India, notes the sacred importance of feeding others for Hindus, making it the "most pleasurable aspect of caring" (133) and deeply distressing when food is refused because of dementia. Driessen (2019, 64–79) and Buch (2018, 137–44) both discuss the ways paid carers employ empathetic attunement to sense clients' dietary needs and desires as well as the ways carers produce "independence" by recognizing the singularity of those needs.

12. Levinas writes, "The need for food does not have existence as its goal, but food." Simon Critchley called this the "world's shortest refutation of Heidegger" (Critchley 2004, 21), because of the way Levinas brings us back to the ethics of vulnerable and embodied existence. As Emiko and other carers remind us, hunger and enjoyment of food are immanently relational, or inter-corporeal; they are about care, or as Levinas puts it, "Only a being that eats can be for the other" (quoted in Critchley 2004, 21). In the context of compassionate care, feeding the other through a careful attunement to the other's pleasure and hunger constitutes the ethical responsibility. See also A. Hirst 2004 for a powerful and detailed discussion of "eating the other" in Levinas's ethics.

13. Just as food links one to others, the denial of food, especially though biomedical nutritional apparatus like PEG tubes (where sustenance is about the delivery of nutrition rather than the act of eating), separates them (Danely 2018). The use of feeding tubes came up frequently as an ethical dilemma for carers and doctors alike, with both in general agreement that they could prolong survival but without any assurances of the quality of that life, especially for patients living with dementia (Nakanishi and Hattori 2014). At the time of my research, there was "no decision-making guide regarding long-term tube feeding that specifically targets individuals making decisions on behalf of cognitively impaired older persons" (Kuraoka and Nakayama 2014).

14. For comparison on the uses of food to create a sense of community in Japan see Kavedžija (2019, 69–73) and Gasparri (2020).

15. *Seishinteki* can refer to mental, emotional, or spiritual states, but is typically an inner experience.

16. While I use the term "facing" (*mukiau*), this should not be confused with the word used to describe one's honor, as in "losing face" (*mentsu ushinau*), or the term for one's physical visage (*kao*).

17. The list here is far from exhaustive, but Levinasian ethics has been central to the work of Judith Butler ([2004] 2020, 131) on precarity; Lisa Guenther's work on solitary confinement (2013); Murakami Yasuhiko's work on mental disorders (2012); Nigel Rapport (2015, 2019) on anthropology of ethics; Throop (2010b) on suffering and compassion in Yap; Trundle (2014, 150–52) on charity in Tuscany; and Kiyokazu Washida (2015) on aging and the life course in Japan, to name a few that have inspired my thoughts.

18. For anthropologists, the notion of "betweenness" immediately calls to mind Victor Turner's (1969) description of ritual "liminality" as "betwixt and between." Indeed, if the carer's journey involves a transformation from responsibility to transcendence, then the fatigue, danger, and existential disorientation that characterize the face-to-face encounter would certainly constitute the middle stage of liminality. The main difference is that carers' journeys, in contrast to rites of passage, are not public events seen as propitiating the values and beliefs of society as in a coming-of-age ceremony or funeral. While individual carers may use the narrative genre of "coming of age" to express the maturity they gain through caring, this departs slightly from the social point that Turner was trying to make.

19. For Levinas, sound offered a means to transcendence beyond the completeness and comfort of the visual. In ethical terms, the sound as event of the word (*verbe*) places me beside my self, or makes me for-the-other (Bruns 2004, 230–33).

5. COUNTER-WORLDS OF CARE

1. "I'm here" resonates with Levinasian interpretations of "Hineni," the response given to Abraham as he was set to fulfill God's command to sacrifice his only son, Isaac. Hineni "performs the speech-act of presenting myself, the speech-act of making myself available to another" with infinite responsibility (Putnam 2004, 37–39). It may also resonate with Arendt's notion of "the disclosure of the agent in speech and action" (1998, 175), which is nothing less than the moment of appearance, a second beginning, or natality. For Jackson (2002, 40) this disclosure of the "I'm here" revealed the recovery of freedom within "contested space of intersubjectivity" or a way for the powerless to regain power by telling their stories. Quoting Arendt, Jackson writes, "when stories fail to effect a transposition of the self-centred (*idion*) to the shared (*koinon*)," they "greatly intensify and enrich the whole scale of subjective emotions and private feelings," but at the expense of our social existence, for it is "the presence of others who see and hear what we hear" that "assures us of the reality of the world and ourselves'" (2002, 40–41).

2. Although it had been almost twenty years since the Tokyo subway attack by members of the religious cult Aum Shinrikyo, the association of new religious groups with dangerous "brainwashing" was still prevalent, and I can't imagine what I might have looked like to her.

3. Akemi's reference to god (*kami*) is not a reference to a Christian God or even a Shinto deity, but to the divine being that this group believes to be the source of an invisible, transformative "light"/"life" with the power to heal both the phenomenal body and the noumenal spirit.

4. "Okage-sama. Chichi Haha no on, ima koko watashi no inochi."

5. Daruma became a code word for prostitute during the Edo period. One explanation is that, like a prostitute, Daruma gets knocked down but keeps coming back up. Another guess is that the nine years Daruma supposedly spent facing a wall in meditation can be compared to the ten years a prostitute's contract was owned by her brothel.

6. England is generally considered one of the most secular countries in the world, with over half the population claiming no religious affiliation. In 2018, about one-third of people in the UK identified as belonging to the Church of England, but less than 5 percent of those attend church weekly (Phillips et al. 2018). Just as Sano-sensei observed in the case of Japan, secular state institutions in England have an even longer history of displacing the role of the church in areas like social welfare, health, and well-being. Church of England–affiliated state schools and Catholic NHS hospitals show the traces of the church's long-standing relationship with charitable social care in the community in ways that one almost never sees in Japanese Buddhism, and yet these institutions are still bound to conform with state regulatory bodies and guidelines for inclusiveness. All my children attended a Church of England–affiliated school, and although church events and Bible lessons were a regular part of the school identity and ethos, multi-faith religious literacy was also a part of the regular curriculum. Particular attention was given to other popular religious groups in England, such as Islam (4 percent), Hinduism (1 percent), and Sikhism (1 percent). More recently, prayer and mindfulness have been introduced as topics.

7. Although a disillusionment with one's faith community following the death of a loved one has been noted in other research on English carers (Coleman et al. 2002), most of the literature on religious coping tends to link religious participation with a faith community to protective effects for psychological well-being, social support, and health, especially in later life (George et al. 2013).

8. Schutz (1970) devised a typology of these "multiple realities" (little, medium, and great), encompassing a range of examples that underlines the ways "we are all entangled

in transcendence all the time" (Robbins 2016). Extending this logic, Robbins suggests that we might consider "values" as a form of transcendence.

9. Anthropologists have mainly examined "utopia" as "utopianism" or the ideology of particular utopian projects such as the Israeli kibbutz (Spiro 2004); the Burning Man Festival (Bowditch 2010); intentional communities (Lockyer 2008); or even space exploration. Not surprisingly, Black and queer anthropology is one area that has come to re-embrace utopia as a source of speculative emergence. Shaka McGlotten (2012), for example, defined utopia as a "genre of unrealized and unrealizable attachments oriented toward the possibility that life might somehow be lived differently and better" (59–60).

10. Ricoeur (1976) goes beyond Mannheim's dialectic pairing of ideology and utopia by looking at the importance of "social imagination" in both. While both modes of thinking are classed by Ricoeur as a form of social imagination, utopia is characterized by its imagination of "another kind of society, of another reality, another world" (24). A carer who is constantly frustrated by the relentless tasks of caring might long for this other reality, but as Ricoeur warns, a utopian imagination can become escapist, or so outside the bounds of reality that it becomes pathological. Cultural and religious tropes, such as notions of suffering, spiritual training, and the interdependence of life, might anchor utopian imagination in more familiar ideas while still allowing carers the flexibility to craft their own narratives.

11. In this way, they might be compared to therapeutic support groups for those in recovery from addiction (Kornfield 2014), mental illness (Myers 2015), or other problematic behaviors (Cubellis 2020). Care might not be considered in the same light morally or socially as, say, addiction or psychiatric crisis, but without meaningful narrative, it can be just as dangerous.

12. In his essay on utopia and heterotopia, Foucault ends with the analogy of the boat: "The ship is the heterotopia par excellence. In civilizations without boats, dreams dry up, espionage takes the place of adventure, and the police take the place of pirates" (1986, 27).

6. LIVING ON

1. *Fukan* in Japanese.

2. Although Ume and Evans (2011) have called this picture "chaos and uncertainty," there are some points of agreement across studies. Caregivers experiencing mental and physical problems prior to the death of the care recipient tend to fare worse after. Yet Boerner, Schulz, and Horowitz (2004) point out that having positive caregiving experience pre-loss is correlated with negative experiences after loss.

3. An interesting finding is that carers who transfer a care recipient to a nursing home do not feel the same relief that bereaved carers do (Crespo, Piccini, and Bernaldo-de-Quirós 2013, 6).

4. This pattern of post-carers continuing to care for those outside their family has been noted in qualitative studies among white British post-carers (Larkin 2009) and African Americans in the US (Ume 2013).

5. Aulino (2019), who examines Thai rituals of care (including elderly care), argues for a critical phenomenology of care (12) that foregrounds the social training of perceptual awareness (13) through habituated actions. This approach allows her to explain the relatively minor role of desires or intentions to care in the enactment of actual practices. Thai carers are habituated to respond to the world in ways that align with local Buddhist notions of mind and merit. In the case of Japan, I would argue similarly that compassion, and its everyday embodied forms of attention and responsiveness, become habituated particularly intensely by family carers. Although Tomomi wonders if she is predisposed to care because of her personality, her descriptions center on bodily states generated through

care rather than on personal wishes or desires. It is almost as if she is compelled to care by her body, and yet for her such a spontaneous way of responding to the world is also a signal of moral maturity and mastery.

6. I had heard similar responses from other carers, mostly in cases of caring for a parent that the carer had felt a strong affection for. It may be that in such cases, the persistence of compassion is intertwined with the need to organize often complex and ambivalent thoughts about a parent one cares for deeply. I do not, in other words, deny that parent-child dynamics of other sorts are likely to be at work beneath the surface, but I do not have the systematic evidence to make such claims. While a more thorough examination of this would be fascinating, it is beyond the scope of this project.

7. In more-developed welfare states like Denmark (Christensen 2020; Grøn 2016) or Sweden these arrangements would be managed and negotiated between paid carers and the care recipient in such a way as to relieve the need for family involvement.

8. According to the 2011 UK census, the only age demographic where there are more men than women providing unpaid care is over eight-five years old (White 2013).

9. On the significance of promises as moral projects in later life see Flaherty 2018.

10. Perhaps we might think of this as a transition from performance to animation (Manning and Gershon 2013) in the sense that past selves, all those characters one has played over one's life, all the scenes that play back repeatedly on the projection screen of memory, are reimagined as elements that have combined to lead up to this moment, this and only this I.

11. Schattschneider (2004) argues that ritual images such as ghost bride dolls used in northern Japan bring up the problem of doubleness (of images and people), that is, the ways they are both signifier and signified, a representation of something that is absent and the thing itself, collectively constituted and a singular entity (143–44). This doubleness allows the images to produce "family resemblances" between people and image that produce a sense of a coherent system of kinship while at the same time producing uncanny and dissonant effects that "fuel their aesthetic, emotive, and ritual power" (144).

7. THE POLITICS OF CARE

1. Aulino (2019, 35–39), working in the context of northern Thailand, frames this routine, embodied activity of care as "ritual," which creates "a shared means by which people can reconcile disparate aspects of their lived experiences through set actions." Aulino's intervention seeks to decenter the individual, internal, cognitive aspects of care in order to open up the possibility of other local understandings. In a similar way, care might open up connections to meaningful counter-worlds.

2. Duclos and Criado (2020, 155) adopt a similar ecological approach to care, stating, "what is needed are more accurate cartographies of the many intersections and frictions between the *enveloping* and the *diverging*, the *protecting* and the *containing*, the *enduring* and the *engendering*, as they play out in care practices."

3. Critical approaches to the politics of care have mainly been applied to paid elderly care, whether in long-term care institutions (McLean 2007; Rodriquez 2014; Stafford 2003) or in paid home care (Broadbent 2014; Buch 2018; Christensen 2020; Danely 2016; Mazus 2013; Shirasaki 2009; Stacey 2011). The widening of global inequality with the rise of neoliberal forms of governance has also prompted anthropologists to look at the disproportionate and largely disadvantageous effects of global political economy (Baars et al. 2006) on paid carers, especially women from countries in the Global South (Amrith 2016; Parreñas 2015; Switek 2016) and the families they leave behind (Yarris 2017). The extensive body of research on the politics of international development and humanitarian aid has also come to inform critical examinations of volunteering, which often occupies a mediating position between paid care and the community (Aulino 2019; Hayashi 2016;

Malkki 2015; Nakano 2005; Read 2019; Trundle 2014). In chapter 1, I argued that in the cases of Japan and England, non-kin-provisioned care institutions have their ethical roots in religious and secular community organizations that provided basic assistance to those without material resources or kin, but the merging of these moral institutions with governmental and economic institutions (e.g., employment-based welfare, pensions) have changed them dramatically.

4. Another place where gender inequality is evident is the government response to carers leaving work (*kaigo rishoku*). This was a topic that was getting close attention both in the mainstream media as well as in Prime Minister Abe's government during my fieldwork, as it was estimated that despite a decade of LTCI, the number of people leaving work to care each year has remained the same (about one hundred thousand). What had changed in that time, however, was that the proportion of men leaving work had doubled (women still accounted for 80 percent of care leavers). Surveys calculate the number of men who are providing care while working at around 2.9 million (about 5 percent of the total workforce); however, experts believe most men are unwilling to admit they are carers and that the actual number is four times this amount (Kojima 2015). The fact that policies change only when men are affected was not lost on everyone. One of the regular attendees of the men's support group meeting was a woman who worked as a consultant. Supporting male carers was part of her pragmatic strategy, since any policies aimed at helping men would likely help women, too. "Women have always been losing their jobs, but no one ever cared. Now we have a chance to make this an issue that changes things for the better for everyone," she told me.

5. In comparison, Skills for Care (2020, 8–9) estimates there are around 1.5 million care workers in England, with 112,000 job vacancies at any one time.

6. The image of *hakidame*, indeed the whole notion of a society of winners and "losing dogs" (*makeinu*), evokes links to medieval notions of exile and banishment (*mura hachibu*) and to class marginalization of those in occupations involving contact with the pollution of aging and dying bodies (Hankins 2013). Scraps are also an increasingly common feature of the life adrift in Japan's disenchanted, post-Fordist "liquid" economy (Allison 2013).

7. On July 26, 2016, Satoshi Uematsu, a twenty-six-year-old former employee of a residence for people with disabilities in Chiba Prefecture, stabbed nineteen people to death before being apprehended. It was the worst mass murder in Japan since World War II. This was still fairly close in memory at the time of our conversation and had brought onto the front pages the issue of the precariousness of people living in care facilities in a time of severe worker shortages. The perpetrator, who had been hospitalized for psychosis and other mental health problems prior to the incident, believed the care of disabled people was a waste of the country's resources. While the victims were not older people, the issues that contributed to the crime (the shortage of workers, the poor conditions of workers, and the discourse of wasted resources) are indistinguishable from those affecting conditions in care homes for older people.

8. For a similar use of these terms in the context of charity see Trundle (2014, 119).

9. A 2018 report on abuse in care homes found 621 confirmed incidents (a 21.8 percent increase from the previous year). Outside of care institutions, there were 17,249 cases of abuse by the carer (a 1 percent increase). See 2018 survey results on the condition of responses based on the "Law for Elder Abuse Prevention and Supporting Older People and Their Carers" (MHLW 2018b)

10. As the lessons from the deinstitutionalization of psychiatric care show, community care does not alleviate the need for extensive welfare services and support (Zegwaard et al. 2011; Brodwin 2013; Friedman 2009).

11. Almost 90 percent of care managers work for companies that provide additional care services, creating what some consider to be an unethical conflict of interest. While care

managers might refer clients to their own company's services because they genuinely feel those services would be best for the client, some have argued that such referrals are used to offset other costs. LTCI fees are not sufficient to ensure income for the companies. The Japan Care Manager Association lists these fees as ¥10,760 (for Care Level 1 and 2) and ¥13,980 (for Care Levels 3–5). If the number of clients for one care manager exceeds forty (very common), the fees paid are reduced to ¥5,390 and ¥6980 respectively. Ishiguro (2021) has used this information to argue that the ideal of a universal provision of long-term care has been undermined by the role-ambiguity and conflicts that arise from the individualization of care demanded from the care manager.

12. Caudill's data come from 1958–1959, but his observations resonate with the descriptions of my informants who were employed as *tsukisoi* or had received care from them as late as the early 1990s, suggesting that there had been little change in the role until the introduction of LTCI.

13. Caudill (1961) notes that the *tsukisoi* role evolved from the practice of family members staying for long periods in hospitals, providing all non-medical care for the patient: "If a family member was not available, the family persuaded or hired someone else to carry out this task. This service gradually became institutionalized in the role of tsukisoi" (206). Caudill, a psychological and psychoanalytically trained anthropologist, is also aware of the importance of dependent transference relationship between the *tsukisoi* and her patient and the cultural correspondence between her role (and it is always a woman) and the figure of the mother (210–11).

14. Baraitser and Brook (2021), drawing on Nancy Fraser, locate this crisis of care in the contradictions of capitalism, which depend on both social reproduction and unlimited accumulation. See also Allison (2013, 33).

15. See Ishkanian and Szreter (2012) for a critical view of the use of charity and voluntarism to substantially replace state-provisioned welfare in the way the "Big Society" idea was meant to. In particular, they predict that investment in volunteer organizations would have limited effect on broadening access to social capital or reducing inequality and that the ideology of the Big Society is based on both a flawed reading of history and an ignorance of the current state of popular citizen participation in political action. Big Society was contrasted with big governments (i.e., Scandinavian welfare states) and thus already presumed a kind of ethical citizenship that had little need of a paternalistic state. This is also similar to US president George W. Bush's call for "compassionate conservatism" (Woodward 2002, 61). According to the Office of National Statistics (ONS 2021), in 2020 there were about one million fewer non-UK-born residents still living in the UK than in 2019.

16. As of 2020, the social care policy still states that anyone who owns a home or has £23,250 in savings will not be eligible for benefits. If individuals who live alone wish to enter a care home, for example, they would not be eligible for benefits as long as they held the house. In a July 2019 survey that made the headlines in several UK newspapers, it was found that about one-third of people with dementia relying on care had to sell their homes to afford that care.

17. Kavedžija (2019) describes a similar kind of community space in a suburb of Osaka, "located in an old townhouse in the shopping arcade" (21–22), and another in a building that used to be a kindergarten.

18. While the term *ibasho* is used to refer to any number of familiar, homelike spaces where people might come together, there is also a more organized "Ibasho Movement" (http://www.ibasho.org), an intergenerational community-building organization with a focus on social integration, sustainability, and valuing elders (elders' leadership and experience are fundamental). While it began as a way to confront elders' loneliness in Japan, it has now established partnerships in Nepal and the Philippines as well.

19. Unlike Sakura-chan, most formal carer support groups are limited to those who are immediately involved in care. Informal groups tend to be more open to anyone who is indirectly related to care.

20. *Iyashi* is typically translated as "healing" but originates in religious contexts as an experience of spiritual and physical soothing. Since the long economic recession of the 1990s, there has been an "*iyashi* boom," where various products, activities, and services were marketed as producing this comforting healing effect. The term has been taken up in contemporary secular therapeutic contexts, as well as in palliative care. Gabriele Koch (2020) has even described how sex workers use the term *iyashi* to describe the rejuvenating effects their white-collar male clients feel, turning this somewhat stigmatized labor into an ethically valuable resource for sustaining and healing the economic malaise of the nation.

21. At the time of writing (2021), lesbian and gay couples in Japan were still not legally allowed to adopt, and lesbian couples are unable to employ IVF and artificial insemination. Being excluded from having children has made care in later life a point of serious concern for aging LGBTQI+ Japanese people.

CONCLUSION

1. Here I paraphrase Mary Douglas's "charity wounds" (1994, 155).

2. In a review of ten years of research on older adults in Japan (1999–2009), Wilińska and Anbäcken (2013) found that "little is known about the lives . . . of older people or how they are constructed and lived" (446), especially in the form of "stories of aging told by older people themselves" (446). In part this is because, as in this book, the focus has been on carers and care policy. I would add that the stories of unpaid carers have been equally missing from the research, and that this gap must also be addressed, particularly as increasing numbers of older people are involved in providing care.

3. In the final paragraph of Lisa Stevenson's ethnography on care and suicide in Nunavut, she writes that her work allows us to "listen differently to the lives and imaginations of people who matter to us. Acknowledging the way our lives are not our own, the way we are called and call others, opens the space for the ethics of care. . . . We are left to work out new ways to love, new ways to imagine the other" (2014, 174).

References

Allison, Anne. 1991. "Japanese Mothers and Obentōs: The Lunch-Box as Ideological State Apparatus." *Anthropological Quarterly* 64 (4): 195–208.
——. 2013. *Precarious Japan*. Durham, NC: Duke University Press.
Al-Mohammad, Hayder. 2010. "Towards an Ethics of Being-With: Intertwinements of Life in Post-Invasion Basra." *Ethnos* 75 (4): 425–46.
Altez-Albela, Fleurdeliz R. 2011. "The Body and Transcendence in Emmanuel Levinas' Phenomenological Ethics." *KRITIKE: An Online Journal of Philosophy* 5 (1): 36–50.
Amrith, Megha. 2016. *Caring for Strangers: Filipino Medical Workers in Asia*. Copenhagen: NIAS.
Anderson, Pamela Sue. 2003. "Autonomy, Vulnerability and Gender." *Feminist Theory* 4 (2): 149–64.
Aneshensel, Carol S., Amanda L. Botticello, and Noriko Yamamoto-Mitani. 2004. "When Caregiving Ends: The Course of Depressive Symptoms after Bereavement." *Journal of Health and Social Behavior* 45 (4): 422–40.
Aneshensel, Carol S., Leonard I. Pearlin, Joseph T. Mullan, Steven H. Zarit, and Carol J. Whitlatch. 1995. *Profiles in Caregiving: The Unexpected Career*. San Diego, CA: Academic.
Arendt, Hannah. 1998. *The Human Condition*. 2nd ed. Chicago: University of Chicago Press.
Arnold, Lynnette, and Felicity Aulino. 2021. "A Call to Care." *Anthropology News* website, June 23, 2021.
Asahara, Kiyomi, Yumiko Momose, and Sachiyo Murashima. 2002. "Family Caregiving of the Elderly and Long-Term Care Insurance in Rural Japan." *International Journal of Nursing Practice* 8 (3): 167–72.
Asai, Masayuki O., and Velma A. Kameoka. 2005. "The Influence of 'Sekentei' on Family Caregiving and Underutilization of Social Services among Japanese Caregivers." *Social Work* 50 (2): 111–18.
Aulino, Felicity. 2016. "Rituals of Care for the Elderly in Northern Thailand: Merit, Morality, and the Everyday of Long-Term Care." *American Ethnologist* 43 (1): 91–102.
——. 2019. *Rituals of Care: Karmic Politics in an Aging Thailand*. Ithaca, NY: Cornell University Press.
Baars, Jan, Dale Dannefer, Chris Phillipson, and Alan Walker. 2006. *Aging, Globalization and Inequality: The New Critical Gerontology*. Amityville, NY: Baywood.
Badone, Ellen. 2021. "From Cruddiness to Catastrophe: COVID-19 and Long-Term Care in Ontario." *Medical Anthropology* 40 (5): 389–403. https://doi.org/10.1080/01459740.2021.1927023.
Baraitser, Lisa, and William Brook. 2021. "Watchful Waiting: Temporalities of Crisis and Care in the UK National Health Service." In *Vulnerability and the Politics of Care*, edited by Victoria Browne, Jason Danely, and Doerthe Rosenow, 230–53. Abingdon: British Academy of Oxford University Press.

Bass, David M., and Karen Bowman. 1990. "The Transition from Caregiving to Bereavement: The Relationship of Care-Related Strain and Adjustment to Death." *Gerontologist* 30 (1): 35–42.

Bateson, Gregory. 2000. *Steps to an Ecology of Mind: Collected Essays in Anthropology, Psychiatry, Evolution, and Epistemology.* Chicago: University of Chicago Press.

Bateson, Mary Catherine. 1989. *Composing a Life.* New York: Atlantic Monthly.

Becker, Gaylene. 1997. *Disrupted Lives: How People Create Meaning in a Chaotic World.* Berkeley: University of California Press.

Behar, Ruth. 1997. *The Vulnerable Observer: Anthropology That Breaks Your Heart.* Boston: Beacon.

Bein, Steve. 2013. *Compassion and Moral Guidance.* Honolulu: University of Hawai'i Press.

Bellah, Robert N. 1957. *Tokugawa Religion: The Values of Pre-industrial Japan.* New York: Free Press.

——. 1999. "Max Weber and World-Denying Love: A Look at the Historical Sociology of Religion." *Journal of the American Academy of Religion* 67 (2): 277–304.

——. 2003. "The Emperor as Mother Figure: Some Preliminary Notes." In *Imagining Japan: The Japanese Tradition and Its Modern Interpretation.* Berkeley: University of California Press.

Ben-Amos, Ilana Krausman. 2008. *The Culture of Giving: Informal Support and Gift Exchange in Early Modern England.* Cambridge: Cambridge University Press.

Benedict, Ruth. 1946. *The Chrysanthemum and the Sword: Patterns of Japanese Culture.* Boston: Houghton Mifflin.

Benedict, Timothy. 2018. "Practicing Spiritual Care in the Japanese Hospice." *Japanese Journal of Religious Studies* 45 (1): 175–99.

Benthall, Jonathan. 2012. "Charity." In *A Companion to Moral Anthropology*, edited by Didier Fassin, 359–75. Hoboken, NJ: John Wiley & Sons.

Berlant, Lauren. 2004. *Compassion: The Culture and Politics of an Emotion.* New York: Routledge.

Berman, Elise. 2019. *Talking Like Children: Language and the Production of Age in the Marshall Islands.* New York: Oxford University Press.

Berman, Michael. 2018. "Religion Overcoming Religions: Suffering, Secularism, and the Training of Interfaith Chaplains in Japan." *American Ethnologist* 45 (2): 228–40.

Berry, Mary Elizabeth, and Marcia Yonemoto. 2019. Introduction to *What Is a Family? Answers from Early Modern Japan*, edited by Mary Elizabeth Berry and Marcia Yonemoto, 1–20. Oakland: University of California Press.

Bestor, Theodore C. 2012. "Cuisine and Identity in Contemporary Japan." In *Routledge Handbook of Japanese Culture and Society*, edited by Victoria Lyon Bestor and Theodore C. Bestor, with Akiko Yamagata, 273–85. New York: Routledge.

Bethel, Diana Lynn. 1992. "Life in Obasuteyama." In *Japanese Social Organization*, edited by Takie Sugiyama Lebra, 109–34. Honolulu: University of Hawai'i Press.

Biehl, João, and Peter Locke. 2017. "Introduction: Ethnographic Sensorium." In *Unfinished: The Anthropology of Becoming.* Durham, NC: Duke University Press.

Bloch, Ernst. 1986. *The Principle of Hope.* Cambridge, MA: MIT Press.

Bloom, Paul. 2017. *Against Empathy: The Case for Rational Compassion.* New York: Random House.

Boekhorst, Selma te, Anne Margriet Pot, Marja Depla, Dieneke Smit, Jacomine de Lange, and Jan Eefsting. 2008. "Group Living Homes for Older People with Dementia: The Effects on Psychological Distress of Informal Caregivers." *Aging & Mental Health* 12 (6): 761–68.

Boerner, Kathrin, Richard Schulz, and Amy Horowitz. 2004. "Positive Aspects of Caregiving and Adaptation to Bereavement." *Psychology and Aging* 19 (4): 668–75.

Böhme, Gernot. 2016. *The Aesthetics of Atmospheres.* Edited by Jean-Paul Thibaud. Abingdon: Routledge.

Bornstein, Erica. 2009. "The Impulse of Philanthropy." *Cultural Anthropology* 24 (4): 622–51.

———. 2012. *Disquieting Gifts: Humanitarianism in New Delhi.* Stanford, CA: Stanford University Press.

Bornstein, Erica, and Peter Redfield. 2011. *Forces of Compassion: Humanitarianism between Ethics and Politics.* Santa Fe, NM: SAR.

Borovoy, Amy. 2005. *The Too-Good Wife: Alcohol, Codependency, and the Politics of Nurturance in Postwar Japan.* Berkeley: University of California Press.

Bourdieu, Pierre. 1984. *Distinction: A Social Critique of the Judgement of Taste.* Cambridge, MA: Harvard University Press.

Bowditch, Rachel. 2010. *On the Edge of Utopia: Performance and Ritual at Burning Man.* Chicago: University of Chicago Press.

Bowie, Katherine A. 1998. "The Alchemy of Charity: Of Class and Buddhism in Northern Thailand." *American Anthropologist* 100 (2): 469–81. https://doi.org/10.1525/aa.1998.100.2.469.

Bows, Hannah. 2019. "Domestic Homicide of Older People (2010–15): A Comparative Analysis of Intimate-Partner Homicide and Parricide Cases in the UK." *British Journal of Social Work* 49 (5): 1234–53. https://doi.org/10.1093/bjsw/bcy108.

Boyles, Miriam. 2017. "Embodying Transition in Later Life: 'Having a Fall' as an Uncertain Status Passage for Elderly Women in Southeast London." *Medical Anthropology Quarterly* 31 (2): 277–92. https://doi.org/10.1111/maq.12320.

Brijnath, Bianca. 2014. *Unforgotten: Love and the Culture of Dementia Care in India.* New York: Berghahn Books.

Broadbent, Kaye. 2010. "Who Cares about Care Work in Japan?" *Social Science Japan Journal* 13 (1): 137–41.

———. 2014. "'I'd Rather Work in a Supermarket': Privatization of Home Care Work in Japan." *Work, Employment & Society* 28 (5): 702–17.

Brodwin, Paul. 2013. *Everyday Ethics: Voices from the Front Line of Community Psychiatry.* Berkeley: University of California Press.

brown, adrienne maree. 2017. *Emergent Strategy: Shaping Change, Changing Worlds.* Chico, CA: AK.

Browne, Victoria, Jason Danely, and Doerthe Rosenow, eds. 2021. *Vulnerability and the Politics of Care: Transdisciplinary Dialogues.* Abingdon: British Academy Press of Oxford University Press.

Brumann, Christoph. 2013. *Tradition, Democracy, and the Townscape of Kyoto: Claiming a Right to the Past.* London: Routledge.

Bruner, Jerome. 1991. "The Narrative Construction of Reality." *Critical Inquiry* 18 (1): 1–21.

Bruns, Gerald L. 2004. "The Concepts of Art and Poetry in Emmanuel Levinas's Writings." In *The Cambridge Companion to Levinas,* edited by Simon Critchley and Robert Bernasconi, 206–33. Cambridge: Cambridge University Press.

Bubandt, Nils, and Rane Willerslev. 2015. "The Dark Side of Empathy: Mimesis, Deception, and the Magic of Alterity." *Comparative Studies in Society and History* 57 (1): 5–34.

Buch, Elana D. 2013. "Senses of Care: Embodying Inequality and Sustaining Personhood in the Home Care of Older Adults in Chicago." *American Ethnologist* 40 (4): 637–50.

———. 2015a. "Postponing Passage: Doorways, Distinctions, and the Thresholds of Personhood among Older Chicagoans." *Ethos* 43 (1): 40–58.

———. 2015b. "Anthropology of Aging and Care." *Annual Review of Anthropology* 44 (1): 277–93.

———. 2018. *Inequalities of Aging: Paradoxes of Independence in American Home Care.* New York: NYU Press.

Bunting, Madeleine. 2020. *Labours of Love: The Crisis of Care.* London: Granta Books.

Butler, Judith. (2004) 2020. *Precarious Life: The Power of Mourning and Violence.* Reprint ed. London: Verso Books. Kindle.

———. 2021. "Bodies That Still Matter." In *Vulnerability and the Politics of Care,* edited by Victoria Browne, Jason Danely, and Doerthe Rosenow, 32–42. Abingdon: British Academy of Oxford University Press.

Butler, Judith, Zeynep Gambetti, and Leticia Sabsay, eds. 2016. *Vulnerability in Resistance.* Durham, NC: Duke University Press.

Caduff, Carlo. 2020. "What Went Wrong: Corona and the World after the Full Stop." *Medical Anthropology Quarterly* 34 (4): 467–87. https://doi.org/10.1111/maq.12599.

Campbell, John C., and Naoki Ikegami. 2000. "Long-Term Care Insurance Comes to Japan." *Health Affairs* 19 (3): 26–39. https://doi.org/10.1377/hlthaff.19.3.26.

Campbell, John C., Naoki Ikegami, and Mary Jo Gibson. 2010. "Lessons from Public Long-Term Care Insurance in Germany and Japan." *Health Affairs* 29 (1): 87–95.

Campbell, Ruth, and Chie Nishimura. 2009. "Does It Matter Who Cares? A Comparison of Daughters versus Daughters-in-Law in Japanese Elder Care." SSRN Scholarly Paper ID 1408440. Rochester, NY: Social Science Research Network.

Candea, Matei. 2018. *Comparison in Anthropology: The Impossible Method.* Cambridge: Cambridge University Press.

Care Collective. 2020. *The Care Manifesto: The Politics of Interdependence.* London: Verso Books.

Carmichael, Fiona, and Marco G. Ercolani. 2016. "Unpaid Caregiving and Paid Work over Life-Courses: Different Pathways, Diverging Outcomes." *Social Science & Medicine* 156 (May): 1–11.

Caudill, William. 1961. "Around the Clock Patient Care in Japanese Psychiatric Hospitals: The Role of the Tsukisoi." *American Sociological Review* 26 (2): 204–14.

Chan, Emily Ying Yang, Nina Gobat, Jean H. Kim, Elizabeth A. Newnham, Zhe Huang, Heidi Hung, Caroline Dubois, Kevin Kei Ching Hung, Eliza Lai Yi Wong, and Samuel Yeung Shan Wong. 2020. "Informal Home Care Providers: The Forgotten Health-Care Workers during the COVID-19 Pandemic." *Lancet* 395 (10242): 1957–59. https://doi.org/10.1016/S0140-6736(20)31254-X.

Chapin, Bambi L. 2014. *Childhood in a Sri Lankan Village: Shaping Hierarchy and Desire.* New Brunswick, NJ: Rutgers University Press.

Charon, Rita. 2009. "Narrative Medicine as Witness for the Self-Telling Body." *Journal of Applied Communication Research* 37 (2): 118–31.

Chattoo, Sangeeta, and Waqar Ahmad. 2008. "The Moral Economy of Selfhood and Caring: Negotiating Boundaries of Personal Care as Embodied Moral Practice." *Sociology of Health & Illness* 30 (4): 550–64.

Cheng, Fung Kei, and Samson Tse. 2014. "A Bodhisattva-Spirit-Oriented Counselling Framework: Inspired by Vimalakīrti Wisdom." *International Journal of Dharma Studies* 2 (1): 1–52.

Christensen, Loa Teglgaard. 2020. "Crafting Valued Old Lives: Quandaries in Danish Home Care." PhD diss., University of Copenhagen.

Coetzee, Siedine Knobloch, and Hester C. Klopper. 2010. "Compassion Fatigue within Nursing Practice: A Concept Analysis." *Nursing & Health Sciences* 12 (2): 235–43.

Cohen, Lawrence. 1994. "Old Age: Cultural and Critical Perspectives." *Annual Review of Anthropology* 24:137–58.

——. 1998. *No Aging in India: Alzheimer's, the Bad Family, and Other Modern Things.* Berkeley: University of California Press.

——. 2020. "The Culling: Pandemic, Gerocide, Generational Affect." *Medical Anthropology Quarterly* 34 (4): 542–60. https://doi.org/10.1111/maq.12627.

Coleman, Peter, Christine Ivani-Chalian, and Maureen Robinson. 2004. "Religious Attitudes among British Older People: Stability and Change in a 20-Year Longitudinal Study." *Ageing & Society* 24 (2): 167–88.

Coleman, Peter, Fionnuala McKierna, Marie Mills, and Peter Speck. 2002. "Spiritual Belief and Quality of Life: The Experience of Older Bereaved Spouses." *Quality in Ageing and Older Adults* 3 (1): 20–26.

Competition and Markets Authority. 2017. Care Homes Market Study: Summary of Final Report. Published online, November 30. https://www.gov.uk/government/publications/care-homes-market-study-summary-of-final-report/care-homes-market-study-summary-of-final-report.

Connell, Patricia. 2003. "A Phenomenological Study of the Lived Experiences of Adult Caregiving Daughters and their Elderly Mothers." PhD diss., University of Florida.

Cook, Joanna, and Catherine Trundle. 2020. "Unsettled Care: Temporality, Subjectivity, and the Uneasy Ethics of Care." *Anthropology and Humanism* 45 (2): 178–83. https://doi.org/10.1111/anhu.12308.

Corwin, Anna. 2017. "Growing Old with God: An Alternative Vision of Successful Aging among Catholic Nuns." In *Successful Aging as a Contemporary Obsession: Global Perspectives*, edited by Sarah Lamb, Jessica Robbins-Ruszkowski, and Anna Corwin, 98–111. New Brunswick, NJ: Rutgers University Press.

Cottam, Hilary. 2019. *Radical Help: How We Can Remake the Relationships between Us and Revolutionise the Welfare State.* London: Virago.

Crapanzano, Vincent. 2003. *Imaginative Horizons: An Essay in Literary-Philosophical Anthropology.* Chicago: University of Chicago Press.

Creed, Barbara. 1996. "Horror and the Monstrous-Feminine: An Imaginary Abjection." In *The Dread of Difference: Gender and the Horror Film*, edited by Barry Keith Grant, 35–65. Austin: University of Texas Press.

Crespo, María, Ana T. Piccini, and Mónica Bernaldo-de-Quirós. 2013. "When the Care Ends: Emotional State of Spanish Bereaved Caregivers of Persons with Dementia." *Spanish Journal of Psychology* 16 (e97): 1–8.

Critchley, Simon. 2004. Introduction to *Cambridge Companion to Levinas*, edited by Simon Critchley and Robert Bernasconi, 1–32. Cambridge: Cambridge University Press.

Csordas, Thomas J. 2008. "Intersubjectivity and Intercorporeality." *Subjectivity* 22 (1): 110–21.

Cubellis, Lauren. 2020. "Sympathetic Care." *Cultural Anthropology* 35 (1): 14–22.

Cwiertka, Katarzyna J. 2006. *Modern Japanese Cuisine: Food, Power and National Identity.* Reaktion Books.

Dalmiya, Vrinda. 2002. "Why Should a Knower Care?" *Hypatia* 17 (1): 34–52. https://doi.org/10.1111/j.1527-2001.2002.tb00678.x.

——. 2009. "Caring Comparisons: Thoughts on Comparative Care Ethics." *Journal of Chinese Philosophy* 36 (2): 192–209.

D'Andrade, Roy. 2008. *A Study of Personal and Cultural Values: American, Japanese, and Vietnamese*. New York: Palgrave Macmillan.

Danely, Jason. 2014. *Aging and Loss: Mourning and Maturity in Contemporary Japan*. New Brunswick, NJ: Rutgers University Press.

——. 2015. "'He Wanted to Eat Eel': Food and End-of-Life Care." *Kyoto Journal* 83:199–202.

——. 2016. "Affect, Infrastructure, and Vulnerability." *Medicine Anthropology Theory* 3 (1): 198–222.

——. 2017a. "Foolish Vitality." In *Successful Aging as a Contemporary Obsession: Global Perspectives*, edited by Sarah Lamb, Jessica Robbins-Ruszkowski, and Anna Corwin, 154–67. New Brunswick, NJ: Rutgers University Press.

——. 2017b. "Carer Narratives of Fatigue and Endurance in Japan and England." *Subjectivity* 10 (4): 411–26.

——. 2018. "Mourning and Mutuality." In *Companion to the Anthropology of Death*, edited by Antonius C. G. M. Robben, 131–43. Hoboken, NJ: Wiley.

——. 2019. "The Limits of Dwelling and the Unwitnessed Death." *Cultural Anthropology* 34 (2): 213–39.

——. 2021. "'It Rips You to Bits!': Woundedness and Compassion in Carers' Narratives." In *Vulnerability and the Politics of Care: Transdisciplinary Dialogues*, edited by Victoria Browne, Jason Danely, and Doerthe Rosenow, 168–85. Abingdon: British Academy Press of Oxford University Press.

Das, Veena. 1997. "Sufferings, Theodicies, Disciplinary Practices, Appropriations." *International Social Science Journal* 49 (154): 563–72.

——. 2006. *Life and Words: Violence and the Descent into the Ordinary*. Berkeley: University of California Press.

Day, Jennifer R., and Ruth A. Anderson. 2011. "Compassion Fatigue: An Application of the Concept to Informal Caregivers of Family Members with Dementia." *Nursing Research and Practice* 2011 (September). https://doi.org/10.1155/2011/408024.

Day, Jennifer R., Ruth A. Anderson, and Linda L. Davis. 2014. "Compassion Fatigue in Adult Daughter Caregivers of a Parent with Dementia." *Issues in Mental Health Nursing* 35 (10): 796–804.

De Antoni, Andrea. 2011. "Ghosts in Translation: Non-human Actors, Relationality, and Haunted Places in Contemporary Kyoto." *Japanese Review of Cultural Anthropology* 12:27–49.

——. 2018. "Steps to an Ecology of Spirits: Comparing Feelings of More-Than-Human, Immaterial Meshworks?" *NatureCulture* (blog), June 20. https://www.natcult.net/steps-to-an-ecology-of-spirits/.

Decety, Jean, and Margarita Svetlova. 2012. "Putting Together Phylogenetic and Ontogenetic Perspectives on Empathy." *Developmental Cognitive Neuroscience* 2 (1): 1–24.

Derrida, Jacques. 1992. *Given Time: 1. Counterfeit Money*. Translated by Peggy Kamuf. Chicago: University of Chicago Press.

Desjarlais, Robert R. 1992. *Body and Emotion: The Aesthetics of Illness and Healing in the Nepal Himalayas*. Philadelphia: University of Pennsylvania Press.

DeVos, George A. 1973. *Socialization for Achievement: Essays on the Cultural Psychology of the Japanese*. Berkeley: University of California Press.

Dewachi, Omar. 2021. "Revealed in the Wound: Medical Care and the Ecologies of War in Post-occupation Iraq." In *Vulnerability and the Politics of Care*, edited by

Victoria Browne, Jason Danely, and Doerthe Rosenow, 126–40. Oxford: Oxford University Press.

De Waal, Frans. 2011. *The Age of Empathy: Nature's Lessons for a Kinder Society*. London: Souvenir.

De Zulueta, Paquita C. 2015. "Suffering, Compassion and 'Doing Good Medical Ethics.'" *Journal of Medical Ethics* 41 (1): 87–90.

Doi, Takeo. (1971) 2001. *The Anatomy of Self: The Individual versus Society*. New York: Kodansha USA.

Douglas, Mary. 1972. "Deciphering a Meal." *Daedalus* 101 (1): 61–81.

——. 1994. *Risk and Blame: Essays in Cultural Theory*. London: Routledge.

Dowling, Emma. 2021. *The Care Crisis: What Caused It and How Can We End It?* London: Verso.

Driessen, Annelieke. E. 2019. "A Good Life with Dementia: Ethnographic Articulations of Everyday Life and Care in Dutch Nursing Homes." PhD diss., University of Amsterdam. Accessed January 13, 2022. https://hdl.handle.net/11245.1/dd0c2b9b-348d-4de8-9747-84363846fdd0.

Drott, Edward R. 2015a. "Aging in Medieval Japanese Buddhism." *Religion Compass* 9 (1): 1–12.

——. 2015b. "'Care Must Be Taken': Defilement, Disgust and the Aged Body in Early Japan." *Journal of Religion in Japan* 4 (1): 1–31.

Duclos, Vincent, and Tomás Sánchez Criado. 2020. "Care in Trouble: Ecologies of Support from Below and Beyond." *Medical Anthropology Quarterly* 34 (2): 153–73. https://doi.org/10.1111/maq.12540.

Dumas, Raechel. 2018. *The Monstrous-Feminine in Contemporary Japanese Popular Culture*. New York: Palgrave Macmillan.

Elisha, Omri. 2008. "Moral Ambitions of Grace: The Paradox of Compassion and Accountability in Evangelical Faith-Based Activism." *Cultural Anthropology* 23 (1): 154–89.

Elliott, Kathryn Sabrena, and Ruth Campbell. 1993. "Changing Ideas about Family Care for the Elderly in Japan." *Journal of Cross-Cultural Gerontology* 8 (2): 119–35.

Engelke, Matthew. 2014. "Christianity and the Anthropology of Secular Humanism." *Current Anthropology* 55 (10): S292–S301.

Farquhar, Judith, and Qicheng Zhang. 2017. "Nurturing Life in Contemporary Beijing." In *Successful Aging as a Contemporary Obsession: Global Perspectives*, edited by Sarah Lamb, Jessica Robbins-Ruszkowski, and Anna Corwin, 168–84. New Brunswick, NJ: Rutgers University Press.

Fassin, Didier. 2005. "Compassion and Repression: The Moral Economy of Immigration Policies in France." *Cultural Anthropology* 20 (3): 362–87.

Faure, Bernard. 2011. "From Bodhidharma to Daruma: The Hidden Life of a Zen Patriarch." *Japan Review* 23:45–71

Ferrarese, Estelle. 2016. "Vulnerability: A Concept with Which to Undo the World As It Is?" *Critical Horizons* 17 (2): 149–59.

Fetzer, Thiemo. 2020. "Did Austerity Cause Brexit?" *Advantage* (Austerity Special), University of Warwick, Summer: 28–33.

Figley, Charles R. 1995. "Compassion Fatigue: Toward a New Understanding of the Costs of Caring." In *Secondary Traumatic Stress: Self-Care Issues for Clinicians, Researchers, and Educators*, 3–28. Baltimore: Sidran.

Flaherty, Devin. 2018. "Between Living Well and Dying Well: Existential Ambivalence and Keeping Promises Alive." *Death Studies* 42 (5): 314–21.

Foucault, Michel. 1986. "Of Other Spaces." *Diacritics* 16:22–27.

Fowler, Edward. 1996. *San'ya Blues: Laboring Life in Contemporary Tokyo*. Ithaca, NY: Cornell University Press.

Frank, Arthur W. 1995. *The Wounded Storyteller: Body, Illness, and Ethics*. Chicago: University of Chicago Press.

Friedman, Jack R. 2009. "The 'Social Case.'" *Medical Anthropology Quarterly* 23 (4): 375–96.

Fujikawa Kōnosuke. 2013. *Haikai to warau nakare* [Don't laugh when I wander]. Tokyo: Chūohōki.

Fujita, Mariko, and Toshiyuki Sano. 1988. "Children in American and Japanese Day-Care Centers." In *School and Society*, edited by H. T. Trueba and C. Delgado-Gaitan, 73–97. New York: Praeger.

Funahashi, Daena Aki. 2013. "Wrapped in Plastic: Transformation and Alienation in the New Finnish Economy." *Cultural Anthropology* 28 (1): 1–21.

Garon, Sheldon M. 1987. *The State and Labor in Modern Japan*. Berkeley: University of California Press.

Gasparri, Duccio. 2020. "Locals, New-Locals, Non-Locals: (Re)mapping People and Food in Post-disaster Ishinomaki, Japan." PhD diss., Oxford Brookes University.

George, Linda K., Warren A. Kinghorn, Harold G. Koenig, Patricia Gammon, and Dan G. Blazer. 2013. "Why Gerontologists Should Care about Empirical Research on Religion and Health: Transdisciplinary Perspectives." *The Gerontologist* 53 (6): 898–906. https://doi.org/10.1093/geront/gnt002.

Gilbert, Paul. 2017. *Compassion: Concepts, Research and Applications*. London: Routledge.

Gill, Harmandeep Kaur. 2020. "Things Fall Apart: Coming to Terms with Old Age, Solitude, and Death among Elderly Tibetans in Exile." PhD diss., Aarhus University.

Gilson, Erinn. 2014. *The Ethics of Vulnerability: A Feminist Analysis of Social Life and Practice*. New York: Routledge.

Glaser, Alana Lee. 2019. "Rationalized Care." *Medicine Anthropology Theory* 6 (2): 79–92.

Glendinning, Caroline. 2012. "Home Care in England: Markets in the Context of Under-Funding." *Health & Social Care in the Community* 20 (3): 292–99.

Glenn, Evelyn Nakano. 2000. "Creating a Caring Society." *Contemporary Sociology* 29 (1): 84–94.

——. 2012. *Forced to Care*. Cambridge, MA: Harvard University Press.

Goetz, Jennifer L., Dacher Keltner, and Emiliana Simon-Thomas. 2010. "Compassion: An Evolutionary Analysis and Empirical Review." *Psychological Bulletin* 136 (3): 351–74.

Goldfarb, Kathryn E. 2016. "'Coming to Look Alike': Materializing Affinity in Japanese Foster and Adoptive Care." *Social Analysis* 60 (2): 47–64.

Goodfellow, Maya. 2019. *Hostile Environment: How Immigrants Became Scapegoats*. London: Verso Books.

Gould, Hannah, Richard Chenhall, Tamara Kohn, and Carolyn S. Stevens. 2019. "An Interrogation of Sensory Anthropology of and in Japan." *Anthropological Quarterly* 92 (1): 231–58.

Grenier, Amanda, Liz Lloyd, and Chris Phillipson. 2017. "Precarity in Late Life: Rethinking Dementia as a 'Frailed' Old Age." *Sociology of Health & Illness* 39 (2): 318–30.

Grenier, Amanda, and Christopher Phillipson. 2018. "Precarious Aging: Insecurity and Risk in Late Life." *Hastings Center Report* 48 (S3): S15–18.

Grøn, Lone. 2016. "Old Age and Vulnerability between First, Second and Third Person Perspectives: Ethnographic Explorations of Aging in Contemporary Denmark." *Journal of Aging Studies* 39 (December): 21–30.

Grøn, Lone, and Cheryl Mattingly. 2018. "In Search of the Good Old Life: Ontological Breakdown and Responsive Hope at the Margins of Life." *Death Studies* 42 (5): 306–13.

Gubrium, Jaber F. 1993. *Speaking of Life: Horizons of Meaning for Nursing Home Residents*. Piscataway, NJ: Transaction.

Guenther, Lisa. 2013. *Solitary Confinement: Social Death and Its Afterlives*. Minneapolis: University of Minnesota Press.

Guyer, Jane I. 2014. "Durational Ethics: Search, Finding, and Translation of Fauconnet's 'Essay on Responsibility and Liberty.'" *HAU: Journal of Ethnographic Theory* 4 (1): 397–409.

Gygi, Fabio. 2018. "Things That Believe: Talismans, Amulets, Dolls, and How to Get Rid of Them." *Japanese Journal of Religious Studies* 45 (2): 423–52.

Hacking, Ian. 1998. *Mad Travelers: Reflections on the Reality of Transient Mental Illnesses*. Charlottesville: University of Virginia Press.

Halifax, Joan, and Ira Byock. 2008. *Being with Dying: Cultivating Compassion and Fearlessness in the Presence of Death*. Boulder, CO: Shambhala.

Hamada Kenji. 2009. *Kaigo/kanbyō tsukare ni yoru satsujin* [Suicides from care exhaustion]. Shakai kōken kōreisha fukushi JA kyōzai sōken repōto No. 106.

Han, Clara. 2018. "Precarity, Precariousness, and Vulnerability." *Annual Review of Anthropology* 47 (1): 331–43.

Hankins, Joseph Doyle. 2013. "An Ecology of Sensibility: The Politics of Scents and Stigma in Japan." *Anthropological Theory* 13 (1–2): 49–66.

Haraway, Donna J. 2016. *Staying with the Trouble: Making Kin in the Chthulucene*. Durham, NC: Duke University Press.

Hardacre, Helen. 1989. *Shintō and the State, 1868–1988*. Princeton, NJ: Princeton University Press.

Hardt, Michael, and Antonio Negri. 2001. *Empire*. New ed. Cambridge, MA: Harvard University Press.

Hareven, Tamara K. 2002. *The Silk Weavers of Kyoto: Family and Work in a Changing Traditional Industry*. Berkeley: University of California Press.

Harris, Phyllis Braudy, and Susan Orpett Long. 1999. "Husbands and Sons in the United States and Japan: Cultural Expectations and Caregiving Experiences." *Journal of Aging Studies* 13 (3): 241–67.

Harris, Tom, Louis Hodge, and David Phillips. 2019. "English Local Government Funding: Trends and Challenges in 2019 and Beyond." IFS (Institute for Fiscal Studies), November 13. https://ifs.org.uk/publications/14563.

Harrison, Paul. 2008. "Corporeal Remains: Vulnerability, Proximity, and Living on after the End of the World." *Environment and Planning A* 40 (2): 423–45.

Hashimoto, Akiko. 1996. *The Gift of Generations: Japanese and American Perspectives on Aging and the Social Contract*. Cambridge: Cambridge University Press.

Hayashi, Mayumi. 2015. *The Care of Older People: England and Japan, a Comparative Study*. London: Routledge.

———. 2016. "The Japanese Voluntary Sector's Responses to the Increasing Unmet Demand for Home Care from an Ageing Population." *Ageing & Society* 36 (3): 508–33.

Held, Virginia. 2006. *The Ethics of Care: Personal, Political, and Global*. Oxford: Oxford University Press.

Hellström, Ingrid, and Sandra Torres. 2016. "The 'Not Yet' Horizon: Understandings of the Future amongst Couples Living with Dementia." *Dementia* 15 (6): 1562–85.

Hillman, James. 1999. *The Force of Character and the Lasting Life*. New York: Random House.

Hirst, Angela. 2004. "Eating the Other: Levinas's Ethical Encounter." PhD diss., University of Queensland.

Hirst, M. 2002. "Transitions to Informal Care in Great Britain during the 1990s." *Journal of Epidemiology & Community Health* 56 (8): 579–87.

Hochschild, Arlie Russell. 2012. *The Managed Heart: Commercialization of Human Feeling*. Berkeley: University of California Press.

Holmes, Jonathan. 2021. "Brexit and the End of the Transition Period: What Does It Mean for the Health and Care System?" King's Fund, January 11. https://www.kingsfund.org.uk/publications/articles/brexit-end-of-transition-period-impact-health-care-system.

Horton, Richard. 2020. "Offline: COVID-19 Is Not a Pandemic." *Lancet* 396 (10255): 874. https://doi.org/10.1016/S0140-6736(20)32000-6.

Hotta, Satoko. 2007. "Toward Maintaining and Improving the Quality of Long-Term Care: The Current State and Issues Regarding Home Helpers in Japan under the Long-Term Care Insurance System." *Social Science Japan Journal* 10 (2): 265–79.

House of Commons. 2015. Debates, September 7. Cols. 23–27. https://publications.parliament.uk/pa/cm201516/cmhansrd/cm150907/debtext/150907-0001.htm.

Hromadžić, Azra. 2015. "'Where Were They until Now?' Aging, Care and Abandonment in a Bosnian Town." *Etnološka Tribina* 45 (38): 3–57.

Ikels, Charlotte. 2004. *Filial Piety: Practice and Discourse in Contemporary East Asia*. Stanford, CA: Stanford University Press.

Ingold, Tim. 2000. *The Perception of the Environment: Essays on Livelihood, Dwelling and Skill*. London: Routledge.

——. 2011. *Being Alive: Essays on Movement, Knowledge and Description*. London: Routledge.

——. 2016. *Lines*. London: Routledge.

Ingold, Tim, and Jo Lee Vergunst. 2008. *Ways of Walking: Ethnography and Practice on Foot*. Burlington, VT: Ashgate.

Ingram, Paul O. 1971. "Shinran Shōnin and Martin Luther: A Soteriological Comparison." *Journal of the American Academy of Religion* 39 (4): 430–47.

Ishiguro, Nobu. 2021. "Care Management of Assistive Technology in Standardized and Marketized Elderly Care." Paper presented at the Transforming Care Conference (online), June 24, 2021.

Ishkanian, Armine, and Simon Szreter, eds. 2012. *The Big Society Debate*. Cheltenham, UK: Edward Elgar.

Itzhak, Nofit. 2020. "Signifiers for the Divine." *American Ethnologist* 47 (3): 276–88. https://doi.org/10.1111/amet.12910.

Ivy, Marilyn. 1995. *Discourses of the Vanishing: Modernity, Phantasm, Japan*. Chicago: University of Chicago Press.

Iwasaka, Michiko, and Barre Toelken. 1994. *Ghosts and the Japanese Cultural Experience in Japanese Death Legends*. Logan: Utah State University Press.

Jackson, Michael. 2002. *The Politics of Storytelling: Violence, Transgression, and Intersubjectivity*. Copenhagen: Museum Tusculanum.

——. 2013. *The Wherewithal of Life: Ethics, Migration, and the Question of Well-Being*. Berkeley: University of California Press.

Jenike, Brenda Robb. 1997. "Home-Based Health Care for the Elderly in Japan: A Silent System of Gender and Duty." In *Aging Asian Concepts and Experiences Past and Present*, edited by Sepp Linhart and Susan Formanek, 329–46. Vienna: Der Osterreichischen Akademie Der Wissenschaften.

Jensen, Casper Bruun, Miho Ishii, and Philip Swift. 2016. "Attuning to the Webs of *En*: Ontography, Japanese Spirit Worlds, and the 'Tact' of Minakata Kumagusu." *HAU: Journal of Ethnographic Theory* 6 (2): 149–72.

Josephson, Jason Ananda. 2012. *The Invention of Religion in Japan*. Chicago: University of Chicago Press.

Kato Etsuko. 2010. *Kaigo Satsujin* [Care murder]. Tokyo: Kress.

Katz, Stephen, and Toni Calasanti. 2014. "Critical Perspectives on Successful Aging: Does It 'Appeal More Than It Illuminates'?" *Gerontologist* 55 (1): 26–33.

Kaufman, Sharon R. 1994. "The Social Construction of Frailty: An Anthropological Perspective." *Journal of Aging Studies* 8 (1): 45–58.

Kavedžija, Iza. 2019. *Making Meaningful Lives: Tales from an Aging Japan*. Philadelphia: University of Pennsylvania Press.

Kawai Katsuyoshi. 2015. *Rōjin ni tsumetai kuni, Nippon: "Hinkon to shakaitekikoritsu" no genjitsu* [Japan, a country that is uninterested in old people: The reality of "poverty and social isolation"]. Tokyo: Kobunsha.

Keltner, Dacher, Jason Marsh, and Jeremy Adam Smith, eds. 2010. *The Compassionate Instinct: The Science of Human Goodness*. New York: W. W. Norton.

King, Martin Luther, Jr. 1968. "I've Been to the Mountaintop." Address delivered at Bishop Charles Mason Temple, Memphis, Tennessee, April 3, 1968. https://kinginstitute.stanford.edu/king-papers/documents/ive-been-mountaintop-address-delivered-bishop-charles-mason-temple.

Kingston, Andrew, Adelina Comas-Herrera, and Carol Jagger. 2018. "Forecasting the Care Needs of the Older Population in England over the Next 20 Years: Estimates from the Population Ageing and Care Simulation (PACSim) Modelling Study." *Lancet Public Health* 3 (9): e447–55.

Kirmayer, Laurence J. 2000. "Broken Narratives: Clinical Encounters and the Poetics of Illness Experience." In *Narrative and the Cultural Construction of Illness and Healing*, edited by Cheryl Mattingly and Linda Garro, 153–80. Berkeley: University of California Press.

Kitanaka, Junko. 2019. "In the Mind of Dementia: Neurobiological Empathy, Incommensurability, and the Dementia Tojisha Movement in Japan." *Medical Anthropology Quarterly* 34 (1): 119–35.

Kittay, Eva Feder. 1999. *Love's Labor: Essays on Women, Equality, and Dependency*. New York: Routledge.

———. 2019. *Learning from My Daughter: The Value and Care of Disabled Minds*. New York: Oxford University Press.

Kiyokawa Takushi. 2020. "'Kaigo herupā fusoku "kuni no sekinin" genyaku 3 nini ga kiki uttae teiso'" ["Elder care worker shortage 'the nation's responsibility,'" three current workers make an emergency appeal]. *Asahi Shinbun Digital*, February 23, 2020 (online). https://www.asahi.com/articles/ASN2F4D7YN2BULZU001.html.

Kleinman, Arthur. 1988. *The Illness Narratives: Suffering, Healing, and the Human Condition*. New York: Basic Books.

———. 2006. *What Really Matters: Living a Moral Life amidst Uncertainty and Danger*. Oxford: Oxford University Press.

———. 2009. "Caregiving: The Odyssey of Becoming More Human." *Lancet* 373 (9660): 292–93.

———. 2014. "How We Endure." *Lancet* 383 (9912): 119–20.

———. 2019. *The Soul of Care: The Moral Education of a Husband and a Doctor*. London: Viking.

Knight, Kelly Ray. 2015. *Addicted. Pregnant. Poor*. Durham, NC: Duke University Press.

Koch, Gabriele. 2020. *Healing Labor: Japanese Sex Work in the Gendered Economy*. Stanford, CA: Stanford University Press.

Kodate, Naonori, and Virpi Timonen. 2017. "Bringing the Family in through the Back Door: The Stealthy Expansion of Family Care in Asian and European Long-Term Care Policy." *Journal of Cross-Cultural Gerontology* 32 (3): 291–301.

Kojima Shigeru. 2015. "'Shigoto to kaigo no ryōritsu' shien ni mukete" [Toward support for "doing work and care together"]. *DIO* 28 (3): 2.

Kondo, Dorinne K. 1990. *Crafting Selves: Power, Gender, and Discourses of Identity in a Japanese Workplace*. Chicago: University of Chicago Press.

Kornfield, Rachel. 2014. "(Re)working the Program: Gender and Openness in Alcoholics Anonymous." *Ethos* 42 (4): 415–39.

Kristeva, Julia. 1982. *Powers of Horror: An Essay on Abjection*. Translated by Leon S. Roudiez. New York: Columbia University Press.

———. 2010. "Liberty, Equality, Fraternity, and . . . Vulnerability." *WSQ: Women's Studies Quarterly* 38 (1–2): 251–68. https://doi.org/10.1353/wsq.0.0203.

Kuraoka, Yumiko, and Kazuhiro Nakayama. 2014. "A Decision Aid regarding Long-Term Tube Feeding Targeting Substitute Decision Makers for Cognitively Impaired Older Persons in Japan: A Small-Scale Before-and-After Study." *BMC Geriatrics* 14 (1): 16.

Laceulle, Hanne. 2017. "Virtuous Aging and Existential Vulnerability." *Journal of Aging Studies* 43 (December): 1–8.

———. 2018. *Aging and Self-Realization: Cultural Narratives about Later Life*. Bielefeld, Germany: Transcript Verlag.

Lamb, Sarah. 2000. *White Saris and Sweet Mangoes: Aging, Gender, and Body in North India*. Berkeley: University of California Press.

Lamb, Sarah, Jessica Robbins-Ruszkowski, and Anna Corwin, eds. 2017. *Successful Aging as a Contemporary Obsession: Global Perspectives*. New Brunswick, NJ: Rutgers University Press.

Lancy, David F. 2015. *The Anthropology of Childhood: Cherubs, Chattel, Changelings*. 2nd ed. Cambridge: Cambridge University Press.

Larkin, Mary. 2009. "Life after Caring: The Post-caring Experiences of Former Carers." *British Journal of Social Work* 39 (6): 1026–42.

Laugier, Sandra. 2009. "Transcendentalism and the Ordinary." *European Journal of Pragmatism and American Philosophy* 1 (1-1/2).

———. 2016. "Politics of Vulnerability and Responsibility for Ordinary Others." *Critical Horizons* 17 (2): 207–23.

———. 2020. "War on Care." Ethics of Care, May 11, 2020. https://ethicsofcare.org/war-on-care/.

Lebra, Takie Sugiyama. 1976. *Japanese Patterns of Behavior*. Honolulu: University of Hawai'i Press.

———. 1979. "The Dilemma and Strategies of Aging among Contemporary Japanese Women." *Ethnology* 18 (4): 337.

Leibing, Annette. 2014. "Heterotopia and Illness: Older Women and Hypertension in a Brazilian Favela." *Anthropology & Aging* 34 (4): 225–37.

Leibing, Annette, and Lawrence Cohen, eds. 2006. *Thinking about Dementia: Culture, Loss, and the Anthropology of Senility*. New Brunswick, NJ: Rutgers University Press.

Lepselter, Susan. 2016. *The Resonance of Unseen Things: Poetics, Power, Captivity, and UFOs in the American Uncanny*. Ann Arbor: University of Michigan Press.

Levin, David Michael. 1999. *The Philosopher's Gaze: Modernity in the Shadows of Enlightenment*. Berkeley: University of California Press.

Levinas, Emmanuel. (1947) 2001. *Existence and Existents*. Translated by Alphonso Lingis. Pittsburgh: Duquesne University Press.

——. (1961) 2003. *Totality and Infinity: An Essay on Exteriority*. Translated by Alphonso Lingis. Pittsburgh: Duquesne University Press.

——. 1996. "Transcendence and Height." In *Emmanuel Levinas: Basic Philosophical Writings*, edited by Adriaan T. Peperzak, Simon Critchley, and Robert Bernasconi, 11–32. Bloomington: Indiana University Press.

Levitas, Ruth. 1990. "Educated Hope: Ernst Bloch on Abstract and Concrete Utopia." *Utopian Studies* 1 (2): 13–26.

Levy, Robert I. 1975. *Tahitians: Mind and Experience in the Society Islands*. Chicago: University of Chicago Press.

Levy-Malmberg, Rika, Katie Eriksson, and Lisbet Lindholm. 2008. "Caritas—Caring as an Ethical Conduct." *Scandinavian Journal of Caring Sciences* 22 (4): 662–67.

Lewis, C. S. 1960. *The Four Loves*. London: G. Bles.

Linger, Daniel T. 2010. "What Is It Like to Be Someone Else?" *Ethos* 38 (2): 205–29.

Livingston, Julie. 2005. *Debility and Moral Imagination in Botswana: Disability, Chronic Illness, and Aging*. Bloomington: Indiana University Press.

Lo, Herman H. M. 2014. "Applications of Buddhist Compassion Practices among People Suffering from Depression and Anxiety in Confucian Societies in East Asia." *Journal of Religion & Spirituality in Social Work: Social Thought* 33 (1): 19–32.

Lock, Margaret M. 1993. *Encounters with Aging Mythologies of Menopause in Japan and North America*. Berkeley: University of California Press.

Lockyer, Joshua. 2008. "From Earthships to Strawbales: Sustainable Housing in Ecovillages." *Anthropology News* 49 (9): 20.

Long, Susan O. 2008. "Someone's Old, Something's New, Someone's Borrowed, Someone's Blue: Changing Eldercare at the Turn of the Twentieth Century." In *Imagined Families, Lived Families: Culture and Kinship in Contemporary Japan*, edited by John W. Traphagan and Akiko Hashimoto, 137–57. Albany: SUNY Press.

Long, Susan O., Ruth Campbell, and Chic Nishimura. 2009. "Does It Matter Who Cares? A Comparison of Daughters versus Daughters-in-Law in Japanese Elder Care." *Social Science Japan Journal* 12 (1): 1–21.

Long, Susan O., and Phillis B. Harris. 1997. "Caring for Bedridden Elderly: Ideals, Realities, and Social Change in Japan." In *Aging Asian Concepts and Experiences Past and Present*, edited by Sepp Linhart and Susan Formanek, 347–67. Vienna: Der Osterreichischen Akademie Der Wissenschaften.

——. 2000. "Gender and Elder Care: Social Change and the Role of the Caregiver in Japan." *Social Science Japan Journal* 3 (1): 21–36.

Lopez, Steven H. 2013. "Culture Change and Shit Work: Empowering and Overpowering the Frail Elderly in Long-Term Care." *American Behavioral Scientist* 58 (3): 435–52.

Lown, Beth A. 2014. "Seven Guiding Commitments: Making the U.S. Healthcare System More Compassionate." *Journal of Patient Experience* 1 (2): 6–15.

Luhmann, Niklas. 1993. "Ecological Communication: Coping with the Unknown." *Systems Practice* 6 (5): 527–39.

Lynch, Caitrin, and Jason Danely, eds. 2013. *Transitions and Transformations: Cultural Perspectives on Aging and the Life Course*. New York: Berghahn Books.

Mahmood, Saba. 2015. *Religious Difference in a Secular Age*. Princeton, NJ: Princeton University Press.

Mainichi Shinbun Osaka Shakaibu Shuzaihan. 2016. *Kaigo satsujin: Oitsumerareta kazoku no kokuhaku* [Care murders: Confessions from family members pushed to the edge]. Tokyo: Shinchosha.

Makita, Meiko. 2010. "Gender Roles and Social Policy in an Ageing Society: The Case of Japan." *International Journal of Ageing and Later Life* 5 (1): 77–106.

Malkki, Liisa H. 2015. *The Need to Help: The Domestic Arts of International Humanitarianism*. Durham, NC: Duke University Press.

Mangion, Carmen M. 2012. "Faith, Philanthropy and the Aged Poor in Nineteenth-Century England and Wales." *European Review of History / Revue européenne d'histoire* 19 (4): 515–30.

Mannheim, Karl. (1929) 1936. *Ideology and Utopia: An Introduction to the Sociology of Knowledge*. London: Routledge & Kegan Paul.

Manning, Paul, and Ilana Gershon. 2013. "Animating Interaction." *HAU: Journal of Ethnographic Theory* 3 (3): 107–37.

Marett, R. R. 1932. *Faith, Hope and Charity in Primitive Religion*. New York: Macmillan.

Marr, Lisa. 2009. "Can Compassion Fatigue?" *Journal of Palliative Medicine* 12 (8): 739–40.

Martin, Peter, Norene Kelly, Boaz Kahana, Eva Kahana, Bradley J. Willcox, D. Craig Willcox, and Leonard W. Poon. 2015. "Defining Successful Aging: A Tangible or Elusive Concept?" *Gerontologist* 55 (1): 14–25.

Mascaro, Jennifer S., Alana Darcher, Lobsang T. Negi, and Charles L. Raison. 2015. "The Neural Mediators of Kindness-Based Meditation: A Theoretical Model." *Frontiers in Psychology* 6 (February). https://doi.org/10.3389/fpsyg.2015.00109.

Mascaro, Jennifer S., Sean Kelley, Alana Darcher, Lobsang Tenzin Negi, Carol Worthman, Andrew Miller, and Charles Raison. 2018. "Meditation Buffers Medical Student Compassion from the Deleterious Effects of Depression." *Journal of Positive Psychology* 13 (2): 133–42.

Mason, Virginia M., Gail Leslie, Kathleen Clark, Pat Lyons, Erica Walke, Christina Butler, and Martha Griffin. 2014. "Compassion Fatigue, Moral Distress, and Work Engagement in Surgical Intensive Care Unit Trauma Nurses: A Pilot Study." *Dimensions of Critical Care Nursing* 33 (4): 215–25.

Masoro, Edward J. 2001. "'Successful Aging'—Useful or Misleading Concept?" *Gerontologist* 41 (3): 415–18.

Matsunaga, Louella. 2000. "Spirit First, Mind Follows, Body Belongs: Notions of Health, Illness, and Disease in Sukyo Mahikari UK." In *Japanese New Religions in Global Perspective*, edited by P. B. Clarke, 198–239. Richmond, UK: Curzon.

Matsuoka Masahiro. 1995. *Furajairu yowasa kara no shuppatsu* [Fragility: Starting out from our weaknesses]. Tokyo: Chikuma.

Mattingly, Cheryl. 2008. "Stories That Are Ready to Break." In *Health, Illness and Culture: Broken Narratives*, edited by Lars-Christer Hydén and Jens Brockmeier, 73–98. New York: Routledge.

——. 2010. *The Paradox of Hope: Journeys through a Clinical Borderland*. Berkeley: University of California Press.

——. 2014a. "The Moral Perils of a Superstrong Black Mother." *Ethos* 42 (1): 119–38.

——. 2014b. *Moral Laboratories: Family Peril and the Struggle for a Good Life*. Berkeley: University of California Press.

——. 2016. "Accounting for Oneself and Other Ethical Acts: Big Picture Ethics with a Small Picture Focus." *HAU: Journal of Ethnographic Theory* 6 (1): 433–47.

———. 2019. "Critical Phenomenology and Mental Health: Moral Experience under Extraordinary Conditions." *Ethos* 47 (1): 115–25.

Mattingly, Cheryl, and Mary Lawlor. 2001. "The Fragility of Healing." *Ethos* 29 (1): 30–57.

Mayer, Mira. 2001. "Chronic Sorrow in Caregiving Spouses of Patients with Alzheimer's Disease." *Journal of Aging and Identity* 6 (1): 49–60.

Mazus, Keren. 2013. "The Familial Dyad between Aged Patients and Filipina Caregivers in Israel: Eldercare, Bodily-Based Practices, and the Jewish Family." *Anthropology & Aging* 34 (3): 126–34.

McGlotten, Shaka. 2012. "Ordinary Intersections: Speculations on Difference, Justice, and Utopia in Black Queer Life." *Transforming Anthropology* 20 (1): 45–66.

McLaughlin, Levi. 2011. "In the Wake of the Tsunami: Religious Responses to the Great East Japan Earthquake." *CrossCurrents* 61 (3): 290–97.

———. 2013. "What Have Religious Groups Done after 3.11? Part 2: From Religious Mobilization to 'Spiritual Care.'" *Religion Compass* 7 (8): 309–25.

McLean, Athena. 2007. *The Person in Dementia: A Study in Nursing Home Care in the US*. Toronto: University of Toronto Press.

McVeigh, Brian. 1991. "Gratitude, Obedience, and Humility of the Heart: The Morality of Dependency in a New Religion." *Journal of Social Science* 30 (2): 107–25.

Mead, George Herbert. 1934. *Mind, Self, and Society*. Chicago: University of Chicago Press.

Meinert, Lotte, and Susan Reynolds Whyte. 2017. "Social Sensations of Symptoms: Embodied Socialities of HIV and Trauma in Uganda." *Anthropology in Action* 24 (1): 20–26.

Melvin, Christina S. 2015. "Historical Review in Understanding Burnout, Professional Compassion Fatigue, and Secondary Traumatic Stress Disorder from a Hospice and Palliative Nursing Perspective." *Journal of Hospice & Palliative Nursing* 17 (1): 66–72.

METI (Japanese Ministry of Economy, Trade and Industry). 2018. *Shōrai no kaigo jukyū ni tai suru kōreisha kea shisutemu ni kansuru kenkyūkai hōkokusho* [Report of the Research Group on the Senior Care System for the Future of Care Demand]. April 9. https://www.meti.go.jp/press/2018/04/20180409004/20180409004-2.pdf.

MHLW (Japanese Ministry of Health, Labour and Welfare). 2016. *Kaigo kyūfu-hi-to jittai chōsa no gaikyō* [Overview of elderly care benefits].

———. 2018a. *Heisei 30 nen kokumin seikatsu kiban chōsa (heisei 28 nen) no kekka kara Gurafu de miru setai no jōkyō* [Graphical review of Japanese household from comprehensive survey of living conditions].

———. 2018b. "Heisei 30 nendo 'Koreisha Gyakutai no Boshi, Koreisha no yogosha ni taisuru shien nado ni kansuru horitsu' ni motodsuku taiou joukyo nado ni kansuru chosa" [Survey about the status of responses based on the 2018 "Laws concerning support for the prevention of senior citizen abuse and support of guardians of senior citizens"]. Accessed September 4, 2020. https://www.mhlw.go.jp/stf/houdou/0000196989_00002.html.

———. 2019. "Kokumin seikatsu kiban chōsa" [Comprehensive survey of living conditions]. Accessed July 30, 2021. https://www.mhlw.go.jp/toukei/saikin/hw/k-tyosa/k-tyosa19/.

Miller, Daniel. 2015. "The Tragic Denouement of English Sociality." *Cultural Anthropology* 30 (2): 336–57.

———. 2017. *The Comfort of People*. Cambridge: Polity.

Ministry of Internal Affairs and Communications. 2021. Rōjin Fukushihō [Act on the welfare of older people]. Accessed June 30, 2021. https://elaws.e-gov.go.jp/document?lawid=338AC0000000133.

Mintz, Sidney W. 1985. *Sweetness and Power: The Place of Sugar in Modern History*. London: Viking.

Mintz, Sidney W., and Christine M. Du Bois. 2002. "The Anthropology of Food and Eating." *Annual Review of Anthropology* 31 (1): 99–119.

Mittermaier, Amira. 2014. "Beyond Compassion: Islamic Voluntarism in Egypt." *American Ethnologist* 41 (3): 518–31.

———. 2019. *Giving to God: Islamic Charity in Revolutionary Times*. Berkeley: University of California Press.

Miura, Takahiro. 2017. "Threshold and Narrative: An Essay on Narrative Community." *Human Relations Studies Research* 15:83–93.

Mol, Annemarie. 2008. *The Logic of Care: Health and the Problem of Patient Choice*. London: Routledge.

Mol, Annemarie, Ingunn Moser, and Jeannette Pols. 2010. *Care: Putting Practice into Theory*. Bielefeld, Germany: Transcript Verlag.

Morisaki Azuma, dir. 2013. *Pecoros no haha ni ai ni iku* [Pecoross's mother and her days]. Surouinn.

Mullan, Joseph T. 1992. "The Bereaved Caregiver: A Prospective Study of Changes in Well-Being." *Gerontologist* 32 (5): 673–83.

Murakami Yasuhiko. 2012. *Revinasu: Kowaremono toshite no ningen* [Levinas: People as fragile beings]. Tokyo: Kawade Books.

Murphy, Michelle. 2015. "Unsettling Care: Troubling Transnational Itineraries of Care in Feminist Health Practices." *Social Studies of Science* 45 (5): 717–37. https://doi.org/10.1177/0306312715589136.

Myers, Neely Laurenzo. 2015. *Recovery's Edge: An Ethnography of Mental Health Care and Moral Agency*. Nashville, TN: Vanderbilt University Press.

Nagel, Thomas. 1986. *The View from Nowhere*. Oxford: Oxford University Press.

Nakamura Hajime. (1954) 2010. *Jihi* [Compassion]. Tokyo: Kodansha.

Nakamura, Karen. 2013. *A Disability of the Soul*. Ithaca, NY: Cornell University Press.

Nakamura, Tamah. 2012. "Fukuoka Butoh: Self-Reflective Identities." *Japan Studies Association Journal* 10:1–16.

Nakanishi, Miharu, and K. Hattori. 2014. "Percutaneous Endoscopic Gastrostomy (PEG) Tubes Are Placed in Elderly Adults in Japan with Advanced Dementia Regardless of Expectation of Improvement in Quality of Life." *Journal of Nutrition, Health & Aging* 18 (5): 503–9.

Nakano, Lynne. 2005. *Community Volunteers in Japan: Everyday Stories of Social Change*. London: Routledge Curzon.

Neilson, Brett. 2003. "Globalization and the Biopolitics of Aging." *CR: The New Centennial Review* 3 (2): 161–86.

———. 2006. "Anti-ageing Cultures, Biopolitics and Globalisation." *Cultural Studies Review* 12 (2): 149–64.

Ngai, Sianne. 2005. *Ugly Feelings*. Cambridge, MA: Harvard University Press.

NHK (Nippon Hōsō Kyoku) Special Shuzaihan. 2017. *Haha oya ni, shinde hoshii: Kaigo satsujin tōjishatachi no kokuhaku* [Mother said, I want to die: Confessions from people involved in care murders]. Tokyo: Shinchosha.

Nippon Keizai Shinbun. 2018. "Kōreisha setai ha 40 nen ni 4 warikoe, Kōseisho suikei, dokui mo kyūsō" [Elderly households to exceed 40% by year 40, Ministry of Health, Labor and Welfare estimates, solo-dwellers also increasing rapidly].

January 12. Accessed September 3, 2020. https://www.nikkei.com/article/ DGXMZO25620520S8A110C1EA4000/.

Nishi, Akihiro, Nanako Tamiya, Masayo Kashiwagi, Hideto Takahashi, Mikiya Sato, and Ichiro Kawachi. 2010. "Mothers and Daughters-in-Law: A Prospective Study of Informal Care-Giving Arrangements and Survival in Japan." *BMC Geriatrics* 10 (1): 61.

Nixon, Rob. 2011. *Slow Violence and the Environmentalism of the Poor*. Cambridge, MA: Harvard University Press.

Noddings, Nel. 1984. *Caring: A Feminine Approach to Ethics and Moral Education*. Berkeley: University of California Press.

Nortvedt, Per. 2003. "Subjectivity and Vulnerability: Reflections on the Foundation of Ethical Sensibility." *Nursing Philosophy* 4 (3): 222–30.

Nozawa, Shunsuke. 2015. "Phatic Traces: Sociality in Contemporary Japan." *Anthropological Quarterly* 88 (2): 373–400.

Nussbaum, Martha C. 1986. *The Fragility of Goodness: Luck and Ethics in Greek Tragedy and Philosophy*. Cambridge: Cambridge University Press.

——. 1996. "Compassion: The Basic Social Emotion." *Social Philosophy and Policy* 13 (1): 27–58.

——. 2003. "Compassion and Terror." *Daedalus* 132 (1): 10–26.

Ochiai, Emiko. 1997. *The Japanese Family System in Transition*. Tokyo: LTCB International Library Foundation.

——. 2009. "Care Diamonds and Welfare Regimes in East and South-East Asian Societies: Bridging Family and Welfare Sociology." *International Journal of Japanese Sociology* 18 (1): 60–78.

Ochs, Elinor, and Lisa Capps. 1996. "Narrating the Self." *Annual Review of Anthropology* 2:19–43.

——. 2002. *Living Narrative: Creating Lives in Everyday Storytelling*. Cambridge, MA: Harvard University Press.

O'Dwyer, Siobhan T., Wendy Moyle, Tara Taylor, Jennifer Creese, and Melanie J. Zimmer-Gembeck. 2016. "Homicidal Ideation in Family Carers of People with Dementia." *Aging & Mental Health* 20 (11): 1174–81.

O'Dwyer, Siobhan T., Wendy Moyle, Melanie Zimmer-Gembeck, and Diego De Leo. 2016. "Suicidal Ideation in Family Carers of People with Dementia." *Aging & Mental Health* 20 (2): 222–30.

Ohnuki-Tierney, Emiko. 1990. "The Ambivalent Self of the Contemporary Japanese." *Cultural Anthropology* 5 (2): 196–216.

Okamoto Taro. (1993) 2002. *Jibun no naka ni doku wo mote* [Bring poison to yourself]. Tokyo: Seishun Bunko.

Okano Yuichi. 2012. *Pekorosu no haha ni aini iku* [Going to meet Pecoross's mother]. Fukuoka: Nishinippon Shinbunsha.

ONS (Office of National Statistics). 2021. "Employment in the UK: March 2021." March 23, 2021. Accessed January 20, 2022. https://www.ons.gov.uk/ employmentandlabourmarket/peopleinwork/employmentandemployeetypes/ bulletins/employmentintheuk/march2021.

Ozawa, Yoshiko. 2014. "Family Strength Caring for the Elderly with Dementia: Engagements and Relationship Changes of Family Members." *Yamagata Hoken Iryō Kenkyū* 17:1–8.

Ozawa-de Silva, Chikako. 2006. *Psychotherapy and Religion in Japan: The Japanese Introspection Practice of Naikan*. London: Routledge.

Parish, Steven M. 2008. *Subjectivity and Suffering in American Culture: Possible Selves*. New York: Palgrave Macmillan.

——. 2014. "Between Persons: How Concepts of the Person Make Moral Experience Possible." *Ethos* 42 (1): 31–50.

Parreñas, Rhacel Salazar. 2015. *Servants of Globalization: Migration and Domestic Work*. 2nd ed. Stanford, CA: Stanford University Press.

Phillips, Daniel, John Curtice, Miranda Phillips, Jane Perry, eds. 2018. *British Social Attitudes 35*. London: National Centre for Social Research.

Phoenix, Cassandra, Brett Smith, and Andrew C. Sparkes. 2010. "Narrative Analysis in Aging Studies: A Typology for Consideration." *Journal of Aging Studies* 24 (1): 1–11. https://doi.org/10.1016/j.jaging.2008.06.003.

Pickard, Susan. 2014. "Frail Bodies: Geriatric Medicine and the Constitution of the Fourth Age." *Sociology of Health & Illness* 36(4): 549–63.

——. 2018. "Health, Illness and Frailty in Old Age: A Phenomenological Exploration." *Journal of Aging Studies* 47 (December): 24–31.

Pickard, Susan, Victoria Cluley, Jason Danely, Hanne Laceulle, Jorge Leon-Salas, Bram Vanhoutte, and Roman Romero-Ortuno. 2019. "New Horizons in Frailty: The Contingent, the Existential and the Clinical." *Age and Ageing* 48 (4): 466–71.

Pinchevski, Amit. 2016. "The Face as Medium." In *Images, Ethics, Technology*, edited by Sharrona Pearly, 193–201. New York: Routledge.

——. 2017. "Echology: The Virtues of Communication under Constraints." Presented at Enhancing Life! A Public Interdisciplinary Conference, Chicago, August 2017.

Pinquart, Martin, and Silvia Sörensen. 2003. "Associations of Stressors and Uplifts of Caregiving with Caregiver Burden and Depressive Mood: A Meta-analysis." *Journals of Gerontology: Series B* 58 (2): P112–28.

Plath, David W. 1964. "Where the Family of God Is the Family: The Role of the Dead in Japanese Households." *American Anthropologist* 66 (2): 300–317.

——. 1975. "The Last Confucian Sandwich: Becoming Middle Aged." *Journal of Asian and African Studies* 10 (1–2): 51–63.

Porter, Elisabeth. 2006. "Can Politics Practice Compassion?" *Hypatia* 21 (4): 97–123.

Povinelli, Elizabeth A. 2011. *Economies of Abandonment: Social Belonging and Endurance in Late Liberalism*. Durham, NC: Duke University Press.

Puett, Michael, and Christine Gross-Loh. 2016. *The Path: A New Way to Think About Everything*. London: Penguin UK.

Puig de la Bellacasa, María. 2012. "'Nothing Comes without Its World': Thinking with Care." *Sociological Review* 60 (2): 197–216.

——. 2017. *Matters of Care*. Minneapolis: University of Minnesota Press.

Putnam, Hilary. 2004. "Levinas and Judaism." In *The Cambridge Companion to Levinas*, edited by Simon Critchley and Robert Bernasconi, 33–62. Cambridge: Cambridge University Press.

Quinter, David. 2008. "Emulation and Erasure: Eison, Ninshō, and the Gyōki Cult." *Eastern Buddhist* 39 (1): 29–60.

Raikhel, Eugene. 2015. "From the Brain Disease Model to Ecologies of Addiction." In *Re-visioning Psychiatry: Cultural Phenomenology, Critical Neuroscience, and Global Mental Health*, edited by Laurence J. Kirmayer, Robert Lemelson, and Constance C. Cummings, 375–99. Cambridge: Cambridge University Press.

Rapport, Nigel. 2015. "Anthropology through Levinas: Knowing the Uniqueness of Ego and the Mystery of Otherness." *Current Anthropology* 56 (2): 256–76.

——. 2019. "Anthropology through Levinas (Further Reflections): On Humanity, Being, Culture, Violation, Sociality, and Morality." *Current Anthropology* 60 (1): 70–90.

Raymo, James M., Jersey Liang, Hidehiro Sugisawa, Erika Kobayashi, and Yoko Sugihara. 2004. "Work at Older Ages in Japan: Variation by Gender and Employment Status." *Journals of Gerontology: Series B* 59 (3): S154–63.

Read, Rosie. 2019. "Caring Values and the Value of Care: Women, Maternalism and Caring Work in the Czech Republic." *Contemporary European History* 28 (4): 500–511.

Reader, Ian. 2012. "Secularisation, R.I.P.? Nonsense! The 'Rush Hour Away from the Gods' and the Decline of Religion in Contemporary Japan." *Journal of Religion in Japan* 30.

Reader, Ian, and George J. Tanabe. 1998. *Practically Religious Worldly Benefits and the Common Religion of Japan.* Honolulu: University of Hawai'i Press.

Reynolds, Joel Michael. 2018. "Killing in the Name of Care." *Levinas Studies* 12 (1): 141–64.

Ricoeur, Paul. 1976. "Ideology and Utopia as Cultural Imagination." *Philosophic Exchange* 7 (1): 17–28.

——. 2007. "Autonomy and Vulnerability." In *Reflections on the Just*, translated by D. Pellauer, 72–90. Chicago: University of Chicago Press.

Robbins, Joel. 2016. "What Is the Matter with Transcendence? On the Place of Religion in the New Anthropology of Ethics." *Journal of the Royal Anthropological Institute* 22 (4): 767–81.

Roberson, James. 2005. "Fight!! Ippatsu!! 'Genki' Energy Drinks and the Marketing of Masculine Ideology in Japan." *Men and Masculinities* 7 (4): 365–84.

Robertson, Jamie. 2018. "Government Accused of Fueling Loneliness Crisis as Day Centres Disappear." ITV News, September 25. https://www.itv.com/news/2018-09-25/government-accused-of-fuelling-loneliness-crisis-as-day-centres-disappear.

Rockwood, Kenneth, and Arnold Mitnitski. 2007. "Frailty in Relation to the Accumulation of Deficits." *Journals of Gerontology: Series A* 62 (7): 722–27.

Rodriquez, Jason. 2014. *Labors of Love: Nursing Homes and the Structures of Care Work.* New York: NYU Press.

Rosa, Hartmut. 2019. *Resonance: A Sociology of Our Relationship to the World.* Cambridge: Polity.

Rosaldo, Renato. 1989. *Culture and Truth: The Remaking of Social Analysis.* Boston: Beacon.

Ross, Fiona. 2010. *Raw Life, New Hope: Decency, Housing and Everyday Life in a Post-Apartheid Community.* Claremont, South Africa: UCT.

Roth, David L., Martinique Perkins, Virginia G. Wadley, Ella M. Temple, and William E. Haley. 2009. "Family Caregiving and Emotional Strain: Associations with Quality of Life in a Large National Sample of Middle-Aged and Older Adults." *Quality of Life Research* 18 (6): 679–88.

Rubinstein, Robert L., and Kate de Medeiros. 2015. "'Successful Aging,' Gerontological Theory and Neoliberalism: A Qualitative Critique." *Gerontologist* 55 (1): 34–42.

Rubio, Doris McGartland, Marla Berg-Weger, Susan S. Tebb, and Lisa A. Parnell. 2001. "Comparing the Well-Being of Post-Caregivers and Noncaregivers." *American Journal of Alzheimer's Disease & Other Dementias* 16 (2): 97–101.

Ryan, Carrie. 2018. "Risk and Care in Aging United States." PhD diss., University of Oxford.

Sahlins, Marshall. 2011. "What Kinship Is (Part One)." *Journal of the Royal Anthropological Institute* 17 (1): 2–19.

Saito, Yuriko. 2010. *Everyday Aesthetics.* Oxford: Oxford University Press.

Sakuma, Ryū. 1994. "Gyōgi (688–749)." In *Shapers of Japanese Buddhism*, 3–13. Tokyo: Kōsei.

Sato Naoki. 2015. *Hanzai no sekengaku: Naze nihon de ha ryakudatsu mo bōryoku mo okinai no ka* [The public study of crime: Why doesn't looting and violence occur in Japan?]. Tokyo: Sekiyūsha.

Schattschneider, Ellen. 2003. *Immortal Wishes: Labor and Transcendence on a Japanese Sacred Mountain*. Durham, NC: Duke University Press.

——. 2004. "Family Resemblances: Memorial Images and the Face of Kinship." *Japanese Journal of Religious Studies* 31 (1): 141–62.

Scherz, China. 2014. *Having People, Having Heart: Charity, Sustainable Development, and Problems of Dependence in Central Uganda*. Chicago: University of Chicago Press.

Schloßberger, Matthias. 2019. "Beyond Empathy: Compassion and the Reality of Others." *Topoi* 39 (4): 771–78.

Schulz, Richard, and Scott R. Beach. 1999. "Caregiving as a Risk Factor for Mortality: The Caregiver Health Effects Study." *JAMA* 282 (23): 2215–19.

Schulz, Richard, Kathrin Boerner, Katherine Shear, Song Zhang, and Laura N. Gitlin. 2006. "Predictors of Complicated Grief among Dementia Caregivers: A Prospective Study of Bereavement." *American Journal of Geriatric Psychiatry* 14 (8): 650–58.

Schulz, Richard, Randy S. Hebert, Mary Amanda Dew, Stephanie L. Brown, Michael F. Scheier, Scott R. Beach, Sara J. Czaja, Lynn M. Martire, David Coon, and Kenneth M. Langa. 2007. "Patient Suffering and Caregiver Compassion: New Opportunities for Research, Practice, and Policy." *Gerontologist* 47 (1): 4–13.

Schulz, Richard, and Paula R. Sherwood. 2008. "Physical and Mental Health Effects of Family Caregiving." *American Journal of Nursing* 108 (9 Suppl): 23–27.

Schutz, Alfred. 1970. "Transcendences and Multiple Realities." In *On Phenomenology and Social Relations*, edited by Helmut R. Wager, 245–62. Chicago: University of Chicago Press.

Seaman, Aaron T., Jessica C. Robbins, and Elana D. Buch. 2019. "Beyond the Evaluative Lens: Contextual Unpredictabilities of Care." *Journal of Aging Studies*, July, 100799.

Shea, Jeanne, Katrina Moore, and Hong Zhang, eds. 2020. *Beyond Filial Piety: Rethinking Aging and Caregiving in Contemporary East Asian Societies*. Life Course, Culture & Aging, Global Transformations. Oxford: Berghahn Books.

Shield, Renée Rose. 1988. *Uneasy Endings: Daily Life in an American Nursing Home*. Ithaca, NY: Cornell University Press.

Shildrick, Margrit. 2015. "'Why Should Our Bodies End at the Skin?': Embodiment, Boundaries, and Somatechnics." *Hypatia* 30 (1): 13–29.

——. "War on Care." Ethics of Care, May 11. Accessed September 13, 2020. https://ethicsofcare.org/war-on-care/.

Shimada Hiromi. 2016. *Mou oya wo suteru shika nai. kaigo/soushiki/isan ha, iranai* [All we can do is abandon our parents: We don't need elder care, funerals, or inheritance]. Tokyo: Gentosha.

Shimizu, Hidetada. 2000. "Japanese Cultural Psychology and Empathic Understanding: Implications for Academic and Cultural Psychology." *Ethos* 28 (2): 224–47.

Shirasaki Asako. 2009. *Kaigo rōdō wo ikiru: Kōmuin herupā kara haken herupā no 22 nen* [Living as an elder-care worker: 22 years from a civil servant aide to an on-call aide]. Tokyo: Gendai Shokan.

Shūkan Asahi. 2018. "Kōreisha hōmu no yūsei wo miyaburu!" [See through the superiority of elderly care homes!]. August 17–24. Pp. 18–27.

Shweder, Richard A. 1996. "1996–97 AN Theme: The Known, Unknown and Unknowable in Anthropology; The View from Manywheres." *Anthropology News* 37 (9): 1–4.

Singer, Tania, and Olga M. Klimecki. 2014. "Empathy and Compassion." *Current Biology* 24 (18): R875–78.

Skills for Care. 2020. "The State of the Adult Social Care Sector and Workforce in England, October 2020." Accessed July 29, 2021. https://www.skillsforcare.org.uk/adult-social-care-workforce-data/Workforce-intelligence/documents/State-of-the-adult-social-care-sector/The-state-of-the-adult-social-care-sector-and-workforce-2020.pdf.

Smith, Robert John. 1974. *Ancestor Worship in Contemporary Japan*. Stanford, CA: Stanford University Press.

Snow, Nancy. 1991. "Compassion." *American Philosophical Quarterly* 28:195–205.

Sokolovsky, Jay, ed. 2020. *The Cultural Context of Aging: Worldwide Perspectives*. Santa Barbara, CA: ABC-CLIO.

Sōmucho Tōkeikyoku. 2017. *Heisei 28 nendo shakai seikatsu kihonchousa, seikatsu jikan ni kansuru kekka yōyaku* [2016 social life general survey, summary of results about lifestyle time]. Accessed January 20, 2022. http://www.stat.go.jp/data/shakai/2016/index.htm.

Sontag, Susan. 2003. *Regarding the Pain of Others*. New York: Farrar, Straus and Giroux.

Soto-Rubio, Ana, and Shane Sinclair. 2018. "In Defense of Sympathy, in Consideration of Empathy, and in Praise of Compassion: A History of the Present." *Journal of Pain and Symptom Management* 55 (5): 1428–34.

Spikins, Penny. 2015. *How Compassion Made Us Human: The Evolutionary Origins of Tenderness, Trust and Morality*. Barnsley, UK: Pen & Sword Books.

——. 2017. "Prehistoric Origins: The Compassion of Far Distant Strangers." In *Compassion: Concepts, Research and Applications*, edited by Paul Gilbert, 16–30. London: Routledge.

Spiro, Melford. 2004. "Utopia and Its Discontents: The Kibbutz and Its Historical Vicissitudes." *American Anthropologist* 106 (3): 556–68.

Stacey, Clare L. 2011. *The Caring Self: The Work Experiences of Home Care Aides*. Ithaca, NY: Cornell University Press.

Stafford, Philip B. 2003. *Gray Areas: Ethnographic Encounters with Nursing Home Culture*. Santa Fe, NM: School of American Research.

——. 2018. *The Global Age-Friendly Community Movement: A Critical Appraisal*. New York: Berghahn Books.

Stamm, Beth H. 2002. "Measuring Compassion Satisfaction as Well as Fatigue: Developmental History of the Compassion Satisfaction and Fatigue Test." In *Treating Compassion Fatigue*, edited by Charles R. Figley, 107–19. New York: Routledge.

Stevenson, Lisa. 2014. *Life beside Itself: Imagining Care in the Canadian Arctic*. Berkeley: University of California Press.

Strathern, Marilyn. 2005. *Kinship, Law and the Unexpected: Relatives Are Always a Surprise*. Cambridge: Cambridge University Press.

Susen, Simon. 2020. "The Resonance of Resonance: Critical Theory as a Sociology of World-Relations?" *International Journal of Politics, Culture, and Society* 33 (3): 309–44. https://doi.org/10.1007/s10767-019-9313-6.

Sutton, David E. 2001. *Remembrance of Repasts: An Anthropology of Food and Memory*. Oxford: Berg.

——. 2010. "Food and the Senses." *Annual Review of Anthropology* 39 (1): 209–23.

Swift, Philip. 2012. "Touching Conversion: Tangible Transformations in a Japanese New Religion." *HAU: Journal of Ethnographic Theory* 2 (1): 269–88.

Switek, Beata. 2016. *Reluctant Intimacies: Japanese Eldercare in Indonesian Hands*. New York: Berghahn Books.

Symonds, Michael, and Jason Pudsey. 2006. "The Forms of Brotherly Love in Max Weber's Sociology of Religion." *Sociological Theory* 24 (2): 133–49.

Tahhan, Diana Adis. 2010. "Blurring the Boundaries between Bodies: Skinship and Bodily Intimacy in Japan." *Japanese Studies* 30 (2): 215–30.

———. 2014. *The Japanese Family: Touch, Intimacy and Feeling.* London: Routledge.

Takeuchi Seiichi. 2009. *"Kanashimi" no tetsugaku: Nihonseishinshi no minamoto wo saguru* [The philosophy of "grief": Searching for the source of Japanese spirit]. Tokyo: NHK.

Tamanoi, Mariko Asano. 2010. "Is 'Japan' Still a Big Family? Nationality and Citizenship at the Edge of the Japanese Archipelago." In *Imagined Families, Lived Families: Culture and Kinship in Contemporary Japan*, edited by Akiko Hashimoto and John W. Traphagan, 111–36. Albany: SUNY Press.

Tamiya, Nanako, Haruko Noguchi, Akihiro Nishi, Michael R. Reich, Naoki Ikegami, Hideki Hashimoto, Kenji Shibuya, Ichiro Kawachi, and John Creighton Campbell. 2011. "Population Ageing and Wellbeing: Lessons from Japan's Long-Term Care Insurance Policy." *Lancet* 378 (9797): 1183–92.

Tanizaki, Jun'ichirō. 1977. *In Praise of Shadows.* Translated by Thomas J. Harper. New Haven, CT: Leete's Island Books.

Taylor, Janelle S. 2008. "On Recognition, Caring, and Dementia." *Medical Anthropology Quarterly* 22 (4): 313–35.

———. 2020. "Tender Idea." In "Post-Covid Fantasies," edited by Catherine Besteman, Heath Cabot, and Barak Kalir, *American Ethnologist* website, August 25. https://americanethnologist.org/features/pandemic-diaries/post-covid-fantasies/tender-idea.

Thane, Pat. 2000. *Old Age in English History: Past Experiences, Present Issues.* Oxford: Oxford University Press.

Thang, Leng Leng. 2001. *Generations in Touch: Linking the Old and Young in a Tokyo Neighborhood.* Ithaca, NY: Cornell University Press.

Thelen, Tatjana, and Cati Coe. 2017. "Political Belonging through Elderly Care: Temporalities, Representations and Mutuality." *Anthropological Theory* 19 (2): 279–99.

Thomas, Günter. 2017. "World and Counter-worlds." Enhancing Life Project. March 14. http://enhancinglife.uchicago.edu/blog/world-and-counter-worlds.

Throop, C. Jason. 2010a. "Latitudes of Loss: On the Vicissitudes of Empathy." *American Ethnologist* 37 (4): 771–82.

———. 2010b. *Suffering and Sentiment: Exploring the Vicissitudes of Experience and Pain in Yap.* Berkeley: University of California Press.

———. 2012a. "Moral Sentiments." In *A Companion to Moral Anthropology*, edited by Didier Fassin, 150–68. Hoboken, NJ: John Wiley & Sons.

———. 2012b. "On the Varieties of Empathic Experience: Tactility, Mental Opacity, and Pain in Yap." *Medical Anthropology Quarterly* 26 (3): 408–30.

———. 2014. "Moral Moods." *Ethos* 42 (1): 65–83.

———. 2017. "Despairing Moods: Worldly Attunements and Permeable Personhood in Yap." *Ethos* 45 (2): 199–215.

Ticktin, Miriam Iris. 2011. *Casualties of Care: Immigration and the Politics of Humanitarianism in France.* Berkeley: University of California Press.

Tokyo Shoko Research. 2018. "2018 Jōhanki 'Rōjin Fukushi Kaigo Jigyō' no Tosan Jōkyō" [First half 2018 "senior citizen welfare / elderly care business" bankruptcy status]. July 9. Accessed July 30, 2021. https://www.tsr-net.co.jp/news/analysis/20180709_06.html.

Tomasello, Michael. 2009. *Why We Cooperate.* Cambridge, MA: MIT Press.

Toshimitsu Mitsuo. 1958. "Ritsuryō Shintai Shōgaisha Hokenhō no Jisshi: Waga kōdai no kyūjustu hō (2)" [Implementation of the Ritsuryo physical disability insurance law: Our ancient aid law (2)]. *Tōyō Hōgaku* 2 (1): 21–47.

Traphagan, John W. 2004. *The Practice of Concern: Ritual, Well-Being, and Aging in Rural Japan*. Durham, NC: Carolina Academic.

——. 2010. "Intergenerational Ambivalence, Power, and Perceptions of Elder Suicide in Rural Japan." *Journal of Intergenerational Relationships* 8 (1): 21–37.

——. 2013. *Rethinking Autonomy: A Critique of Principlism in Biomedical Ethics*. Albany: SUNY Press.

Trautwein, Fynn-Mathis, José R. Naranjo, and Stefan Schmidt. 2016. "Decentering the Self? Reduced Bias in Self- vs. Other-Related Processing in Long-Term Practitioners of Loving-Kindness Meditation." *Frontiers in Psychology* 7 (November). https://doi.org/10.3389/fpsyg.2016.01785.

Tronto, Joan C. 1993. *Moral Boundaries: A Political Argument for an Ethic of Care*. London: Routledge.

Trundle, Catherine. 2014. *Americans in Tuscany: Charity, Compassion, and Belonging*. Oxford: Berghahn Books.

Tsing, Anna Lowenhaupt. 2015. *The Mushroom at the End of the World: On the Possibility of Life in Capitalist Ruins*. Princeton, NJ: Princeton University Press.

Tsuji, Yohko. 2002. "Death Policies in Japan: The State, the Family, and the Individual." In *Family and Social Policy in Japan: Anthropological Approaches*, edited by Roger Goodman, 177–99. Cambridge: Cambridge University Press.

Tsukamoto Renpei. 2019. *Kyō mo iyagarase bentō* [Bento harassment]. Django Film.

Turner, Victor. 1969. *The Ritual Process: Structure and Anti-structure*. Chicago: Aldine.

Twigg, Julia. 2000. *Bathing—the Body and Community Care*. London: Routledge.

Ume, Ebere P. 2013. "Post-Caregiving Transition in African American Caregivers." PhD diss., Arizona State University.

Ume, Ebere P., and Bronwynne C. Evans. 2011. "Chaos and Uncertainty: The Post-caregiving Transition." *Geriatric Nursing* 32 (4): 288–93.

Vimalakirti. 1976. *Vimalakirti Nirdesa Sutra*. Translated by R. A. F. Thurman. Pennsylvania State University. Accessed February 15, 2015. http://www2.kenyon.edu/Depts/Religion/Fac/Adler/Reln260/Vimalakirti.htm.

Wall, John. 2005. *Moral Creativity: Paul Ricoeur and the Poetics of Possibility*. Oxford: Oxford University Press.

Washida Kiyokazu. 2015. *Oi no kūhaku* [The void of senescence]. Tokyo: Iwanami Shoten.

Washington, Keahnan. 2019. "Love Politics and the Carceral Encounter." *Anthropology News* 60 (1): 20–22.

Weber, Max. (1920) 1946. "Religious Rejections of the World and Their Directions." In *Max Weber: Essays in Sociology*, translated by Hans H. Gerth and C. Wright Mills. Oxford: Oxford University Press.

——. (1934) 2002. *The Protestant Ethic and the "Spirit" of Capitalism and Other Writings*. New York: Penguin.

Weng, Helen Y., Andrew S. Fox, Heather C. Hessenthaler, Diane E. Stodola, and Richard J. Davidson. 2015. "The Role of Compassion in Altruistic Helping and Punishment Behavior." Edited by Pablo Brañas-Garza. *PLOS ONE* 10 (12): e0143794.

Wentzer, Thomas Schwarz. 2014. "'I Have Seen Königsberg Burning': Philosophical Anthropology and the Responsiveness of Historical Experience." *Anthropological Theory* 14 (1): 27–48.

White, Chris. 2013. "2011 Census Analysis: Unpaid Care in England and Wales, 2011 and Comparison with 2001." Office of National Statistics. Accessed September 4, 2020. https://www.ons.gov.uk/peoplepopulationandcommunity/healthandsocialcare/healthcaresystem/articles/2011censusanalysisunpaid careinenglandandwales2011an dcomparisonwith2001/2013-02-15.

WHO (World Health Organization). 2021. "Ageing." Last modified August 6, 2021. https://www.who.int/health-topics/ageing/.

Wijngaarden, Els van, Hugo van der Wedden, Zerline Henning, Rikke Komen, and Anne-Mei The. 2018. "Entangled in Uncertainty: The Experience of Living with Dementia from the Perspective of Family Caregivers." *PLOS ONE* 13 (6): e0198034.

Wikan, Unni. 2013. *Resonance: Beyond the Words*. Chicago: University of Chicago Press.

Wilińska, Monika, and Els-Marie Anbäcken. 2013. "In Search of the Everyday Life of Older People in Japan: Reflections Based on Scholarly Literature." *Journal of Cross-Cultural Gerontology* 28 (4): 435–51.

Wilkinson, Eleanor, and Iliana Ortega-Alcázar. 2019. "The Right to Be Weary? Endurance and Exhaustion in Austere Times." *Transactions of the Institute of British Geographers* 44 (1): 155–67.

Woodward, Kathleen. 2002. "Calculating Compassion." *Indiana Law Journal* 77 (2): 223–45.

———. 2009. *Statistical Panic: Cultural Politics and Poetics of the Emotions*. Durham, NC: Duke University Press.

———. 2013. "A Public Secret: Assisted Living, Caregivers, Globalization." *International Journal of Ageing and Later Life* 7 (2): 17–51.

Wu, Yongmei. 2004. *The Care of the Elderly in Japan*. London: Routledge.

Yamaguchi Michihiro. 2016. *Kaigo hyōryū: Ninchishōjiko to sasaekirenai kazoku* [Care adrift: Dementia accidents and family who cannot give enough support]. Tokyo: Gendai Shokan.

Yamamoto-Mitani, Noriko, and Margaret I. Wallhagen. 2002. "Pursuit of Psychological Well-Being (Ikigai) and the Evolution of Self-Understanding in the Context of Caregiving in Japan." *Culture, Medicine and Psychiatry* 26 (4): 399–417.

Yamashita, Junko, and Naoko Soma. 2016. "The Double Responsibilities of Care in Japan: Emerging New Social Risks for Women Providing Both Childcare and Care for the Elderly." In *New Life-Courses, Social Risks and Social Policy in East Asia*, edited by Raymond K. H. Chan, Jens Zinn, and Lih-Rong Wang, 95–112. London: Routledge.

Yanagiya Keiko. 2011. *Edo Jidai no oi to mitori* [Aging and end-of-life care in the Edo period]. Tokyo: Yamagawa.

Yarris, Kristin Elizabeth. 2017. *Care across Generations: Solidarity and Sacrifice in Transnational Families*. Stanford, CA: Stanford University Press.

Yates-Doerr, Emily. 2020. "Antihero Care: On Fieldwork and Anthropology." *Anthropology & Humanism* 45 (2): 233–44.

Yuhara Etsuko. 2017. *Kaigo satsujin no yobō: Kaigo shien no shiten kara* [Preventing care murder: From the perspective of care supporters]. Tokyo: Kress.

Yuki Yasuhiro. 2012. *Kaigo: Genba kara no kenshō* [Eldercare: Inspection from the ground]. Tokyo: Iwanami Shoten.

Zahavi, Dan, and Philippe Rochat. 2015. "Empathy ≠ Sharing: Perspectives from Phenomenology and Developmental Psychology." *Consciousness and Cognition* 36 (November): 543–53.

Zarit, Steven H., Karen E. Reever, and Julie Bach-Peterson. 1980. "Relatives of the Impaired Elderly: Correlates of Feelings of Burden." *Gerontologist* 20 (6): 649–55.

Zegwaard, Marian I., Marja J. Aartsen, Pim Cuijpers, and Mieke H. F. Grypdonck. 2011. "Review: A Conceptual Model of Perceived Burden of Informal Caregivers for Older Persons with a Severe Functional Psychiatric Syndrome and

Concomitant Problematic Behaviour." *Journal of Clinical Nursing* 20 (15–16): 2233–58.

Zigon, Jarrett. 2007. "Moral Breakdown and the Ethical Demand: A Theoretical Framework for an Anthropology of Moralities." *Anthropological Theory* 7 (2): 131–50.

——. 2010. *HIV Is God's Blessing: Rehabilitating Morality in Neoliberal Russia.* Berkeley: University of California Press.

——. 2013. "On Love: Remaking Moral Subjectivity in Postrehabilitation Russia." *American Ethnologist* 40 (1): 201–15.

Zimmermann, Ruben. 2015. *Puzzling the Parables of Jesus: Methods and Interpretation.* Minneapolis, MN: Augsburg Books.

Index

www.ingramcontent.com/pod-product-compliance
Lightning Source LLC
Chambersburg PA
CBHW030356270326
41926CB00009B/1124